SPIRITUAL WARFARE Q&A

SPIRITUAL WARFARE Q&A

PRIESTS AND *LAITY*

DAN SCHNEIDER, PHD & JESSE ROMERO

TAN Books
Gastonia, North Carolina

Cover design by David Ferris, www.davidferrisdesign.com

ISBN: 978-1-5051-3346-2
Kindle ISBN: 978-1-5051-3699-9
ePUB ISBN: 978-1-5051-3698-2

Published in the United States by
TAN Books
PO Box 269
Gastonia, NC 28053
www.TANBooks.com

Printed in the United States of America

CONTENTS

Introduction 1

Chapter I: Exorcism & Deliverance Basics 5

From the Field: "You have no authority here."

1. What is exorcism? Is that the same as deliverance?
2. What is the difference between "imprecatory" and "deprecatory" prayer?
3. Why can't I just take authority in the name of Jesus and drive out demons?
4. What does the authority structure have to do with exorcism and deliverance?
5. What happens when someone steps out of the authority structure?
6. What are the most common sins which lead to possession?
7. What are the levels of diabolic affliction?
8. Why does God allow us to be tempted?
9. What do exorcist and exorcism mean? Is an exorcist's mandate "just a piece of paper" as some claim?
10. You say an exorcist needs a mandate from the local bishop. Do we see that concept anywhere in the Bible where an apostle gives a mandate to a subordinate?

11. Sometimes exorcists on the internet report on what the demon says in session. But doesn't the demon lie?
12. Should every diocese have an exorcist?
13. Can a bishop do prayers of exorcism over the city of his diocese? What else can he do to fight off evil?
14. What do you mean that "the most powerful force in the world is the human will"? Can you give an example of what that looks like?
15. What do you mean in saying that "all liberation is self-liberation"?
16. What is the Phase One Prayer Regimen? Why is it helpful in spiritual combat?
17. I was reading an exorcism from Matthew's Gospel and saw that the verse stating "this kind is not cast out but by prayer and fasting" is missing from some versions. Why was this removed?
18. I'm worried about you looking at occult websites to prepare for your radio show. I don't want you to get attacked by demons. Isn't curiosity dangerous? Didn't Eve get in trouble for curiosity?

Chapter II: General Questions 45

From the Field: "My habit is falling off of me."
1. What about the seventy apostles in Luke chapter ten? They were lay people, right?
2. I am part of an exorcism team, and I am getting emotionally invested in the case of this petitioner. I feel like I should counsel her and personally invest myself in her case and help her get liberated. Thoughts?
3. Can other religions conduct exorcisms? I thought that the "gods of the Gentiles are demons" (Psalm 96:5)?

4. I was at a conference where someone manifested. The priest came over and people prayed until he calmed down. Does that mean the person was delivered?
5. Why is the prologue in John 1:1–14 used during the rite of Exorcism? It's also read at the end of the Latin Mass.
6. Why do demons hate Gregorian Chant and Latin?
7. Is it ok to watch horror movies?
8. If I pray prayers outside a Planned Parenthood abortion facility, what prayer protocol is recommended?
9. I'm going to an abortion clinic to inspect it as part of my job. What sacramentals do I wear? What prayers do I pray?
10. I am a police detective working major crime cases including assaults, sex assaults, and homicides. Is there an appropriate binding prayer that I can use before going into an interview?
11. Can a Catholic practice yoga? I am not sure this is something that any Christian should be doing.
12. What do I pray if I am being attacked by things like back pain, neck pain, and headaches (physical) as well as anxiety (psychological). I think it may be demons projecting these attacks. How do I pray against these attacks?
13. A priest told me that I should not pray deliverance or binding prayers for my family. He strongly advised me against this practice. I listen to War College, and I hear quite the opposite.

Chapter III: The Occult and Mystical Phenomena . . 69

From the Field: "But I am not being retaliated against."

1. I know the diabolical can mimic anything. How can we tell the difference between true and false visions?
2. I purchased a house and found out that a murder-suicide took place there years ago. Sometimes I think the house is haunted. Can that happen?
3. What do I do when I awake at three o'clock in the morning with a sense of evil? Is that just a coincidence or is there more to that hour?
4. I have dreams that often seem very symbolic. Is it wrong to interpret dreams?
5. Is there such a thing as a Chucky doll?
6. What are "satanic" rosaries?
7. How do I dispose of objects which I believe may be cursed? Can't I just throw them away?
8. What is wrong with going to haunted houses?
9. My father and grandfather were Freemasons. What prayers do I need to pray to break any curses? What do I do with his ring and apron?
10. What is a "demonic matrix?"
11. What does Liber Christo mean when they say that a person has "fractured thoughts"?
12. Can a demon take on a physical body?
13. What makes the Rosary such a powerful weapon against Satan?

Chapter IV: Breaking a Vice, God's Providence, and Evil 95

From the Field: "Leave."
1. I need to work harder to stop being in mortal sin so much. My Achilles heel is lust. Any advice on what I can

do to stay in a state of grace for longer periods and hopefully for good?

2. What does the battle with lust look like practically? What is "custody of the mind"?
3. I have heard you recommend that people who struggle with lust should gaze upon the crucified feet of Jesus. Will you give me instructions or ideas on how to proceed with this?
4. What do you mean by "the demon enters through sin but holds through heresy"? How does that relate to removing obstacles to grace?
5. What does it mean to live in a state of grace? How does that help in spiritual combat?
6. My son tries to practice his faith, but his speech is very vulgar. Is this dangerous for spiritual life, and what is the best way to break that habit?
7. I am a twenty-two-year-old that is on fire for my Catholic faith, but my parents are consulting a wizard and go to Mass as well. What can I do? I still live with them.
8. I keep hearing of the efficacy of the novena to Our Lady of Sorrows, but how exactly is this novena made? By praying the Rosary, by other special prayers?
9. I am under spiritual attack. What should I do?
10. What are "generational spirits"? Is this the same as "healing the family tree" and "generational sin"?
11. I know IVF (in vitro-fertilization) is a grave sin, but is it a satanic ritual?
12. What is the most effective protocol for decommissioning tattoos, especially those in which the ink might have been cursed, or the image itself might be evil?

13. Is all magic evil? Didn't Saint John Bosco do magic tricks?
14. Megan Fox recently said that she and her boyfriend drink each other's blood. Is that satanic? Vampirism?
15. If you renounce God and Our Lady and even sign a pact with the devil, can you ever come back?
16. My adult son does not go to Mass anymore. Where do I begin?
17. I think my husband is possessed. Can you help me?
18. Should a Catholic use "healing rocks" for physical, spiritual, or emotional healing of self? Did St. Hildegard of Bingen use healing rocks or stones?
19. Is burning sage in your home OK with the Catholic Church?
20. What is the role of sacramentals in spiritual warfare?

Chapter V: Questions from Priests—General. 143

From the Field: "What is your name?"
1. How does the ministry of exorcism relate to me as a parish priest? What does it have to do with the *tria munera*?
2. What is "exhausting the pastoral response"? Phase zero?
3. I had a good formation in the seminary, especially regarding sacramental theology, but we never learned anything about praying deliverance prayers after sacramental absolution. Wouldn't it be best for the diocesan exorcist to pray these types of prayers?
4. I was told by a priest-mentor not to pray deliverance prayers/minor exorcisms, since only the diocesan exorcist has the authority of the Church behind him, and

therefore I would be spiritually vulnerable engaging the demons on my own. How do I respond to him?

5. When do you recommend that I use exorcised oil in deliverance ministry?
6. I see many priests and exorcists being taken down in this ministry by women. Why is this seemingly more common among those who engage in spiritual warfare?
7. Some of my brother priests think that when it comes to deliverance, we should just leave well enough alone, or at least let the diocesan exorcist deal with it. What should I say to that?
8. I am hesitant to engage in deliverance ministry because of fear of transference. Am I as a priest vulnerable to this, especially if I pray with my hand on the person's head?
9. Doesn't the Bible show us that lay people can impose hands as well?
10. Someone showed up at my parish and said he is possessed. What should I do?
11. I have a deacon at my parish. What can deacons do in deliverance ministry? Can they lay hands? Can they pray imprecatory prayers?
12. Some parishioners want to set up a deliverance team at my parish. Is that safe?
13. What do modern exorcists say about the imposition of hands by the laity? Don't sponsors impose hands during the Rite of Confirmation?
14. A group from our diocese wants to lead a retreat doing "impartation" at my parish. I have never heard of it. What is impartation?
15. What about Vatican II's "active participation" of the laity

in deliverance ministry? Isn't that part of the rights of their universal priesthood as baptized Christians?

16. I recently preached on the priesthood and cautioned lay people against imposing hands. A woman accosted me after Mass and accused me of clericalism. How is that clericalism?
17. I did not learn anything about spiritual warfare in the seminary. How can I use it to help my parishioners and protect my parish?

Chapter VI: Questions from Priests—Specific 187

From the Field: "Look at the Anointed Hands of a Priest of the Living God."

1. Who can pray Chapter Three? How often should I pray it over my parish property?
2. I am an exorcist, and I noticed that when possessed people see me, they get fidgety and struggle to make eye contact. Why is that?
3. Is it true that deliverance prayers are most effective following the words of the absolution in the sacrament of confession, and if so, why?
4. If I pray deliverance prayers in the sacrament of confession, am I protected by that sacrament from demonic retaliation?
5. I have been considering praying deliverance prayers in the confessional following sacramental absolution, but what prayers should I begin with?
6. If a penitent manifests in the confessional, then the demons try to attack the priest physically, but it goes away after the priest does binding prayers, what's their end game in attempting to attack? (e.g., panicking, retalia-

tion, affirming the priest that he's getting them angry because you're about to absolve, etc.?)

7. I was recently ordained, and after one of my first Masses, a woman manifested right outside the sacristy right after Mass. A group of lay people jumped in to help, but it seemed to make things worse. When I raised my hands in prayer, the demon seemed to be in pain. Why did this happen and how do I shut it down?
8. A parishioner says she is hearing voices. How can you tell if this is demonic?
9. I started doing some deliverance prayers and now things are lighting up. I hear that a priest will get his toughest case up front. Why is that?
10. I am doing minor exorcisms, and another priest told me I needed to find a "sensitive" to help me. What is that?
11. I serve in an area where the charismatic movement and also laying on of the hands has been widespread for decades. It is expected that eventually a charismatic, usually a woman, will come back into the sacristy and say something like, "Father, I have gifts. Can I pray over you?" I'm not sure how to respond to her.
12. What is "saturation prayer"? Some people want to teach this at my parish.
13. I had always had the impression that a general confession should not be made because it would foster scrupulosity. Why then is a general confession especially recommended before deliverance prayers are prayed?
14. In my pastoral experience, breaking soul ties is very effective with regard to sexual sins and even sins of abortion, but some priests think breaking soul ties is not in Catholic tradition and has Protestant or New Age

origins and therefore is a suspicious pastoral practice at best. How do I respond?

Chapter VII: Conclusion—
Smashmouth Catholicism 213

From the Field: Prayer begets what it signifies
An Historical Note: A Lesson from the 82nd Airborne

Appendix A: Authority Charts 225
Appendix B: The Liber Christo Thirty-Day Prayer Regimen. 229
Appendix C: Prayers of Protection for Praying at an Abortion Clinic 233
Appendix D: Destroying Cursed Objects. 237
Appendix E: Instructions for Breaking Freemasonic Curses. 243
Appendix F: Protocol for Decommissioning of Tattoos . 249
Appendix G: Suggested Prayers for Priests 251
Bibliography 255

INTRODUCTION

"THE WHOLE OF man's history has been the story of dour combat with the powers of evil," states the Catechism of the Catholic Church, "stretching, so our Lord tells us, from the very dawn of history until the last day." Thus, the life of man is one of "battle" where he finds himself "in the midst of the battlefield" and he must contend and struggle for victory in this life (CCC 409). While most Catholics recognize this as true, very few set about learning the rules of engagement so that they can attain that victory which, in the words of Saint Peter, is "the goal of your faith, the salvation of your souls" (1 Pt 1:9).[1] This book is designed with that purpose in mind and the additional purpose of bringing some objectivity to an otherwise elusive and subjective—at times, even outright speculative—field of spiritual warfare.

What is needed today is a return to Catholic norms in an apostolate that has been largely influenced by Protestant and charismatic modalities that emerged in the wake of the charismatic renewal of the previous generation. Although these have had some effect, such modalities are not equipped to meet the emerging needs of today's post-Christian and increasingly pagan world. Too often, that influence has meant

[1] Unless otherwise noted, all Scripture references will be taken from the New American Bible. My own translations are taken from the Nestle-Aland *Novum Testamentum Graece* (NA28), Alfred Rahlfs, ed., *Septuaginta* (LXX), and *Biblia Sacra: Iuxta Vulgatam Versionem*, 5th edition (VUL).

an overemphasis on the devil and freedom from affliction and temporal suffering to the exclusion of Jesus Christ and the intricacy of the human person as a body-soul composite created in the image and likeness of God. As Pope Benedict XVI insisted as inherently self-evident, Christianity is, after all, about Christ. Liberation is not static, therefore, nor is it merely the cessation of pain and suffering but a movement towards Him: "For freedom Christ set us free; so, stand firm and do not submit again to the yoke of slavery" (Gal 5:1). The first movement, therefore, is one of *freedom from* disordered attachments and sin which expose the soul to the slavery of the diabolic. This requires, however, a second movement, or *freedom for* a life of virtue, sanctifying grace, and ultimately, union with Christ.

The pathway to that union, indeed, one of "dour combat" and the "battlefield" in which we find ourselves, as if air-dropped behind enemy lines, is largely an interior one. Thus, our safe return homeward—that is to say, heavenward—means a return to authentic Catholic theology and philosophy, to include Christian anthropology. The Christian understanding of the human person can be gleaned from the words of Saint Augustine: "Inasmuch as the mind itself is the image of God, in that (reality) he is *capable* of God." Sometimes translated "partaker of," the Latin *capax* means *capable*, in the sense of *able, apt, suitable for, able to conceal,* and *the right to inherit*. In the Catholic tradition, our "partaking" of God (*capax Dei*) encompasses all of those realties. Man's *telos* is God, which means the definition of liberation also encompasses much more than simply an absence of darkness. On the contrary, true and lasting "liberation" means reconciliation with God the Father, the full actualization of man's divine filiation, his baptismal dignity.

What we have attempted here in this book is to provide in laymen's terms how to defeat the infernal enemy through adherence to the teachings of the Catholic Church, a renewed prayer life, and radical return to the sacraments. Accordingly, this is not merely an informational treatise on the topic for the curious seeker but a "how-to" manual for the Church Militant. We chose the question-and-answer format for this book to help flesh out the rules of engagement for today's Catholics. On average, across our platforms, we receive approximately eight thousand emails a year inquiring on spiritual warfare. Over time, certain questions come in on a regular basis, patterning in a certain way, if you will. We include here many of the most common and recurring questions. Some are more theological, and others quite practical. Some answers have been expanded and others shortened, but overall, the astute reader will see the same pattern emerge.

We fight an ancient enemy, and therefore, our best weapons are those that are ancient, tried, and tested. The sacraments and liturgical life of the Church are both the means and the end of true and lasting liberation. You have them at your disposal, but the enemy does not want you to learn how to use them. Most Catholics, then, need someone to take them to the gunnery range so they can learn how to use their spiritual weapons safely and effectively.

We begin with a principle set forth by Saint Irenaeus of Lyon who first spoke of the "unbending Rule of faith." This second-century Father and Doctor of the Church gave a principle with which to check both doctrine and practice by asking whether it is consistent with (1) that faith which the successors to the apostles taught and handed down to apostolic witnesses and (2) the unity of Sacred Scripture. "The Rule" not only helps us to know true doctrine but also serves as a guide for holiness of life. Thus, we lean upon the living Tradition of the Church in formulating a systematic and institutional response for this "dour combat with the powers of evil" with whom we are now engaged. May this book bring you closer to Him and to that freedom which only He can give.

Dan Schneider, PhD
Jesse Romero, MA

Chapter I

EXORCISM & DELIVERANCE BASICS

"A PRIEST—ONE WHO is expressly and particularly authorized by the Ordinary—when he intends to perform an exorcism over persons tormented by the devil, must be properly distinguished for his piety, prudence, and integrity of life. He should fulfill this devout undertaking in all constancy and humility, being utterly immune to any striving for human aggrandizement, and relying, not on his own, but on the divine power. Moreover, he ought to be of mature years and revered not alone for his office but for his moral qualities.

"In order to exercise his ministry rightly, he should resort to a great deal more study of the matter (which has to be passed over here for the sake of brevity), by examining approved authors and cases from experience; on the other hand, let him carefully observe the few more important points enumerated here.

"Especially, he should not believe too readily that a person is possessed by an evil spirit; but he ought to ascertain the signs by which a person possessed can be distinguished from one who is suffering from some illness, especially one of a psychological nature. Signs of possession may be the following:

ability to speak with some facility in a strange tongue or to understand it when spoken by another; the faculty of divulging future and hidden events; display of powers which are beyond the subject's age and natural condition; and various other indications which, when taken together as a whole, build up the evidence."

—*Praenotanda to the Rite of Exorcism, nos. 1, 2, 3*

From the Field: "You have no authority here."

Power and authority are not the same thing. Simply stated, power is the ability to effect change, and authority is the right to command change. What is known as "Chapter Three" is a restricted prayer (the third chapter of the Rite of Exorcism) that requires a priest to attain permission from his bishop to pray publicly.[2] The demon knows the rules of engagement and will try to seduce priests out of their lane of authority. Make no mistake, priests can also become afflicted or even possessed (and we have had several cases of possessed priests over the years). A newly formed team in another country, for example, reported their initial case load as including four priests and a permanent deacon. What was common to all five? Each was praying Chapter Three without permission from their bishop, using ecstatic forms of adjuration (including praying in tongues over the possessed), blending of the roles between priest and lay team members, and generally

[2] This is a "slang reference to Title 12, Chapter 3 *Rituale Romanum*, also known as the Leonine 'Prayer against Satan and his fallen angels.' Pope Leo XIII incorporated this prayer into the solemn rite of exorcism, which had previously contained Chapter 1 (Praenotanda), Chapter 2 (Solemn Exorcism), and now by inclusion, Chapter 3, the above-mentioned prayer. By recent proclamation from the Congregation for the Divine Faith, this prayer is now regulated and only available to priests for public use with episcopal permission." Schneider, *The Liber Christo Method*, 23–24.

following a Protestant model found in a popular book used in some Catholic circles.

Closer to home, a young man in his twenties presented himself to a priest in his hometown. The man reported that he had been involved in Satanism at some level, and so the priest decided to pray over him immediately. They were not in the confessional, and the priest knew nothing of the man's background. The man simply came to the office and told the priest of his affliction. Without asking anything regarding the man's sacraments or anything of his current situation, this well-meaning young priest began to pray the Chapter Three in Latin over this young man.

The demon immediately began to manifest; that is, he appropriated the senses of the young man, and a diabolical presence took over his body. The demon spoke to the priest in English, and the first thing that the voice said was "Your Latin is deplorable."

The priest had just enough training to know that this does not detract from the power of his office as priest, so he replied to the demon,

"Yes, but you must yield to it."

In this, by dialoging with the demon, the priest departed the protection of his authority. The demon lured him out, as if easing him onto the edge. The priest then returned to the Ritual and prayed, "and I command you."

The young priest later reported that at those words, he immediately experienced a shift. The Praenotanda, or Preface, to the Rite of Exorcism delimits the rules for engagement and right use of this powerful prayer. Specifically, the preface gives guidelines on how the priest must be vested and what sacramentals which he must have on hand, in addition to the interior preparation through prayer before deploying the Rite. Notably, the young priest did not possess the things requisite to praying Chapter Three. For starters, he did not have a crucifix in his hand, nor was he wearing a stole, nor had he been fasting.

The priest reports that in the moment when he simply said, "I command you" to the demon, he felt a chill come over the room. First his fingers, he said, went numb. Then his feet went numb. His nose became icy cold. His tongue became, in his words, "frozen to the top of my mouth," and he could not speak. Then the eyes of the young man, now appropriated by the demon, held him. The priest said they "pierced" him, as the demon's voice then said, "You have no authority."

And in that moment, the priest was absolutely devastated, terrified. He says that he does not know how long the eyes held him, but eventually feeling started to come back to his fingers and feet. Meanwhile, the young man recovered and had no clue what had just happened. This priest, however, knew. He had enough schooling to know that he had the power over the demon but despite being a priest, he lacked the proper authority.

In this section, we discuss this in depth, specifically what it means to be "authorized by the Ordinary" as a mandated exorcist, as well as the importance of holiness ("piety, prudence, and integrity of life") and other rules for spiritual combat.

1. What is exorcism? Is that the same as deliverance?

According to the *Catechism*: "Exorcism is directed at the expulsion of demons or to the liberation from demonic possession through the spiritual authority which Jesus entrusted to his Church" (CCC 1673). Thus, as explained in *The Liber Christo Method: A Field Manual for Spiritual Combat*, exorcism is "the expelling of evil spirits in cases of possession and obsession according to the rite prescribed in the Roman ritual, and presently performed by a priest with the permission of his bishop." Exorcism, moreover, can be "*major* (with use of the Solemn Rite of the Church) or *minor* (deliverance prayers, prayer of minor exorcism using various rites and not requiring permission of the local Ordinary)."[3] This liturgical action is "the Church's formal response on behalf of the energumen[4] . . . whereby the Church asks publicly and authoritatively in the name of Jesus Christ that the person be protected from the evil one and withdrawn from his domination."[5]

Deliverance is a broader term and is related to exorcism, referring to "prayers of minor exorcism, typically in the deprecatory form, which address primarily the affliction, its effects, and entreat the Lord, His angels, His saints, the Holy Spirit, the Blessed Virgin Mary, etc. to intervene and to bring relief to the penitent/energumen suffering affliction."[6] This is significant in that many lay practitioners have blurred the distinction between exorcism and deliverance and who, while claiming to do "deliverance from evil spirits," are, in effect, performing minor exorcism without the requisite authority (to wit, "through the spiritual authority which Jesus entrusted to his Church" as per CCC 1673). Unless one has the proper authority over the person, place, or object, he should not bind any demons.

2. What is the difference between "imprecatory" and "deprecatory" prayer?

The imprecatory form of prayer is the direct commanding of a demon. The imprecatory form ("In the of Jesus Christ, I

3 Schneider, *The Liber Christo Method,* 24.
4 A technical term for one who is possessed.
5 Liber Christo, *Mentors, Case Facilitators, and GP Priests,* 7–8.
6 Liber Christo, *Mentors, Case Facilitators, and GP Priests,* 8.

command *x*") is dictated not simply by the ability to command, but also implied is the right to do so. This means that to command a demon, you have to have authority over the realm where the nefarious activity is found. Whenever someone prays, "In the name of Jesus, I bind *x*" (note the "I bind"), he is using the imprecatory form. Because man has been given by God the right of self-determination, anyone can bind any demons afflicting himself. To bind (Latin, *ligare*) means to place under oath, and therefore what is referred to as a "binding prayer" means to place a demon under oath and command him to do this or that (the cessation of nefarious activity). To bind another (whether another person or a demon) means you first have the right of disposition over the person, place, or object. The purpose of adjuration is to place another under obligation. Authority, then, is the right over another to command and place him or her under an obligation.

The deprecatory form is petitioning God for this or that intention or desired effect. While not directly commanding the demon, deprecatory prayer is asking the Lord, the Blessed Mother, Saint Michael, our guardian angel, etc. to bind the demon. One is a command; the other is a petitioning. Both are effective, but we often fall into the trap that we need to bring out the "big guns" and pound the demon, which is not always the case. The use of the Divine Name is rightly exercised as imprecatory (command) or deprecatory (beseeching) according to one's relation to the other person, place, or object. Deprecatory prayer should not be seen as the backup plan in case the imprecatory cannot be used. Petitioning the Lord in the deprecatory form is an act of faith in the providence of God, something which requires trust and, at times, even suffering. Thus, when someone prays "May the Lord bind x" (note the language of "may the Lord do this or that"), he is petitioning, which is perfectly safe and legitimate.

Saint Thomas Aquinas explains how the use of the Divine Name can be exercised as either imprecatory (command) or deprecatory (beseeching) according to one's relation by natural law vis-à-vis a person, place, or object that desires the demonic activity to cease.[7] A priest shares in the jurisdictional authority of his bishop and can use the imprecatory command as needed within his sacred office. A husband can also command the demon by merit of the office of head of household. Husbands and wives can command the demon in relation to each other's body by merit of the marital debt and one-flesh union. Every Christian has the right to command the demon over himself and his temporal goods.

3. Why can't I just take authority in the name of Jesus and drive out demons?

A common mistake today among practitioners in the field of deliverance is to equate (or collapse, actually) power and authority. These are two different things. Power is the ability to effect change, and authority is the right to adjure or command another. The right to command, moreover, follows the right to bless, which is based on office. For example, we read in the *Book of Blessings*: "The ministry of blessing involves a particular exercise of the priesthood of Christ and [is exercised] *in keeping with the place and office within the people of God belonging to each person*." The *Book of Blessings* further explains

[7] See *ST* II–II, q. 90. On the distinction between the use of the Divine Name in solemn and private adjurations and the application of this section of the *Summa*, see McHugh and Callam, *Moral Theology*, 360–62. The authors make note of special charisms among the laity to drive out demons, citing two saints as examples: the monk and Desert Father Saint Anthony of Egypt and the consecrated religious and Doctor of the Church Saint Catherine of Sienna. Notably, they cite here saints who were also consecrated celibates. One must always exercise prudence and guard against the sin of presumption.

that "laypersons exercise this ministry [of blessing] *in virtue of their office*," citing as an example "parents on behalf of their children" (emphasis mine). Elsewhere, the document lists those individuals in the Old Testament who administered an office from which they blessed (or prayed over) others: "patriarchs, kings, priests, Levites, and parents—by allowing them to offer blessings in praise of His name and to invoke His name."[8] Thus, those who had the right to bless held an office, either patriarchal or priestly.

The right to command follows the right to bless. Baptism does not give you the right to drive out every demon. Baptism removes original sin and places supernatural grace in the soul, by which God recreates you as is child and member of the Church. The right to bless (and also command) flows from that orientation towards the Church, as well as natural law. As Father Chad Ripperger states with regard to lay people, "spouses . . . by virtue of the marital contract . . . have right over each other's bodies by virtue of the conceding of those rights to each other on the day of their marriage. For this reason, wives may command the demons to leave their husbands' bodies and the husbands, their wive's bodies. For the husband, it is a twofold authority, the one as the head of household and the other by virtue of the rights over his wife's body."[9] Since by natural law, everyone has the right of self-determination, you can command the demon to leave you or your temporal goods, and husbands over wives, wives over their husbands' bodies, parents over children, etc. But to "take" authority and command demons outside of what the Church has delimited can be dangerous.

Rather than "taking" authority (which is common, Protestant language), you assert what is yours by right given through

8 USCCB, *Book of Blessings*, nos. 18, 6.

9 Ripperger, *Deliverance Prayers for the Laity*, 8.

natural or divine law (i.e., your office within the Church) by God the Father. The two ends of an authority-based-on-office are to provide and to protect.[10] When we work within that structure, we are generally protected. When we step outside of that, we expose ourselves and our families to retaliation.

For more on the right to command and bless, see Appendix A.

4. What does the authority structure have to do with exorcism and deliverance?

This ties into a previous question, as field experience suggests that certain demons, specifically in case of possession, will require an exorcist with a mandate to be driven out. On multiple occasions, we have heard the demon tell a well-intended visiting (and, therefore, not incardinated into the diocese) priest performing an exorcism, "You have no authority here." We have also heard this reply to deacons who were praying priestly prayers of minor exorcism. As Father Ripperger notes, moreover, a demon is a "lawyer from hell" who intimately knows who has the right to adjure him under oath. We have also seen a demon reveal that he knows whether the exorcist or bishop is in the diocese or not, which he voices through the possessed person. "You have a different priest coming today, huh? Father so-and-so is out of town, isn't he?" We have also noted that the energumen will often have an aversion both to the mandated exorcist and his or her parish priest, while showing no such reaction to other priests. In addition, we have seen the same aversion to the prayers of a husband over his wife (often with the effect equal to the exorcist). This suggests

10 As Father Ripperger writes, these two are "the final cause of authority." *Dominion*, 156. For the structure of authority within the various offices (husband, wife, mother, father, owner, etc.), see *Dominion*, 154–72.

that he responds to the intrinsic nature of the authority structure which flows from office (divine positive law with regard to the mandated exorcist, pastor, and natural law with regard to the husband as head of household).

Once the person has gone through our protocol, moreover, he generally has sufficient willpower over the demon, whose power has also been weakened by the imposition of order. In fact, we have found it sufficient for the exorcist to punish the demon when he manifests with a simple command, "In the name of Jesus Christ, I command you to stop this now and be quiet!" For example, when a demon attempts to bash the person's head against the wall, the simple command of the exorcist to stop hurting the person will cause the violence to stop as if there were an invisible hand preventing the head from hitting the wall, stopping one inch from striking. We have also witnessed cases where a demon is completely subdued during a manifestation by the imposition of hands of the husband upon his wife's head. This reinforces that the demon knows the authority structure under which he must yield.

There is a difference between *deliverance* and *liberation,* which means to "set free." The latter can be done without adjuration (and the ordinary means of liberation is the sacraments). In the milieu of the spiritual life, liberation means freed from the influence of evil spirits and is often used interchangeably with exorcism. Because we believe as Catholics that the power to "bind and loose" is given to the apostolic office of Peter and the Apostles (cf. Mt 16:18; Jn 20:21–23), then the ritual of exorcism properly speaking is reserved to the local bishop, and only to those (priests) to whom he has given formal permission (and therefore authority) to perform.

Accordingly, we have also found that certain entry points of particularly grave matter, such as institutional evil, will require an institutional response from the Catholic Church. Perhaps this is a matter of justice, whereby the Church authority is invoked to make satisfaction for the first commandment violations. Grave sexual sins such as incest also often requires a sacerdotal response.

An institutional entry point (the result of membership in a satanic coven, personal membership in a masonic lodge, etc.) will generally require an institutional response by the Catholic Church. There are times when there is not an institutional element present and nonetheless the authority of the Church is needed to bind the demon by her ecclesial authority so as to expel him from a person. The normal response of the Church is the "administering of the oaths" by adjuration to expel the demon by recourse to the authority given by Christ to the Apostles and their successors, the Catholic bishops and their appointed exorcists.

5. What happens when someone steps out of the authority structure?

Many parishes offer deliverance ministry, staffed by lay people, for parishioners or for anyone seeking deliverance. The pastor may approve, endorse, or even promote such a ministry as a "stewardship" and or a "collaborative" approach to the laity. This is usurpation of authority on the part of the laity and abdication of authority on the part of the priest. That is, the duty to sanctify and govern at the parish belongs to the pastor by virtue of his sacerdotal office.

The authority structure provides protection. Retaliation is the barometer by which we can discern whether we operate under the protection of authority with respect to commanding the demon. As Father Ripperger explains: "For it is when we remain under the authority structure that God has established by the divine law (i.e., the authority of the Church) the natural law, that we remain protected. For this reason, if the laity always remain within the confines of the authority that God has given to them by the natural law, such as commanding the demons to leave their own bodies or those over whom they have authority by natural law (such as their children or wife, etc.), then they will experience little to no retaliation, as a general rule."[11]

If you step out from under the protection provided by the authority structure, demons can retaliate against you, your marriage, or your children by exploiting any area of weakness. Father Ripperger states that, "Most experienced exorcists have had to do exorcisms over people who suffer from oppression, obsession, and even possession because of the fact that they prayed over people whom they did not have authority."[12] This principle applies even if the parish priest endorses a lay deliverance ministry at his parish, because authority cannot be granted by permission. For example, a bishop cannot decide to give a lay person the authority to say Mass because he has more theological training, or is a better public speaker, than the parish priest. Authority is based on office, not charism, and the ability to command a demon is not the same as the right to do so. As former president of the International Association of Exorcists Father Giancarlo Gramolazzo, affirms, "I always use this phrase: the prince of disobedience is the devil and you beat him by being obedient, not by your own personality, or charisms."[13] "The obedience," writes Father Ripperger, "is due to the natural law and divine positive law and the structure of authority that God has established within these two."[14] In those cases where the pastor abdicates his authority and

11 Ripperger, *Deliverance Prayers for the Laity*, 8.
12 Ripperger, *Dominion*, 140.
13 Cited in Baglio, *The Rite*, 196.
14 Ripperger, *Dominion*, 140.

outsources, in a sense, the work of expulsion of demons, both the priest and the lay practitioners are exposed to retaliation.

The demon's main target of retaliating is against the sacrament that orients you to God—for the married person, his or her marriage. Father Vincent Lampert echoes this and warns the laity, "Demons recognize the authority of bishops and the Church. If you claim authority on your own, it can get you into trouble." He cites the retaliation against the Sons of Sceva who were attacked by demons in Acts of the Apostles as proof that invoking the name of Jesus in command can be dangerous without requisite authority (Acts 19:13–20). He notes that an exorcist possesses a power not of his own but "the power and authority of the Church that comes from Jesus Christ." Lay Catholics, however, "don't have that power."[15]

Matt Baglio relates one story which reinforces this point as told by an Italian exorcist about a charismatic prayer group. This group, the priest recounts, "thought they had a special 'gift' to cast out evil spirits." As Baglio recounts:

> During the exorcism, the charismatics were laying on hands and talking to the demon, ordering it to comply. Without warning, the demon turned on them saying, "who are you?" Then he launched a bookcase at them, sending them all to the emergency room with injuries.[16]

Like the sons of Sceva, they learned that authority is based on office, not charism.

See Appendix A for charts on the authority structure.

---

[15] Quoted in *Catholic World Report*, "US Exorcists: Demonic Activity is on the Rise."

[16] Baglio, *The Rite*, 79.

6. What are the most common sins which lead to possession?

The most common sin leading to possession is participation with the occult and witchcraft. As the *Catechism* states: "All forms of divination are to be rejected: recourse to Satan or demons, conjuring up the dead or other practices falsely supposed to 'unveil' the future. Consulting horoscopes, astrology, palm reading, interpretation of omens and lots, the phenomena of clairvoyance, and recourse to mediums all conceal a desire for power over time, history, and, in the last analysis, other human beings, as well as a wish to conciliate hidden powers. They contradict the honor, respect, and loving fear that we owe to God alone" (CCC 2116).

While a single mortal sin is sufficient to open a person to diabolical affliction (and even possession), God, in His mercy, gives a person ample opportunities for repentance and conversion before allowing the demon's claim to a person. We have found, moreover, that certain grave sins generally require the help of the Church. As mentioned above, sins against the first commandment where someone ritually participates in institutional evil in giving worship to a false god (worship, or *latria,* is due to God alone) will often require an institutional response from the Church. In those instances, the Church, through her priests, assists the person by asserting her authority over a soul to force the demon to leave. The same goes for sins against the sixth commandment, especially grave sins such as incest, rape and child molestation, and sexual deviancy. Thus, we have seen that witchcraft, superstition, and other occult activity, when combined with sexual immorality, are like a "one-two punch" which opens one up to extraordinary diabolic activity.

The demon knows us by our sins and is attracted to any behavior inconsistent with the indelible mark of Baptism. We have found, nonetheless, that certain secondary sins do appear particularly to attract the demon. In addition to occult practices and sexual deviancy, other sins often found in cases of possession include a deep-seated unforgiveness (of God, self, or others); sins of the speech (blasphemy, detraction, slander, gossip); heresy (the demon often holds here); and despair (grave sins against hope). This is not to say if someone holds a heretical belief, for example, that he will become possessed. Rather, these sins are the common warning flags which signal to the demon that a person has certain vulnerabilities which the demon is more than happy to exploit. Although not exhaustive, these sins are commonly found in cases of possession, perhaps because each of these reflects something of the demon's own fallen, existential state: unforgiving of God and remorse, cursing and reviling God and others (the Greek word *diabolos* means slanderer or reviler), the rejection of reveal truths, leading to a state of eternal despair.

7. What are the levels of diabolic affliction?

Diabolic activity is divided into ordinary and extraordinary.[17] The ordinary activity of the devil is called temptation, which Father John Hardon defines as:

> Solicitation to sin, whether by persuasion or offering some pleasure. It may arise from the world, the flesh, or the devil. Temptation from the world is the attractiveness of bad example and the psychological pressure to conform. Temptations from the flesh are all the urges of concupiscence, whether carnal or spiritual, where man's fallen nature has built-in tendencies to the seven capital sins. Demonic temptations arise from instigations of the evil spirit, whose method is to

[17] Definitions here are excerpted from Schneider, *The Liber Christo Method*, 19–20. Used with permission.

encourage every form of avarice or selfishness, in order to lead one to pride, and through pride to all other sins.[18]

Temptation is part of the human condition after the fall of Adam and Eve, which means we will battle with temptation as long as we are alive. While ordinary temptation remains exterior to the person, extraordinary diabolic activity becomes increasingly interior. The latter has three levels and can be seen along a continuum of oppression, obsession, and possession whereby the enemy gains increasing access to, and control over, one's interiority. Spiritual oppression is the first stage in the progression toward classic possession and has three discernible levels. Oppression can be heaviness, malaise, melancholy, or depression. As the influence of the diabolical increases during this phase, the individual begins to lose focus, especially on vocational obligations. Spiritual oppression can also cause interior afflictions, such as darkness, despair, and sorrow. This lowest level of extraordinary diabolic activity is generally experienced as an affliction upon one's externals (finances, relationships, temporal goods, etc.).

Obsession can be spiritual or psychological. Spiritual obsession is the second stage in the progression toward classic possession and is often seen in marked neurotic and abnormal mental symptoms due to the persevering efforts of an evil spirit to gain mastery over a person; where one is besieged psychologically—that is, intellectually and emotionally—by demons. The demon is becoming increasingly interior (and present in a menacing way) to the person. Father Francisco Bamonte, former president of the IAE (International Association of Exorcists), cites Father Antonio Royo Marín in describing the experience as "profound and unsurmountable repugnance for his duty or an intense desire to do what is

[18] Hardon, *Modern Catholic Dictionary*, 534.

prohibited, proposing to the mind all sorts of illicit and indecent fantasies which continue regardless of one's efforts to reject . . . a sense of anger, doubt, anguish, desperation, rebellion and antipathy."[19] The experience is generally a disproportionately affective interior emotional state. At this level of affliction, there will be both psychological and physical indicators of the diabolical presence where the enemy exhibits an increased and persistent activity in the interiority of a person. A psychological obsession is experienced as recurrent and persistent thoughts, urges, or images that are experienced as intrusive and unwanted. Of importance is that a psychological obsession can expose the soul to a spiritual oppression or even spiritual obsession. For this reason, working on good mental health and stabilizing the interior through mental prayer is very important spiritual combat.

Possession is the phenomenon in which the devil invades the body of a living person and moves the faculties and organs as if he were manipulating a body of his own. There are three types of possession. Classic is usually a gradual progression through the stages of oppression and obsession. Partial possession occurs generally when there has been a pact made in exchange for a favor with a demon such that the demon is present to that activity, and when the person seeks God, demonic affliction arises. Sometimes this can be ethnic/cultural related. Transient possession is where rights are given by someone else, usually familial, such as in Freemasonry or other witchcraft, and the demon becomes present when the rights are challenged. This is sometimes seen as akin to a "peanut allergy" in that that the effects arise situationally. The

19 Bamonte, *Diabolical Possession*, 67. These can also find their origin in psychological causes, which our protocol is designed to discern.

demonic claim will (as a rule) spike when the activity associated with the possession/curse is performed.[20]

The introduction to the solemn rite of exorcism is attributed to Saint Charles Borromeo, who lists three primary signs as indicative of possession: speaking/understanding languages unknown to the person, or other occult knowledge, such as making known distant or hidden events, knowledge of things beyond one's state in life; display of power, superhuman strength (or strength beyond one's age or condition), to include shapeshifting; aversion to the sacred, such as a vehement aversion to God, the Holy Name of Jesus, the Blessed Virgin Mary or the saints, blessed objects, sacred ritual, sacred images, etc.[21]

It is important to note that you cannot "catch" a demon like you catch a cold, nor is it random. The ordinary pathway for the diabolic is sin, and the protection against diabolic activity is avoiding temptation by the practice of virtue and by staying in a state of grace.

8. Why does God allow us to be tempted?

The *Catechism* defines a *temptation* as "an attraction, either from outside oneself or from within, to act contrary to right reason and the commandments of God" (CCC 538). As an astute predator, the demon knows our individual weaknesses and vulnerabilities and seeks to lay traps for us on a regular basis. The enemy draws upon habits, inclinations, and the weakness of our fallen human nature. He does so, however, not just to take us out of the battle, but he wants to take out as many other people in our circle as possible.

---

[20] Schneider, *The Liber Christo Method*, 20.
[21] See Weller, *Roman Ritual*, 160–73.

According to Saint Thomas Aquinas, God allows a certain amount of temptation against evil so that we may progress in the spiritual life and grow in holiness. To that end, the demons serve God's plans by becoming the means of our sanctification. Thus, the Angelic Doctor explains that God allows the devil to tempt us and put us to the test for a threefold end. Our struggle against evil, says Saint Thomas, makes "our merits greater, our virtues purer and higher, and our spiritual progress more rapid."[22] Similarly, Saint John Chrysostom says that God allows the devil to be "useful" to us because through our "courageous resistance," we can "turn his evil deeds to [our] advantage."[23]

Father Jordan Aumann explains, moreover, that when we participate with the grace of God and overcome the enemy's temptations, we actually "humiliate" the devil.[24] Thus, while the demon is the instrument of our salvation, we are the instrument of his punishment. How can this be? Simply stated, the more little battles we win, the more Christ grows in us and His glory emanates from within us. Our willful resistance through prayer and sacrifice punishes the demon. Father Aumann affirms that our spiritual victories over temptation have many positive effects. In addition to glorifying God, our souls grow in purity as we discover the weapons against temptation—the virtues of humility, self-denial, repentance, and a greater dependence upon God's constant help.[25] In these struggles, moreover, we become more alert to the enemy's tactics and grow in the holy desire for not only liberation but also true holiness and deeper union with God. When the devil's punch "lands," however, even that is to the

22 Saint Thomas Aquinas, *Commentary on the Letter to the Hebrews*, 12:6.
23 Saint John Chrysostom, *Third Homily on Demons*, 2.
24 Aumann, *Spiritual Theology*, 157.
25 Aumann, *Spiritual Theology*, 157–58.

glory of God because it reveals to us areas of weakness and vulnerability. We pick ourselves up and Charlie Mike—that is—continue the mission toward heaven.

This is affirmed by Saint Paul when he writes, "No trial has come to you but what is human. God is faithful and will not let you be tried beyond your strength; but with the trial he will also provide a way out, so that you may be able to bear it" (1 Cor 10:13). While the Latin *tentatio* means "an attack," it also implies a trial or proof. The Greek word for "to be tested" here means not just to be tempted but "an attempt, experiment" and therefore "to be proven" in one's resolutions. In our struggles, then, God is glorified by the conformity of the mind to the truth and the resolution of the will toward the good. Thus, elsewhere Saint Paul affirms that "all things work for good for those who love God" (Rom 8:28), for even our struggles become occasions for growing in merit and holiness. Accordingly, Father Ripperger states, "For demons, no good deed goes unpunished. Therefore, if the person is on the right track with his life and doing the good, the fact that he is under diabolic attack is a witness to the goodness of what he is doing. If what he was doing were evil, the demons would not attack but would encourage it."[26] Ultimately, as Jesus says, "without me, you can do nothing" (Jn 15:5), so our struggles reveal our weakness and defects and, therefore, total dependence on Jesus to attain victory.

9. What do exorcist and exorcism mean? Is an exorcist's mandate "just a piece of paper" as some claim?

Good question. Some charismatics and Protestants wrongly claim that being an exorcist is "just a piece of paper" and that

[26] Ripperger, *Dominion*, 216.

there is no difference between a lay person and a priest, or even an exorcist, when commanding a demon. In addition, there are instances where a priest claims to be an exorcist when, technically speaking, he is not. An exorcist has a written mandate which means he has been given an office of special authority by his bishop. The word "mandate" itself is derived from the Latin *mandatum*, which means "one charged with a commission" or "one sent with imperial command."[27] Simply stated, any priest has the authority to command the demon in minor exorcism (prayers of deliverance), but to be an exorcist, one must be given faculties by his bishop.

There are two ways to attain these faculties and jurisdictional authority of the bishop over demons. When a priest has faculties for a case, and only for that case and during the time of that case, he is an exorcist *ad actum* (which basically means "for this action or deed") while he processes that case. There are some dioceses which designate a priest as the one who will receive the faculties *ad actum* should a case arise, but outside that timeframe, he is not an exorcist. Other dioceses will have an appointed exorcist with stable faculties. If a priest has stable faculties, then he is an ongoing exorcist and has the title of exorcist continually—that is, as long as he still has the designation as stable exorcist from his bishop. Thus, the one will have a mandate for a particular case and in that case alone he possesses the full authority of his bishop, and he is an exorcist while he has that case. The other will have faculties for all cases in his diocese during the duration of his appointment. Whether on a case-by-case basis or stable, moreover, both appointments are generally given in writing with a date of termination of office, and the former containing the name of the specific individual for whom the priest has been given

[27] Latin definitions taken from Lewis and Short, *An Elementary Latin Dictionary*.

temporary faculties.[28] "In either case [whether permanent mandate or temporary *ad actum* appointment]," states the USCCB, "the exorcist should work closely with, and under the direction of, the bishop."[29]

The Greek word *exorkizo* means "to adjure," with the root meaning of "to administer an oath to" and thus binding another by oath.[30] *Exorcism,* then, is the adjuration and expulsion of demons whereby they are bound by oath by the one who adjures, whether solemnly in the name of the Church or privately. Implied within that right to bind by oath is a relationship of authority—that is, the right to command, or adjure, the demon. The local Catholic bishop is the chief exorcist in his diocese and, due to the apostolicity of that office, he holds jurisdictional authority over the demons. While a mandate is conferred in writing (the demon is, after all, legalistic), it is more than a "piece of paper." A mandate is a written commissioning of a priest to act (to wit, "bind by oath") on behalf of the local bishop. Thus, "Whoever listens to you, listens to me" (Lk 10:16). An *exorcist* is one who bears the apostolic authority of that local bishop, and binds on his behalf, specifically as it relates to the demon.

Thus, properly speaking, an exorcist is a Catholic priest who has an official *mandate* from his bishop to perform exorcisms.[31] The Congregation of the Divine Faith (headed by then-Cardinal Jospeh Ratzinger) clarified this in 1985: "Canon 1172

---

[28] This terminology can be confusing because there can be found priests who may have had faculties at one point for a case but who still retain the title of exorcist and give the impression that he has always been an exorcist and continually does exorcisms, etc. when, in fact, his authority ceased at the end of his appointment.

[29] USCCB, "Exorcism." https://www.usccb.org/prayer-and-worship/sacraments-and-sacramentals/sacramentals-blessings/exorcism.

[30] Greek definitions taken from Liddell, Scott, and Jones, *A Greek-English Lexicon.*

[31] *Code of Canon Law,* no. 1172.

of the *Code of Canon Law* states that no one can legitimately perform exorcisms over the possessed unless he has obtained special and express permission from the local Ordinary (§ 1), and states that this permission should be granted by the local Ordinary only to priests who are endowed with piety, knowledge, prudence and integrity of life (§ 2). Bishops are therefore strongly advised to stipulate that these norms be observed."[32]

Anyone with any time in the field knows that to reduce an exorcist's mandate to a mere "piece of paper," as if a child passing a note in school, is laughable to the demon. The demon knows the levels of priestly authority and will react differently whether confronted by a visiting priest versus the person's canonical pastor, or the diocesan exorcist. Accordingly, the "piece of paper" is a legal document that asserts that a given priest is charged with a commission, given jurisdictional authority, qualified for the task, and has been properly trained.

Perhaps causing confusion today are itinerant, self-trained priests (and even Catholic laity) who claim to be exorcists. Properly speaking, to be called an "exorcist," one must be "expressly and particularly authorized by the Ordinary" according to the Praenotanda (and echoed in canon law). There is ancient wisdom in this precept. Also seen in the Praenotanda is how a bishop's mandate will help to prevent self-promotion, as the bishops generally pick mature priests who are "revered for their moral qualities" and are "utterly immune to any striving for human aggrandizement." For this reason, an exorcist, to be an exorcist formally, has a mandate from his bishop to perform this office. He also shares in the protection of the office of bishop. A priest (or anyone who

[32] CDF 1985, *Letter to Ordinaries regarding norms on Exorcism*. Can. 1172 states: §1. "No one can perform exorcisms legitimately upon the possessed unless he has obtained special and express permission from the local ordinary. §2. The local ordinary is to give this permission only to a presbyter who has piety, knowledge, prudence, and integrity of life."

engages in this arena, for that matter) who does not operate under authority, who lacks moral qualities, and who seeks human praise presents a huge vulnerability to the enemy.

The International Association of Exorcists (IAE) recently published guidelines for the safe practice of deliverance grounded in Catholic tradition due to the presence of self-stylized "rogue operators both clerical and lay" who perform "do-it-yourself" exorcisms without proper authority. Many well-intended Catholics unwittingly fall into the category of "rogue operators" today because they draw from Protestant Pentecostalism and not Catholic tradition. The IAE warns that "unauthorized priests and laity who attempt to perform exorcisms without authorization actually may open the door to further demonic influence over the people they are trying to help."[33] Demons are lawyers from hell, and they often retaliate when priest or laity step outside of the protection of authority. The IAE noted a situation in which a rogue priest, who did not have the proper authority, sexually abused vulnerable women that sought help. If demons retaliate against a Catholic priest who steps outside of the protection of authority, what do you think they will do to a lay person who commands demons without the requisite authority? Working within the authority structure provides a layer of protection not afforded to those who choose to create their own rules of engagement.

10. You say an Exorcist needs a mandate from the local bishop. Do we see that concept anywhere in the Bible where an apostle gives a mandate to a subordinate?

Yes. One example is found in the book of Acts:

> The apostles and the presbyters, your brothers, to the brothers in Antioch, Syria, and Cilicia of Gentile origin: greetings.

[33] IAE, *Guidelines for the Ministry of Exorcism,* 14.

> Since we have heard that some of our number [who went out] without any mandate (*non mandavimus*, in the Latin Vulgate) from us have upset you with their teachings and disturbed your peace of mind, we have with one accord decided to choose representatives and to send them to you along with our beloved Barnabas and Paul, who have dedicated their lives to the name of our Lord Jesus Christ. (Acts 15:23–26)

We have also been present when a visiting priest invoking the authority of his priesthood in minor exorcism was told, "You have no authority here." Lawyers from hell know it is not a piece of paper but the legal right to adjure the demon, to bind (evil spirits) by oath or adjuration.

11. Sometimes exorcists on the internet report on what the demon says in session. But doesn't the demon lie?

As Our Lord tells us, "the devil is a liar and the father of lies" (Jn 8:44), and accordingly, a priest should be cautious lest he follow a trail of lies and be led down a proverbial rabbit hole. Admittedly, some priests with little or no formal training will tell vivid stories, and even Hollywood-type reenactments, from their prayer sessions. While undoubtedly such focus on the external actions of the devil may draw an audience, it does little for souls. In fact, this can lead to a "satanic panic" which merely feeds an unholy curiosity in people and diverts our gaze from Jesus Christ. Moreover, when an exorcist builds his ministry around insights which come out of sessions (whether seemingly from the demon or a so-called "sensitive" on his team), the demon will quickly (and subtly) draw him away from the safest path, found in the approved formulae of the rubrics of the liturgical rites of the Church.

As seen above, the root meaning of the word *mandatum* is to hand over, in the sense of to command, but also means "one who executes an order or command, agent" and from this sense, we get the word "mandatory." Accordingly, when a mandated exorcist commands a demon, the demon is bound to comply. Make no mistake, the demon in an exorcism is under extreme duress. Although disembodied, they are pure intellect and will in their being and have psychological limits which can be broken. Against his will, he will reveal things pertaining to the case. To see the Solemn Rite of Exorcism performed by a Roman Catholic priest with proper faculties is as if watching a demon being spiritually waterboarded. The demon is bound there until God mines the maximum amount of grace out of the situation. In the meantime, when a demon manifests through the bodily senses of the energumen, he suffers acute pain in hearing the prayers of the priest (even when prayed silently). The demon traffics in the senses and shrills at the application of sacramentals such as holy water, exorcised salt, sacred bells, and incense. (Pull these out of the sacristy, Fathers, and use them because the "smells and bells" of traditional Catholicism cause the demons to shriek in pain.)

The most amazing stories, however, are not the parlor tricks often found in manifestations, such as levitations and the like, but rather when the demon admits, under duress, some facet of the Catholic faith. Sometimes this is gleaned in his visceral response during the Litany of Saints to certain known saints like Saint Mary Magdalene (who usually indicates a demon of impurity), or Saint Padre Pio (stigmatists acutely punish the demon since they defeated him in the flesh and bore the marks of Christ physically, and thus call the afflicted soul to the deep waters of redemptive suffering), or Saint Joseph (usually seen when there is abandonment or abuse by the earthly father), or almost forgotten ones like the

Fourteen Holy Helpers or Saints Comas and Damian. These give insight into the nature of the demon, his entry and holding points, and what virtues the energumen needs to develop along the path towards liberation.

Spend enough time downrange on this battlefield and the glories of the Virgin Mary inevitably shine forth. We have heard the demon, under duress of the Solemn Rite, give insights into the Virgin Mary. In response to a deacon quietly reading the wedding feasts of Cana (Jn 2:1–12), for example, we have observed a demon covering the energumen's ears and screaming, "Stop reading that, I command you! Stop! She is the Spouse of God!" Or, crying in pain in response to the priest praying the Litany of Loretto with, "O her! Whenever you call on her, she comes; she wraps her mantle around you!" There is a substantial difference between relating what the demon says under duress and retelling his parlor tricks. The former serves a salvific purpose by giving specific intel for a case and always taps into the richness of the Catholic faith. The latter draws attention to the demon and away from Christ.

When an exorcist uses examples, therefore, to teach the Catholic faith grounded in good theology and philosophy, and he stays focused on Christ (not the devil), then his teachings can be salutary and even catechetical. When in the context of the lawfully executed liturgical life of the Church, these statements affirm Catholic tradition on Mary and the saints and strengthen the faith of the exorcist and his team. What becomes evident is an expanded ecclesiology and functional theology that brings into *bas-relief* what the *Catechism* states about the relationship between dogma and the spiritual life: "There is an organic connection between our spiritual life and the dogmas. Dogmas are lights along the path of faith; they illuminate it and make it secure. Conversely, if our life is upright, our intellect and heart will be open to welcome the light shed by the dogmas of faith" (CCC 89).

The Mystical Body—militant, suffering, and triumphant—takes on a dimensionality when the enemy proclaims certain truths about Mary and the saints against his will. The enemy's reluctant admissions, moreover, also reveal his weaknesses. God is forcing him to reveal this battlefield intel, so the energumen knows what he or she needs to do to achieve liberation. This usually means increased devotion to certain saints, and always a call to increase devotion to the Blessed Mother, Mediatrix of All Grace.

As Father Ripperger has remarked, moreover, being an exorcist is like being on the end of a sewage pipe. The exorcist spends most of his time being hit with cosmic sewage, but every so often the proverbial diamond ring that some lady dropped into the kitchen sink comes through, which far outshines the banality of the grime and filth of the job. To be clear, the most amazing stories that come from exorcisms—the true diamonds in the sewage—are the conversions and heroic levels of holiness achieved by the afflicted souls as they fully embrace the unadulterated truths of the Roman Catholic faith.

What comes out in session, therefore, is the battlefield intel which always reinforces the truths of the Catholic faith if it is to be trusted. If the demon says anything against the revealed truths of the Catholic faith, you know it is a lie. If he claims to be a saint, angel, or a purgative soul (which often happens in session, where the demon claims to be someone's Aunt Tilley, etc.) recall the words in the Praenotanda attributed to Saint Charles Borromeo: "Neither ought he to give any credence to the devil if the latter maintains that he is the spirit of some saint or of a deceased party, or even claims to be a good angel."[34] This is the wisdom of the saints. If the demon knows that you are curious about such things and possess an unhealthy curiosity towards the supernatural, he will exploit you and begin to work on you and your team members.

When a mandated exorcist commands the demon to tell the truth, however, the demon knows that the mandate is more than "just a piece of paper," as a previous question asked. The demon is bound by the rules of engagement to comply. He does not have to comply, however, if the priest does not have faculties, requisite authority, or is morally compromised. He will take a priest (and the team who no longer have his protection) to the proverbial woodshed, particularly in cases of the latter.

The demon can also at times answer in compliance but still be deceptive in some way. For example, in the Solemn Rite, the exorcist demands in Latin, *Dicas mihi nomen tuum* ("Tell me your name!"). Sometimes the demon will use hand or bodily gestures (as in the case of a mute spirit) not unlike gang symbols, or he will speak in language that has been extinct for three thousand years. He complied, but now it is up to the exorcist and team to figure it out. The veracity quotient of demons is low, to be sure, but when exorcists compare notes with other exorcists and cases across the country, things pattern out.

This is not unlike prisoners of war being interrogated in different parts of the battlefield who reveal enemy secrets consistent with each other. In law enforcement, this is akin to multiple gang members being interrogated in separate rooms who will reveal consistent (or inconsistent) stories. The interrogation may begin with lies, but when the pressure (and pain) of the prayer session bears upon him (because of the authority of the exorcist), he will eventually "spill the beans"

---

34 Weller, *Roman Ritual,* 381.

like any prisoner of war. Over time, however, he may also be under such duress so as to say whatever he thinks the priest wants to hear, also not unlike a tortured prisoner of war. So, the window for reliable intel is small, but very fruitful when it occurs.

In that sense, then, it is good for the lay faithful to hear real stories from the experience of authentic exorcists so they can be encouraged in their pursuit of holiness, affirmed in their adherence to Catholic tradition and practice, and more learned in their understanding of the enemy's tactics. Nonetheless, when a priest uses it to promote his apostolate or himself, particularly when that priest in not mandated by his bishop, the lay faithful should look for more stable voices.

12. Should every diocese have an exorcist?

The 1917 *Code of Canon Law* required that each diocese appoint an official exorcist, but this requirement was removed in the 1983 revision. In 2004, however, Pope Saint John Paul II (and then-Cardinal Ratzinger, prefect of the Congregation for the Doctrine of the Faith) reiterated that every diocese should appoint an exorcist. Exorcism is part of the *munus regendi* of a bishop—that is, the responsibility to rule and govern. The local bishop rules by office, and not by merit, as successor to the Apostles. For a diocese to neglect this important aspect of Christianity, out of fear or denial of the reality of evil, is detrimental to the flock entrusted to it. That many bishops today, moreover, do not have a designated exorcist in their dioceses suggests a failure to discharge their office as chief exorcist in their diocese, a sacred trust handed over to each bishop by Our Lord.

13. Can a bishop do prayers of exorcism over the city of his diocese? What else can he do to fight off evil?

Yes, a bishop is the exorcist of his diocese, and he has full jurisdictional authority as a successor of the apostles over everyone (Catholic or not) in his diocese. As a prince of the Church, the Catholics in his diocese are his flock, and he can (and should) regularly pray imprecatory prayers, prayers for blessings and protection. He should also pray Chapter Three (the "Saint Michael the Archangel Prayer Against the Apostate Angels") over the diocese as a routine practice. Putting exorcised salt blocks buried in the four corners of the diocese is also very effective; this marks the geographical corners of the diocese with an exorcised sacramental. Moreover, an annual Eucharistic procession in the diocese is very powerful spiritual warfare. As Father Philip Weller notes concerning the Rite of Exorcism, "Whereas the preceding rite of exorcism is designated for a particular person, the form given here is meant especially to be employed to expel the devil's sway over a locality (parish, city, etc.)."[35]

14. What do you mean that "the most powerful force in the world is the human will"? Can you give an example of what that looks like?

A priest can rush too quickly to pray for someone, and sometimes this can do more harm than good. A woman once emailed that she brought her husband, whom she thought was possessed, to a local priest (not her pastor) for prayer. His grandfather was a Freemason, she reported, and this must be the reason their marriage was failing. She told the priest what

35 Weller, *Roman Ritual*, 223–29.

prayers of minor exorcisms to pray for him, but she failed to inform the priest that her husband did not want to be prayed over, that they had fought about it the entire way to the prayer session, and that their marriage was falling apart. He needed exorcism now, she explained, and that would fix the marriage (or so she presumed).

First of all, imagine if this were in the physical and medical realm. She diagnosed her husband's illness by researching on the internet, then took him to the doctor and told the doctor what medicine to prescribe and what procedure to perform. And, amazingly, he complies! This would *never* happen in the medical system, but because many well-intended clergy desire to be "pastoral," this priest did what the woman asked, and the results were devastating. The husband quietly let the priest pray over him, but within weeks, he left his wife, a deep division soon came upon her and her children, and she found herself rife in legal and spiritual problems.

She then reached out to Liber Christo for help, hoping we would intervene and somehow have *another* priest pray over her now-estranged husband so she could save her marriage. Simply stated, she overstepped her bounds of authority and was retaliated against quite fiercely. Rather than speaking to an exorcist, the couple should have made an appointment with their parish priest, sought a Catholic counselor or program for troubled marriages, and worked on the requisite virtues for a successful marriage. The husband should have also worked with their parish priest and not allowed his wife to go searching for any priest willing to pray prayers of exorcism. There are many self-styled, self-trained, and even rogue exorcists and lay-practitioners out there willing to pray over anyone, so one must always work within the local system (parish and diocesan).[36] The woman usurped her husband's (and her

[36] See IAE, *Guidelines for the Ministry of Exorcism*, 21.

pastor's) authority and manipulated a well-intended priest by convincing him her husband needed exorcism. The result was that she, her husband, their marriage, and their children, paid the price.

Manipulation is the lowest form of witchcraft. Here we also have an example of subverting the normal channels of grace and using the office of priesthood for deliverance prayers in a superstitious way. "The most powerful force in the world is the human will" means that you cannot force your husband, or anyone else, to seek help. God also honors our free will and will not force our conversion. The husband himself needs to seek help because, as stated above, all liberation is self-liberation. A person must make an act of the will to be free. Deliverance prayers are not magic. The priest's stole is not simply our version of a Harry Potter magic wand. A person must desire to be free and have an active agency—that is, willful participation—in his own liberation. A simple prayer session with a priest will not fix something deeply wounded and disordered. Sometimes it even makes things worse, as this woman discovered.

Rather than asserting her own will, she should have increased her traditional devotions and prayers for his conversion, offering her suffering with the intention that he desire to seek liberation. Better to stick to the old, known ways of obtaining grace which are the sacraments, prayer, mortification, and penance. She should have also fixed the marriage with a critical first step: yield to her husband's authority as head of household. This is the first movement and one which allows sacramental grace to flow again into the home. Then ask Our Lady of Sorrows in a special way for the graces of conversion and step onto the path of the deep waters of redemptive suffering that our Lord and Our Lady walked.

15. What do you mean in saying that "all liberation is self-liberation"?

In every case of affliction, the afflicted person must desire to be liberated. This often requires a prolonged act of the will in which he becomes an active agent in his own liberation. In a sense, then, all liberation is self-liberation, even in cases of full possession. Part of that active agency is the imposition of authority of the natural law rights over the person—over himself or herself, and husband over his wife, the parents over children, or priest over laity. The only exception is possession of children who cannot make voluntary acts yet. In those cases, the priest may be the one whose agency Christ uses to drive the demons out, but this is also contingent on the will of the person.

The demon will often claim a right to be present to the person, which is generally untrue if the person is baptized. The Christian, by right, belongs to God through the indelible mark of Baptism. Through sin, however, the Christian grants permission to the demon. He is an interloper, of sorts, but once he receives permission, he quickly moves from tempter to accuser, as we read in Revelation, the "accuser of our brothers . . . accuses them before our God day and night" (Rv 12:10). Accordingly, the spade work of deliverance ministry is the revoking of these permissions, beginning with sacramental confession, to remove the obstacles to grace (that is, divine life) so that grace can go to work again. From there, we begin to force compliance upon the demon who, although bound by natural law, will resist and claim a legal right to be there. In a sense, then, all liberation is self-liberation. Part of that active agency, therefore, is the rejection of the sinful choices and defects which attracted the demon, beginning with confession, but also through prayer and penance. Then he can begin to impose his authority of the natural law rights—over himself or herself, and husband over his wife, the parents over children, or priest over laity.

16. What is the Phase One Prayer Regimen? Why is it helpful in spiritual combat?

Many men have done Exodus 90 and learned that the imposition of order is important to getting his life reordered to prayer and the assertion of the will. The Liber Christo Thirty Day Protocol works in the same way. We have found that the demon responds to the imposition of order as much as to the prayers themselves. Many Catholics think that all that is needed is the "right prayer" to push the demon away, but the prayer regimen brings many benefits to spiritual battle because it teaches you to pray regularly and often. The media fast helps to eliminate unnecessary distractions while at the same time, the focus on the daily Mass readings helps to tap into the liturgical and prayer life of the Church. This means that over time, you learn how to move from vocal prayer to mental prayer, which is key to gaining custody of the mind (where the battle takes place). This weakens the demon and strengthens your will to take back your interiority. When combined with weekly confession, moreover, we have had many people report being liberated from low level afflictions, to include lifelong addictions to pornography or struggles with alcohol abuse.

For a description of the prayer regimen, see Appendix B.

17. I was reading an exorcism from Matthew's Gospel and saw that the verse stating "this kind is not cast out but by prayer and fasting" is missing from some versions. Why was this removed?

There are multiple copies of the New Testament text in the original Greek, some complete and some only fragments (and everything in between). Most of our manuscripts contain quite substantive portions of the New Testament, and all of these copies represent a wealth of evidence for the reliable preservation of the New Testament.

Since handwritten copies were reproduced by human scribes, however, these manuscripts can contain differences from one to another. Mistakes like spelling a word differently, accidentally skipping a word or a line, copying the same line twice, and other normal mistakes in handwriting can be found throughout the manuscript tradition. In addition, there are various manuscript traditions which contain slight variants from one to another. For these and other reasons, we have minor differences between various copies. Such differences between manuscripts are known as "textual variants," for they are places where the text "varies" between some manuscripts and others. The editors of most editions will place such verses in brackets [ ] and leave a footnote for the reader. See, for example, John 20:31, which has two equally reliable and ancient manuscripts, one which reads "these things were written so that you come to believe" and another reading "so that you continue to believe." We simply do not know, based on the manuscript evidence, which Jesus said, and both are valid translations.[37]

[37] See Metzger, *A Textual Commentary on the Greek New Testament*, 256.

The Douay Rheims, which is based on Saint Jerome's Latin Vulgate, is a good place to find some clarity in such disputes. That the Vulgate translation includes Matthew 17:21 ("This kind is not cast out but by prayer and fasting") means he attests to its authenticity. Some modern translations, however, are based on ancient manuscripts that contain the verse, while others on equally ancient manuscripts that do not. The same can be said about Mark 9:29, which reads in some versions, "This kind can only come out through prayer" and others (like the Vulgate) add "and fasting." The New American Bible that most Catholics use is based on what is called the Nestle-Aland Greek New Testament, which does not contain Matthew 15:21 or the phrase "and fasting" in Mark 9:29. Other equally ancient and reliable extant manuscripts contain them, and that is noted in the footnotes.

That being said, Saint Jerome is reliable, and that is sufficient to make note of both the historicity of the texts and also the ancient weapon of fasting. The formula of "through prayer and fasting" is central to driving out the demon (with "fasting" not limited to diet but also various forms of self-denial to include fasting from sleep, the marital act, abstinence from meat on Fridays, etc.). Jesus showed us, moreover, how to engage with the body when he battled the devil in the temptation narrative. To combat Satan, Jesus withdrew from food and also the world for a time of prayer and combat (see Mt 4:1–11; Mk 1:12–13; Lk 4:1–13). The Liber Christo prayer regimen is a form of fasting (from social media, sleep, etc.) and is a prayerful engaging of the body designed to break demonic strongholds found in unholy thoughts and patterns of behavior. As Saint Peter writes, "Therefore, since Christ suffered in the flesh, arm yourselves, also with the same attitude, for whoever suffers in the flesh has broken with sin" (1 Pt 4:1). People who live clean and ordered lives are harder for the demon to compromise (see Mt 5:8; Col 2:5). In general, demons are resisted by faith (see 1 Pt 5:8–9) and some driven out by prayer and fasting (see Mt 17:21; Mk 9:29).

Who does this prescription to "prayer and fasting" apply to, the priest or the energumen (the person afflicted by demons)? Some interpret Matthew 17:21 as the prayer of the Church for the energumen, but not the energumen as one fasting and praying for liberation. The Praenotanda, however, says both need to fast, because fasting is a powerful weapon in the spiritual life. The fasting by the priest (and others in the church, especially monks and cloistered nuns, in union with him) increases the merit of his prayers. This discipline also provides a layer of protection from evil for the priest. The fasting on the part of the energumen does the same but also serves to strengthen his will (much needed for liberation) and, significantly, serves as reparation for his own sins (sins which often have opened the door to the diabolic). It gives him a competitive edge, if you will, over the enemy for, like Jesus in the desert for forty days (see Lk 4:1–13), he battles through prayer and fasting. The priest does fast and do penance, but not instead of the afflicted person, as if vicariously, but to prepare for battle.

We fight an ancient enemy, and the ancient weapons are best. Listen to the words of Saint Cyprian, who was preparing his followers for martyrdom. He himself was martyred (in AD 258) shortly after he wrote this:

> Your unity, your strength have become shining examples of these virtues to the rest of the brethren. Divine providence has now prepared us. God's merciful design has warned us that the day of our own struggle, our own contest, is at hand. By that shared love which binds us close together, we are doing all we can to exhort our congregation, to give ourselves unceasingly to fastings, vigils and prayers in common. These

> are the heavenly weapons which give us the strength to stand firm and endure; they are the spiritual defenses, the God-given armaments that protect us.[38]

Notably, "fastings, vigils and prayers in common" are not mere pious devotions, he says, but are "heavenly weapons which give us the strength to stand firm and endure." They are our spiritual body armor, "the spiritual defenses, the God-given armaments that protect us." Thus, all who do battle need to fast.

18. I'm worried about you looking at occult websites to prepare for your radio show. I don't want you to get attacked by demons. Isn't curiosity dangerous? Didn't Eve get in trouble for curiosity?

Thank you for your concern; we truly appreciate that. Looking at occult websites out of curiosity is spiritually dangerous, but when a researcher is working in his field, he practices studiosity. The FBI has technicians who assist in proving the guilt of alleged child sex offenders by scouring their computers for evidence. This is also a dangerous job which should be approached with proper studiosity. Whenever we research the occult, the purpose is to study and prepare an accurate presentation for our listeners.

Saint Thomas Aquinas also clearly states that curiosity is a vice.[39] Usually the distinction (and blurring of lines) lies in one's vocation and apostolic works. Studiosity is not knowledge for the sake of knowledge, however, but the right ordering of a pursuit of knowledge. Saint Thomas also noted the pride of knowledge when its pursuit becomes detached from

---

38 Cyprian of Carthage, *Epist. LVI*, in *ANF*, 352.
39 Saint Thomas Aquinas, *ST* II-II, q. 167.

truth. When we bump up against evil in our research, we must stay focused on the truth of Jesus Christ and the salvation of souls and not give in to the curiosity of evil itself. This is why the demon will often bait us to dive deeper into this or that evil, especially out of curiosity if we are not steeped in our faith, the sacraments, and a daily life of prayer. We always pray first by binding any demons who would try to afflict us, any curses associated with the opening of the site, and do our research. Bind, pray, stick to the facts.

Chapter II
GENERAL QUESTIONS

"Therefore, he [the priest] will be mindful of the words of our Lord (Mt 17:20), to the effect that there is a certain type of evil spirit who cannot be driven out except by prayer and fasting. Therefore, let him avail himself of these two means above all for imploring the divine assistance in expelling demons, after the example of the holy fathers; and not only himself, but let him induce others, as far as possible, to do the same.

"The subject, if in good mental and physical health, should be exhorted to implore God's help, to fast, and to fortify himself by frequent reception of penance and holy communion, at the discretion of the priest. And in the course of the exorcism, he should be fully recollected, with his intention fixed on God, whom he should entreat with firm faith and in all humility. And if he is all the more grievously tormented, he ought to bear this patiently, never doubting the divine assistance.

"Finally, after the possessed one has been freed, let him be admonished to guard himself carefully against falling into sin, so as to afford no opportunity to the evil spirit of returning, lest the last state of that man become worse than the former."

—*Praenotanda to the Rite of Exorcism, nos. 10, 12, 21*

From the Field: "My habit is falling off of me."

A priest called to consult on a case. He lives in an inner city, and people from the area go to him for exorcism, and he has a long list of regulars who come to him for exorcism. An energumen had done a specific satanic ritual in a cemetery and joined a coven. Now he wanted out. The priest went into detail about the ritual, the type of bodily gestures and rituals performed and incantations prayed. He concluded with his question:

"What prayer do I pray to drive this demon out?"

"I dunno."

"What do you mean, you don't know? You're the expert."

What the priest was looking for is a quick fix, a special ritual or prayer that he can use to counteract this specific type of witchcraft this individual had engaged in. The problem was that the priest was not using any protocol or any preparation of the energumen before praying prayers of exorcism. Nor does he ask that the people who come to him for prayer go to confession and be in the state of grace. People show up, he prays a diagnostic prayer, and if they manifest, he goes straight into exorcism. Many come back week after week. Most experience manifestations of the diabolic, but very few are actually liberated. This is a common model, however, and can be effective—or at least light up the cosmos a bit. There is a difference between a manifestation, an extraction, and an actual liberation. The latter are rare and, as a general rule, require a state of grace, some ascesis and penance on the part of the energumen to include development of virtue, and a reordering of one's life to prayer.

"I mean" I told him, "there are myriads of ways to apostatize, but one way to reconcile with God."

"But what prayers should I pray to help him?"

"It's hard to tell exactly what's going, as there are generally no quick fixes. But I read about this Jewish carpenter who was also an exorcist, and he once said, 'This type only comes out through prayer and fasting.'"

"I am fasting so much," the priest said, "my habit is falling off of me."

"I'm not talking about you, Father. I'm talking about the guy. He's the one who did the stuff at the cemetery, ritual prostitution, abandoned his Catholic faith, committed apostasy, and worshipped a false god. There has to be some satisfaction for these grave sins. He has to get his house in order. This kind only comes out through prayer and fasting. Put him on the protocol and you will get clarity on what to do next."

Many priests fail to discern the psychological or whether the individual is in a state of grace, which often does more harm than good. This man did not want to be reconciled with God the Father, but rather, he wanted to be demon-free. He was never liberated, and the priest was eventually removed and sent to a retreat center for health reasons.

In this section, we field questions which address the broader picture of spiritual warfare.

1. What about the seventy apostles in Luke chapter ten? They were lay people, right?

If you have a low ecclesiology and place the priesthood of the laity as equal to that of the ordained, as do Protestants, then, yes, those are lay people. If you read the text as Saint Luke presents, and through the lens of the received tradition of the Church Fathers, however, then these represent the expansion of the authority of the Apostles into the presbytery.

The number seventy recalls the appointment of seventy *presbuteroi* (where we get the word "priest") who received "a portion of the spirit" of Moses who would share the burden of administration (Nm 11:6). Because they have also been "sent," Jesus reminds them of the import of what being sent means: "Whoever listens to you listens to me. Whoever rejects you rejects me. And whoever rejects me rejects the one who sent me" (Lk 10:16). In the Catholic tradition, these were not lay people. Thus, Saint Augustine concludes that "no one doubts that the twelve Apostles foreshadowed the order of Bishops, so also we must know that the seventy-two represented the presbytery, that is, the second order of priests."[1] Thus, the twelve are the first tier of the hierarchy (the episcopacy), and the seventy are the second tier (the priests in union with their bishops).

Saint Luke also says, "After this the Lord *appointed* seventy others whom he sent ahead of him" (Lk 10:1). As the mission expands now to seventy, Saint Luke notes that these men were "appointed" by Jesus in Luke 10:1, a word used in the Bible only here and the "appointing" of Judas's successor in Acts 1:24. The Greek word means "to commission, dedicate for a purpose, and appoint to an office." This invokes the language of the hierarchical office of ordination (notably, being on the parish council or a lay prayer team leader are not offices in the Catholic Church to which one is "appointed" in this sense). That the seventy share in the apostolic and prophetic office is implied in the parallel instructions Jesus gave to the twelve ("carry no money bag," etc.; Lk 9:3; Lk 10:4). To the seventy, however, he added the command to "greet no one on the way," echoing Elisha's command to his servant whom he sent in 2 Kings 4:29. In addition, only Luke recounts the words of Jesus in reference to "hand to the plow" (Lk 9:61) for would-be disciples, suggesting the Elijah-Elisha paradigm of

[1] Cited by Saint Thomas Aquinas in *Catena Aurea,* 344. For more, see Schneider, "Sacerdotal Office, Invisible Fire."

prophetic sending as the contextualization of the expansion from the twelve now to seventy. Notably, Elisha was behind a "plow" of twelve oxen when Elijah threw his cloak over him and called him to the prophetic ministry (1 Kgs 19:19). Thus, the seventy are to the twelve as the presbytery (priests) will be to the episcopy (bishops), in the same manner the great prophets of old called and sent disciples.

This is affirmed by the earliest and most comprehensive list of the seventy Apostles as found in the writings of Saint Hippolytus of Rome (c. 170–235 AD), who includes such notable figures as Saint Luke himself, Saint James, the brother of the Lord, Saint Matthias who replaced Judas, and Saint Barnabas. Even Demas, who Paul tells Timothy "deserted me" (2 Tm 4:10), Saint Hippolytus recounts as having apostatized "and became a priest of idols." One detail to which Saint Hippolytus gives each of the seventy is important: they were all ordained, and he recounts that nearly all were bishops of early apostolic sees.[2]

2. I am part of an exorcism team, and I am getting emotionally invested in the case of this petitioner. I feel like I should counsel her and personally invest myself in her case and help her get liberated. Thoughts?

Stay in your lane. The demon is trying to draw you out of your lane and has already triggered your emotions in a disordered way. Here is the set up: he draws you in emotionally by exploiting your paternal instinct to help, to fix things, and perhaps even projected thoughts to you such as, "I can help

[2] Hippolytus of Rome, *On the Seventy Apostles of Christ*, in *ANF*, 254–57.

her better than Father can. He doesn't see what is really going on." That slight usurpation of authority is the angle he will use to get inside your guard. The demon also knows that if you have not completely mastered your sexual desire, and now that your guard has been lowered, he can come inside striking range. His second move is to alter the images of this woman in your imagination, and images of you in her imagination, at the same time distancing you from your wife, creating division in your marriage to slow down the flow of sacramental grace. Once you and the woman both appropriate those projected distorted images, he then begins to gradually romanticize (and sexualize) them. Now he just needs to wait for the opportune moment. We have seen many priests being taken out with this exact scenario.

Father Ripperger once asked a demon why he kept doing the same things to tempt humans, and the demon responded, "Because they work." Part of the reason the Church restricts who can perform exorcisms comes from experience. From as early as the fourth century are found accounts of itinerant exorcists who were getting emotionally and eventually sexually involved with possessed women.[3] Many holy exorcists have lost their priestly faculties, and have even been removed from the priesthood, because their emotions were inflamed and they began improperly touching the possessed woman with lust.

This door can be opened when, during the prayer sessions, lay associates touch an energumen's body as handlers. That skin-to-skin contact can also be taken as a permission by the demon, which opens a door to you (which is why we do not

---

3 As Bishop Jeffrey Grob noted: "It seems that not only inappropriate advances were being made by the exorcists, especially when men were exorcising women, but the possessed were sometimes even being charged for the services of the exorcist." Grob, "Discipline on Exorcism," 57.

have handlers in our system). Besides serving in prayer support during sessions, the primary job of a layperson on the team is catechizing the possessed person during the second phase in preparing them for prayer. In addition, you should never be alone with a person of the opposite sex. The fact that you are emotionally invested in her should be a huge warning flag, so tell your exorcist what is happening. He should remove you from the case and pray specific prayers over you to sever any clinging and/or retaliating spirits. Go to confession as well, because the demon of impurity may very well be "inside your wire." God is allowing you to see your defects so that you work on your own virtue and holiness.

3. Can other religions conduct exorcisms? I thought that the "gods of the Gentiles are demons" (Ps 96:5)?

That ancient peoples such as the Egyptians and the Jews performed exorcisms is well attested. Jewish exorcists, for example, existed at the time of Christ, and presumably before (see Acts 19:13; Mt 12:27). Although not found in the Old Testament, in intertestamental Judaism (historical evidence from the time of Hellenistic Judaism around the Second Temple period, 516 BC–70 AD), we find that the title "son of David" was invoked as evidence of the belief that Solomon's wisdom included the power to cure disease and drive out demons. This may be part of what is behind the title "son of David" as applied to Jesus in the New Testament (see Lk 18:38; Mt 12:22–24, et al.). In the early Church, as the Gospel was being spread, the name of Jesus was invoked to drive out demons from pagan converts. This continues today, and eventually the Rite of Exorcism developed for use by the ordained only.

We know that non-Christian exorcists, however, exist to this day. How can modern non-Christians have power if the name of Jesus and the power and jurisdictional authority were given to the Church/apostles (cf. Lk 9:1; Mk 16:17) and through them, to us Christians? The answer lies in our understanding of natural law and the authority structure granted therein. For example, through natural law, a person (of any or no religion) has natural law spiritual authority over himself (i.e., man has the right of self-determination, as shown above), the space he occupies, his temporal goods, his wife and children (or a wife over her husband's body and also over her children and temporal goods). Thus, if a demon is afflicting what a person has natural law authority over, he must yield to the commands of that person when those rights are asserted. When a non-Christian exorcist assists a person in driving out a demon, he is tapping into the natural law structure established by God and leading him or her to self-deliverance. They are, in effect, invoking the rules of the engagement set by God and the demon yields, as he is bound by the construct of the natural law. So, if the demon has no legal claim, then a *de jure* appeal to natural law is sometimes sufficient to diminish nefarious activity.

The divine law (or also known as divine positive law) is a further layering of juridical authority and includes constructs such as the moral, ecclesial, canonical, and sacramental law of the Catholic Church. This additional layering builds upon the natural law which was embedded into humanity from the beginning. The experience of Catholic exorcists, however, is that many of these non-Catholic exorcists (including Protestants) often reach a stopping point in many cases where they cannot lead a person to self-deliverance through an assertion of rights or through conversion. Where there is an institutional element to the entry point, for example, there generally must be an institutional response by the Church which Christ established and granted juridical authority over all demons.

At times, where there is grave evil present, or deeply rooted sin and the like, only the authority of the Catholic priest (who alone and uniquely stands *in persona Christi*) with the mandate from the local bishop can drive the demon out. That is, when it is a "big one," only the Catholic exorcist has the requisite power and authority to drive the demon out. The smaller demons can be driven out, even among pagans and non-Catholics, because the rules of engagement (i.e., natural law) have been set by our merciful God.

4. I was at a conference where someone manifested. The priest came over and people prayed until he calmed down. Does that mean the person was delivered?

A manifestation (from the Latin *manifestare,* meaning "to show clearly, exhibit, manifest, or reveal") is when a demon shows himself, normally in some physical manner. The demon traffics in the senses, so what you saw was the demon appropriating the bodily senses of someone in response to something he did not like (perhaps just getting too close to a priest and the Blessed Sacrament, or he sensed interior movements of metanoia in the person).

There is a difference, however, between a manifestation, an extraction, and a liberation. In a *manifestation,* the demon appropriates the senses of the afflicted person and comes forth in some way. Demons tend to be either opened or closed, meaning some will be very talkative and even violent, while others "go deep" and are not inclined to come to the surface. The fact that a demon manifested at a prayer meeting or church event does not necessarily mean he was extracted. An *extraction* means a demon is expelled from the person. The demon does not want to show himself, and when he manifests, it is by God's command for some salvific purpose. That is, God wants to reveal to a priest or the family or the individual that there is a deeper problem so that they will ultimately seek conversion. The demon may manifest because the person was too close to the sacred or he sensed conversion. The demon acts like a pit bull does when someone gets too close to its master's property.

Thus, some people go to a charismatic prayer meeting, or other spiritual retreat, and seemingly "all hell breaks loose." People who pray over others can experience raw, spiritual power when the name of Jesus is invoked, but this can deceive them into thinking they have spiritual superpowers of some kind. We have found that what they actually did was draw the demon out through prayer and invoking the name of Jesus in the context of a conversion experience. This does not mean the demon was expelled; rather, he reacted to the prayers which forced a manifestation. This may sometimes mean the demon will retaliate against everyone involved, or attach themselves to participants, which we have seen in consistent patterns with our cases.

In addition, a manifestation, or even an extraction, does not mean that the person was liberated. Remember, the Gerasene demoniac's name was Legion, he explained, "because we are many" (Mk 5:9). A Roman legion consisted of roughly six thousand legionaries. This means you may extract one or two or even take out an entire cohort, but in the case of possession, the primary possessing demon (in cases of possession) is going nowhere until the hierarchical Church weighs in and the individual has grown in sufficient virtue and desire to be free. *Liberation*, therefore, means not only have demons been extracted but also all the impediments to grace which are blocking reconciliation with God the Father have been removed. The person is not only "demon free" but his soul is reconciled to God through the sacraments.[4] What you likely saw was a manifestation. That person will need to see his parish priest for further help.

5. Why is the prologue in John 1:1–14 used during the rite of Exorcism? It's also read at the end of the Latin Mass.

In the end of the Latin Mass, the priest faces the altar, places his hands in the *orans* position, turns to the people, and gives the blessing and distributes the merits of the Mass through the final blessing. *Ite, missa est*: "Go, it [the sacrifice] has been sent." The laity are also now sent into the world to bring Christ to every corner of the secular sphere where they live and work.

The priest then carries the Lectionary to the left side of the altar and reads the Prologue of Saint John. There is symbolism in that movement. As Monsignor George Moorman explains: "The Jews, to whom the 'Gospel of the Kingdom' was first preached, rejected it. It was then carried to the Gentiles. This is symbolized by carrying the Missal to the other side of the altar. Transferring the Missal from one side of the altar to the other also recalls to our minds how Our Lord was led about from one iniquitous judge to another."[5] By reading the Prologue, the priest is proclaiming the creation narrative from the perspective of Christ, "the Word made flesh" (Jn 1:14). Through the merits of the Holy Sacrifice of the Mass, Christ makes all things new. The liberation and salvation of the world through divinity of Christ, the eternal Word who "became

4 Liber Christo, *Mentors, Case Facilitators, and GP Priests*, 7–8.
5 Moorman, *The Latin Mass Explained*, 110.

flesh and dwelt among us" (Jn 1:14), is now proclaimed to the nations and into the cosmos.[6]

The solemn rite of Exorcism starts with psalms, imprecatory prayers, and then the priest signs the possessed person in the forehead, lips, and breast, and then also proclaims the Prologue of John. This is, in a sense, the priest punching the devil right in the nose, reminding the demon of his expulsion from paradise as well as the restoration of humanity by the Incarnate Word in the new creation. For us, the Prologue is a message of hope; for the demon, it is a reminder of his eternal damnation. The demons, along with the damned who reject Christ, will hear these words thunderously proclaimed at their final judgment.

6. Why do demons hate Gregorian Chant and Latin?

The famous exorcist Father Gabriele Amorth once quipped that "the devil hates Latin." The field experience of most exorcists confirms his observation. We have often seen the demon mock a priest's Latin in an attempt to dissuade him from using the primitive language. He knows what we assert: we fight an ancient enemy, and the ancient weapons are best, including the ancient language of the Roman Catholic Church.

There are three sacred languages—Hebrew, Greek, and Latin. Each is sacred because each is linked to the cross of Jesus Christ. When Jesus was crucified, Saint John noted that Pilate had placed upon the cross the words "Jesus the Nazarene King of the Jews" in those three languages (Jn 19:20). Hebrew is the language of the God's People of the Old Covenant (and Masoretic text of the Old Testament), Greek is

---

6 This is also why it is salutary for Catholics to pray the Angelus at 6:00 a.m., noon, and 6:00 p.m., as they join voices with the Church universally in proclaiming these salvific realities.

the language of the New Testament and Septuagint Old Testament. Latin is the common language of the Church, and its sacred character is found also in Latin's use in the sacred liturgy, and the Vulgate Bible. All Church documents are written in Latin.

Because of the connection to the cross and because it is the common language of the Church, Latin is more pleasing to God than other languages. This fact is suggested in the phenomenon *de facto* that the Latin exorcism is more efficacious than in the vernacular. The Catholic Church has been using this language in exorcisms to drive the demon out for centuries. When the priest pulls out the Solemn Rite in Latin, it is as if the demon hears the famous fight announcer Michael Buffer saying, "Let's get ready to ruuuumble!" The demon sees the entire connection with the cross of Christ and the Mystical Body.

The same can be said for Gregorian chant. In fact, we have seen that the use of Gregorian chant often causes a demon to manifest instantly. For this reason, we recommend playing chant (specifically, the monks of Santo Domingo de los Silos) on low level continually in the home. Just as the Latin language is ancient and sacred (used for sacred purpose for centuries in the liturgical life of the Church), Gregorian chant is ancient and sacred and used for centuries in monasteries (and sacred liturgy) throughout the world.

At the beginning of the Rule of Saint Benedict, the father of Western monasticism who lived in the fifth century reminds monks that "this is how you have chosen to do battle."[7] The demon can tell, moreover, the difference between the chant of consecrated celibate monks or consecrated virgins and that of a concert by a choir of well-trained lay people. While the voices may sound the same, the former is prayed from the

7 *Rule of Saint Benedict*, Prologue.

heart of the Church as part of her liturgical worship. It is not just *what* is chanted (sacred hymns and psalms) but also *by whom* (consecrated virgins), *from where* (the sacred space of a monastery or cloister), and *when* (the liturgical calendar) is significant. His cosmic hearing knows that the liturgical chant of consecrated monks or nuns bears with it the weight of the Church and the monastic tradition. Gregorian chant, therefore, is an offensive weapon in spiritual battle.

Conversely, Protestant praise and worship may have God as its subject and even give you an emotional high (which is its goal), but that does not make it sacred music. A religious themed (even high energy) music may create an emotional experience, but that does not make it liturgical music—that is, part of the sacred liturgy of the Church. In the Benedictine tradition, this liturgical action is referred to as the *opus Dei*, or the work of God. Because Gregorian chant is used (in Latin) by consecrated religious as part of the sacred liturgy, it is also sacred. The demon knows the difference between that and music sung by lay people.

We have even seen the demon manifest at the sound of Gregorian chant and decidedly not manifest with similar, seemingly sacred, music. The former, it was discerned, was chanted by Benedictine monks and the latter by a lay choir. Both sounded equally pleasing to the ear, but one made the demon fall to the floor and the other had zero effect. The difference is not simply the words themselves but the context in which the chant is sung and by whom it is chanted.

7. Is it ok to watch horror movies?

Listen to the words of Jesus: "The eye is the lamp of the body. So, if your eye is sound, your whole body will be full of light; but if your eye is not sound, your whole body will be full of darkness. If then the light in you is darkness, how great is the darkness!" (Mt 6:22–23). The point of this passage is that much of our lifestyle is determined by how we use our eyes—what we choose to allow into our interiority through what we watch and read. What people see with their eyes shapes their soul because the eyes are the windows to the soul. As stated in a question above, demons traffic through the senses. Accordingly, Saint John Vianney warned, "We must watch over our mind, our hearts, and our senses, for these are the gates by which the devil enters in."[8] We become what we experience through our senses, or as the old saying goes: "Garbage in garbage out."

Three things can happen when you watch a horror movie. On rare occasions, you see the reality of evil which causes you to examine your life and your conscience and have compunction in your heart. This drives you to repentance and back into a right relationship with God. This is extremely rare and unwise to experiment. Two, and more commonly, curiosity leads you to the rabbit hole of the diabolic and you become focused on the demon and enamored by the phenomena. Three, watching horror movies opens you to the diabolic. If you have other openings through past sinful behavior or are in a state of mortal sin, you expose yourself and your home to diabolic influence.

Because the demon has access to what is contained in your imagination and memory, watching horror movies builds up stock footage in your brain that demons can use to harass you, often at the most inopportune of times. Father Ripperger highlights the vulnerabilities created by viewing unholy images and advises that Catholics

> must be sure to avoid not only sinning themselves but of watching the sins of others. By viewing the sins of others,

---

[8] Saint John Vianney, *Sermons*, 120.

> e.g. watching someone commit fornication on TV or killing someone in a graphic fashion on TV, they provide the sense data for the demons to make suggestions to them by forming images in their imagination. In fact, the more programs one watches on TV, the more demons can influence a person's actions since they have more data to use. The more we become familiar with the imagery of sin, the easier it is for the demons to coax us into sinning because we have lost our inhibitions with respect to the sin because we are comfortable with it.[9]

Similarly, Father Amorth said, "I oppose the viewing of horror films, and I advise people, particularly the young, not to patronize them. If the demon's mission is to tempt man, then viewing these films—which tend to normalize brutal situations, particularly, where the demon is the protagonist—can seriously upset fragile minds and stir others to sadistic emulation. Why voluntarily subject oneself to evil temptations?"[10] The disordered curiosity with demons and viewing evil can become an entry point for the diabolic to begin to work on you. The words of the Psalmist are good counsel for us in deciding what movies to watch: "I follow the way of integrity; when will you come to me? I act with integrity of heart within my royal court. I do not allow into my presence anyone who speaks perversely. Whoever acts shamefully, I hate; no such person can be my friend" (Ps 101:2–3).

For a Christian to watch a horror movie is like walking into a bad neighborhood at night, by yourself, and with a big sign on your chest that says, "I'm unarmed, and I have a pocket full of money."

Rather than horror films, watch good, Catholic filming and wholesome movies.

---

9 Ripperger, *Science of Mental Health*, 535.
10 Amorth, *Exorcist Explains the Demonic*, 56–7.

8. If I pray prayers outside a Planned Parenthood abortion facility, what prayer protocol is recommended?

First of all, know that when anyone steps out in protest to stop women from having an abortion, they had better be in a state of grace and have a vibrant prayer life. This is the unholiest of ground, and when Christians protest there in quiet prayer, the demons animating the actions in that facility will take notice. You are lobbing prayer bombs into their perimeter and helping save babies in the process. Thus, the demon will assess the protestors and probe those with vulnerabilities. In addition, you do not own the property and should not plant Saint Benedict medals there, as this could cause retaliation. Use sacramentals like holy water and exorcized salt on yourself for spiritual protection.

If you are contracepting at home but militating against offenses of the generative principle, you may get taken to the proverbial woodshed. If the demon sees a priest there who neglects praying the office daily, or skips Mass on his day off, or lacks spiritual discipline, he may also be tested. Defending the unborn is highly noble and gravely needed, but those who militate against this evil must be sure to have their spiritual house in order.

See Appendix C for the suggested prayer regimen for those who pray in front of an abortion clinic.

9. I'm going to an abortion clinic to inspect it as part of my job. What sacramentals do I wear? What prayers do I pray?

You do not have any authority at the abortion clinic other than over yourself and by virtue of the office of your particular job. What you want to do is pray prayers of protection against any clinging spirits (evil spirits which may attach to you and retaliate). Before you go, be sure to be in a state of grace and also pray prayers of protection before and after. If you haven't already been invested in the brown scapular, that is a good sacramental to wear. Have the Miraculous Medal and the Saint Benedict medal on you somewhere. Praying the Chaplet of Saint Michael beforehand would also be helpful for protection. Before you enter your home that evening, say a simple binding prayer to block any clinging spirit from entering into your home and sprinkle your home with holy water that evening before going to bed.

See the appendix for suggested prayers. The same regimen can be used for law enforcement, military personnel, teachers, counselors, therapists, etc. before and after work.

10. I am a police detective working major crime cases including assaults, sex assaults, and homicides. Is there an appropriate binding prayer that I can use before going into an interview?

You may use imprecatory prayers over yourself and your workspace but not over the body of the criminal. You can pray a "perimeter prayer" over the interview room, just like a teacher can over his/her classroom. If you are not in a state of grace, your prayer has no power. Thus, know that demon will try to compromise you so that your prayer has no merit. Do the "Light of Christ" prayer for the defendant before praying the perimeter prayer.

Light of Christ Prayer (modified for this situation: cop to suspect)

> Heavenly Father, I ask You in the name of Jesus, and through the precious blood of Jesus Christ to rebuke Satan for taking captive that which is your creation. And I ask You Lord Jesus, to place your crown of thorns around [name] and draw [him/her] to Your Sacred Heart under your mantle of Love. May the Light of Christ be upon [name], so that [he/she] sees [himself/herself] as the Heavenly Father sees [him/her]; and that I see [name] as the Heavenly Father sees [name]. Mother Mary most Holy, please hold [name] in the mantle of your motherly protection and cover [name] with the veil of your holiness and bring [name] to a knowledge of the truth. Amen.

See Appendix C for Perimeter Prayer.

11. Can a Catholic practice Yoga? I am not sure this is something that any Christian should be doing.

Two principles apply here. First, certain bodily actions are imbued with symbolic and spiritual significance from which they cannot be separated.[11] A baseball player, for example, who makes the sign of the cross before taking the plate evokes a Christian and Trinitarian symbolism regardless of his intention. Bodily gestures have meaning. This works in the negative as well. Would you walk down parts of Chicago, Detroit, or Los Angeles, for example, wearing the known colors of an opposing gang out of curiosity to see what happens? You would likely learn very quickly that what we do with our bodies has consequences.

---

[11] For basic principles, see USCCB, *Evaluating Reiki.*

Sacred objects as well cannot be separated from their sacred use. King Belshazzar learned this lesson the hard way when he used the sacred vessels from the temple for profane purposes (see Dn 5:1–30). Conversely, certain objects used for evil cannot be "decommissioned" or "blessed" and the evil associated with them suddenly removed. A healthy person would not, for example, take the forceps used at an abortion clinic and place them on their fireplace mantle. We are a body-soul composite, and certain bodily actions take on a deeper significance. Both bodily actions and inanimate objects can act as agents of preternatural power. Catholics know this instinctively, as demonstrated in the bodily actions in Holy Mass and the inanimate agency of the divine in sacramentals such as holy water and exorcised salt.

A second principle builds upon the first and is found in the psalms, one of which states: "The gods of the Gentiles are demons" (Ps 96:5). As Father Mitch Pacwa notes, *yoga* "can refer to physical (hatha), mental (raja), sexual (tantra), or other disciplines to achieve enlightenment."[12]

The Pontifical Council for Culture and the Pontifical Council for Interreligious Dialogue, moreover, list yoga as one of many neo-gnostic, New Age practices which are inconsistent with Christian beliefs and practices. With regard to New Age, the document states:

> It is difficult to separate the individual elements of *New Age* religiosity—innocent though they may appear—from the overarching framework which permeates the whole thought-world on the *New Age* movement. The gnostic nature of this movement calls us to judge it in its entirety. From the point of view of Christian faith, it is not possible to isolate some elements of *New Age* religiosity as acceptable to Christians, while rejecting others. Since the *New*

[12] Pacwa, *Catholics and the New Age*, 225.

> *Age* movement makes much of a communication with nature, of cosmic knowledge of a universal good—thereby negating the revealed contents of Christian faith—it cannot be viewed as positive or innocuous.[13]

As in other New Age practices, the bodily poses in yoga, therefore, cannot be "isolated" from their religious meaning, as the postures invoke the various deities towards that goal of spiritual enlightenment. In Hinduism, the religious system from which yoga is derived, the general category of various kinds of disciplines is meant to unite a person with the divine. To achieve that end, the exercises and stretches are representations of various deities. That presents a problem for Catholics, particularly since we believe that we are temples of the Holy Spirit and that God dwells in us through Baptism. Saint Paul reminds us that "whoever is joined to the Lord becomes one spirit with him" (1 Cor 6:17). Is this not the same when someone becomes "joined" (or yoked, or united) by bodily forms which invoke other spirits? What we do in the body has consequences. Thus, "do you not know that your body is a temple of the Holy Spirit within you, whom you have from God, and that you are not your own? For you have been purchased at a price. Therefore, glorify God in your body" (1 Cor 6:19–20).

We have seen cases of possession where the primary entry point was yoga, and the manifestations were consistent with the type of yoga the individuals had done over a period of time (that is, their bodies manifested in the same shape as the yoga poses). Playing Christian music in the background or praying the Rosary beforehand cannot change the essence of what yoga is at its core. There is no baptizing of this and

[13] Pontifical Council for Culture and Pontifical Council for Interreligious Dialogue, *Jesus Christ, the Bearer of the Water of Life: a Christian Reflection on the "New Age,"* no. 4.

isolating it from its pagan roots. Yoga can be an open door to the demons and should be avoided.

12. What do I pray if I am being attacked by things like back pain, neck pain, and headaches (physical) as well as anxiety (psychological). I think it may be demons projecting these attacks. How do I pray against these attacks?

Try the Judo Prayer:

> *Lord, I am experiencing (n.). If this is not from you and is diabolic in origin, I ask you to send it back to its source with a tenfold blessing. If, however, you want me to carry this cross, I willfully accept it, I ask you for the grace to carry it, and I offer it for (insert your intention here).*

If this is a spiritual attack, you now have used the demon's momentum against him, like a spiritual judoka. He will either flee or the Lord will give you the grace to bear the affliction and apply its merits to your intention. This is consistent with Scripture:

- "But to you who hear I say, love your enemies, do good to those who hate you, bless those who curse you, pray for those who mistreat you" (Lk 6:27–28).
- "If your enemy be hungry, give them food to eat, if thirsty, give him to drink. For live coals you will heap on his head, and the Lord will vindicate you" (Prv 25:21–22).
- "A mild answer calms wrath, but a harsh word stirs up anger" (Prv 15:1).

13. A priest told me that I should not pray deliverance or binding prayers for my family. He strongly advised me against this practice. I listen to War College, and I hear quite the opposite.

It is good to work with your parish priest because he knows you and your family best. To what extent you engage is best determined, therefore, within your own vocation and in consultation with your confessor, spiritual director, or parish priest. Many priests, however, were not given any instruction on spiritual warfare in the seminary and, as a result, some have apprehensions about it. You may have to educate yourself first as to why you want to engage at this time.

Bear in mind, however, that the two ends of the authority structure are provision and protection. If you are the husband and head of the household, that means you bear the responsibility to provide for and defend your wife and your children. This includes spiritually, to include their Christian formation (provision) and when you suspect nefarious activity by the enemy in your domestic church (protection). Failure to engage, particularly when your family is under attack, would be a neglect of your vocational obligations. That being said, work with your pastor, but also spiritually clean before anything else. Learn the rules of engagement so that you can safely and effectively defend your home.

Chapter III

THE OCCULT AND MYSTICAL PHENOMENA

"At times, moreover, the evil spirits place whatever obstacles they can in the way, so that the patient may not submit to exorcism, or they try to convince him that his affliction is a natural one. Meanwhile, during the exorcism, they cause him to fall asleep, and dangle some illusion before him, while they seclude themselves, so that the afflicted one appears to be freed.

"Some reveal a crime which has been committed and the perpetrators thereof, as well as the means of putting an end to it. Yet the afflicted person must beware of having recourse on this account to sorcerers or necromancers or to any parties except the ministers of the Church, or of making use of any superstitious or forbidden practice."

—*Praenotanda to the Rite of Exorcism, nos. 7, 8*

From the Field: "But I am not being retaliated against."

Why does Monsignor Stephen Rosetti (see below) refer to "pastoral prudence" with regards to laity imposing hands on others outside of their immediate family? As stated above, experienced exorcists have noted that the barometer [as to whether one stepped outside of his lane of authority] is retaliation. Simply stated, for lay people to impose hands on other lay people outside of their familial construct has no standing in either Scripture or Tradition. As Father Ripperger notes, exorcists have noted cases which arise in individuals who claim a particular charism for healing others or casting out demons. "In some of these cases," he notes, "the people who believed that they had a charism also came under diabolic attack and were perplexed as to why." What is often discerned as a charism may, in fact, be of their own "personal judgment about the matter."[1] The imposition of hands is the gesture of a priest or of a father over his domestic church, or parents blessing their children. Done outside of that, you can open yourself to diabolic retaliation because in so doing, you step outside your lane of authority. But what does that retaliation look like?

A woman reported that after receiving a miraculous healing, she now has the charismatic gift of healing. In her words, she said, "I can raise my hand and command, for example, that 'knee be healed' and it will be healed. It's a gift from Jesus."

"That may be, but unless that's your own knee or your husband's or your children's knee, I would not recommend it."

"Why not? It's my gift."

"First of all, the *Catechism* teaches that all charismatic gifts need to be subjected to the local bishop. Plus, you could be opening yourself up to retaliation if you impose hands outside of your own authority structure."

"I have been doing this safely for years," she replied, "and have not experienced any retaliation at all."

"Sure," I said, "but the power to do something—even something good like healing—does not give you the right to do it.

1 Ripperger, *Dominion*, 140.

That is determined by office, not charism. Even if we don't know, the demon knows, and we can be retaliated against for not staying in our lane."

"What do you mean by retaliation? I haven't experienced anything demonic. Jesus uses me to help others."

"Right, but sometimes the demon can move laterally."

"Laterally?"

"Rather than attacking you, he will move to your spouse or children. You step outside of the protection of authority, and he comes in sideways and works within your authority structure. Tit-for-tat."

"That has not happened to me."

"Tell me about your relationship with your husband."

At that, the woman paused and exhaled. "He doesn't go to Mass anymore. About ten years ago, he started sleeping in the basement. We have not been intimate," she said, "for a long time. Now we have a living arrangement more than a marriage. But he knows I have this gift and pray over people."

It was evident that the woman genuinely wanted to help others.

"How long have you been praying over people?"

"It started about ten or twelve years ago after I was healed."

"About the same time your relationship with your husband became strained. But there's no retaliation?"

"No."

"How about your children?"

At the mention of her children, she again paused.

"I have two grown children," she said, "but they are not married in the Church. They both live with their significant others."

"Any grandchildren?"

"Yes," she replied, "but they are not baptized. That really hurts me."

"But there isn't any retaliation for your healing ministry?"

"I didn't think so, but what do you recommend?"

"Stop praying over other people," I told her, "and fix your marriage."

She then said that Jesus would be disappointed if she did not use the gift that He gave her. This inordinate attachment to a form or gift is a common sign of the presence of the demonic. I recommended that she discuss this with her husband and take this to her spiritual director or parish priest.

"Jesus gave me this gift to heal," she explained.

"He first gave you your husband in the sacrament of Holy Matrimony. Heal your marriage first so you can then together work to bring your children back to the Church. The spiritual healing is far greater—and much more difficult—than the physical."

"I can't disappoint Jesus," she said as she walked away.

Many Christians are naïve to how subtle the demon can be and are blind to his movements. The demon is as the lawyer from hell. Jurisdiction is always an issue. If you have proper jurisdiction and you have proper authority, then power may be rightly (and safely) exercised.

In this chapter, we answer questions on the supernatural and the occult.

1. I know the diabolical can mimic anything. How can we tell the difference between true and false visions?

An apparition is a supernatural vision, which Father Hardon defines as a "psychical experience in which a person or object not accessible to normal human powers is seen and ordinarily also heard."[2] These generally can have three sources. They can

[2] Hardon, *Modern Catholic Dictionary*, 37.

be of divine origin, a psychological hallucination, or a diabolic projection. For this reason, the Church's position on mystical phenomena can be summarized as "open but cautious." Because many people have been led astray (and have led others astray) by false visions or locutions, we offer as advice: *obedience trumps gift.* This is consistent with what the *Catechism* states about charismatic gifts: "It is in this sense that discernment of charisms is always necessary. No charism is exempt from being referred and submitted to the Church's shepherds. 'Their office [is] not indeed to extinguish the Spirit, but to test all things and hold fast to what is good,' so that all the diverse and complementary charisms work together 'for the common good'" (CCC 801).

Saint John Vianney and Saint Padre Pio are examples of saints who had (false) visions of angels, Our Lady, etc. which actually turned out to be demons. These saints, however, were able quickly to discern this because once they started praying, the visions disappeared like a puff of smoke. Other saints have been tempted by false apparitions, locutions, and consolations. We must always be on guard and not rely on consolations and visions as indicators of our relationship with God; as Saint Paul reminds us: "even Satan masquerades as an angel of light" (2 Cor 11:14). Saint John of the Cross warns that the devil can present false, but convincing, images to the memory, and accordingly, the soul should be very suspicious, even rejecting extraordinary phenomena such as visions, locutions, and the like.[3] We encourage the rejection of all mystical phenomena for this simple reason: it is too easy to be deceived.

Look no further than so-called visionaries (and some who even falsely claim to be exorcists) who claim to receive regular communication from heaven about all sorts of matters,

---

3 See Saint John of the Cross, *Ascent of Mt. Carmel,* 227, in Kavanaugh and Rodriguez, trans., *Collected Works of St. John of the Cross.*

including the end times. Some people are more sensitive to the spiritual realm of existence, especially after experiencing an interior conversion. We have found that in most high-level cases of affliction, as the person approaches liberation, the demon often changes tactics and will begin to appear to the person (either through visual or auditory illusions) as Saint Michael or the Blessed Mother, etc. We have found the same with interior locutions (i.e., "God is telling me this or that"). The devil is a good ventriloquist, and his goal is to distract the person from the ordinary path of conversion. The less exciting, but safest, path is prayer, penance, and the sacramental life.

Saint Paul talks about the authentic spiritual gift of the "discernment of spirits" (1 Cor 12:10). God allows certain temptations and trials in order to purify us. He wants us to discern His voice (through the ordinary means) and to love Him for who He is—and not for the spiritual candy He may give us. The best way to discern whether a consolation is from God is to look at the fruit of prayer. Am I growing in virtue, self-denial, and the ability to suffer for Christ? Am I better living my vocation? These indicators are much more secure than emotional consolation. The demon can work on a soul who sees emotional satisfaction as an indicator of God's love, or one who desires "special gifts" rather than a humble path of sanctity and self-denial.

Be prayerful, continue living in a state of grace, and be holy. Do not become curious about these things; rather, keep your "eyes fixed eyes on Jesus, the leader and perfecter of our faith" (Heb 12:2). If you receive a spiritual consolation in prayer, praise God. If you are on a dry path and He seems far away, praise God. As the prophet Habakkuk says: "For though the fig tree blossom not, nor fruit be on the vines, though the yield of the olive fail and the terraces produce no nourishment, though the flocks disappear from the fold and there is no herd in the stalls, yet I will rejoice in the Lord and exult in my saving God" (Hb 3:17–18). This simple trust is the safest path.

2. I purchased a house and found out that a murder-suicide took place there years ago. Sometimes I think the house is haunted. Can that happen?

Some states require these things to be disclosed, and others are *caveat emptor*: let the buyer beware. Every act of grave evil has diabolic accompaniment. There is a difference, however, between a purgative soul (that is, a soul in purgatory seeking prayers) and an infestation of a place by demons. On rare occasion, God allows the former to appear in a place, usually where the person committed some serious sin and is permitted to ask for prayers of reparation. The latter is when generally where a demon lays claim to a locale due to a grave evil occurred at a place. At first sight, they may appear the same, there is a marked difference between the two:

Purgative soul	Demon
non-destructive	destructive
tied to location; can cause a natural fear but not increase in sinful behavior	negative energy; usually accompanied by strife, calumny, detraction
there for prayers (decreases with prayer)	gets worse with prayer
does not follow person	will follow the person
does not speak	sometimes speaks

The first distinction is that purgative souls are not destructive, while demons are destructive, often knocking things off walls (especially religious items). The purgative soul is always silent and there for a single purpose—he seeks prayers to help him make satisfaction for sins he committed which are holding him in purgatory. The demon, conversely, often speaks or communicates and is destructive, causing as much fear and sin as possible. His goal is to drive you away if you offer any opposition, or to lead you to sin if you choose to stay.

You can also tell the difference between a demon and a purgative soul by the response to prayer. The preternatural activity will decrease with prayer if it is a purgative soul but increase if it is a demon. The purgative soul will not follow the person (renter or homeowner) but is bound to a location by God's permission for his singular purpose. The demon, however, can cling to a person and follow him when he leaves, especially if the individual committed grave sins at the house while living there. In grave cases, such as a murder-suicide, satanic rituals, and the like, the demon will also stay bound to the place until forced to leave. Remember, the demon has no rights, *per se*, but will take permissions that we grant him though our sinful behavior. In his mind, it is *his* house because someone in the past consented to the evil that he was animating to take place there or he was ritually summoned there by someone with right authority. Either way, he is claiming title to the property which has now become unholy space, desecrated grounds.

Two stories illustrate this point. The first is recounted by a colleague who recalls when a young priest moved into a new rectory after the previous pastor had died. The rectory, the young priest reported, was "haunted," with doors slamming, cabinets doors opening and closing, etc. While it caused fear in the priest, the presence was not destructive. The diocesan exorcist was called in and eventually found that the previous pastor's desk was filled with Mass requests for the deceased. The deceased priest, it was discovered, had for years accepted

Mass stipends but never actually said the Masses. The local bishop then distributed Mass requests to several priests throughout the diocese, and in thirty days, all the Masses for the dead were said. At that, all preternatural activity in the rectory immediately ceased.

The second is a young man who reported getting awakened at night, being scratched and harassed by demons, and other preternatural activity. He also had a general malaise and sense of fear/dread and restlessness. It was further discovered that the house (a rental property) had previously been rented by the local *curandera*, a woman who practices witchcraft (a witch for hire). To make sure he had the right authority to drive any demon out, the priest had the property owner accompany the house blessing. In addition to mysterious noises, the tenant's two television sets had simultaneously burst into smoke while they were watching movies. When the priest was blessing the house, a cache of horror movies and drug paraphernalia were found. The young man was instructed during the home blessing to destroy the objects and return to the Church by going to confession and never missing Mass. As soon as he returned to the sacraments and the state of grace, the phenomena ceased. He reported later that the issues would recur only when he missed Mass and fell out of the state of grace.

The moral is to work on holiness, fulfill your vocational duties, and always have your new home blessed. Regularly sprinkle the house with holy water and claim it for Jesus Christ. Exorcized salt on the outside perimeter of the property is very effective, as also is blessed oil (smeared in the sign of the cross) over the windows and doors of the house. Once a year, on the feast of the Epiphany each January, the house can be blessed using the Epiphany Blessing. This feast is traditionally celebrated the twelfth day after Christmas, January 6, and marks the end of the liturgical season of Christmas (also known by the popular carol The Twelve Days of Christmas).

This blessing is best performed by a priest but can also be done by the head of household. If you suspect more at work, see your local parish priest. Having Mass said (in the house, if possible, with permission) for the souls in purgatory is often sufficient to make proper satisfaction. Praying the Office of the Dead in the home is also effective to assist purgative souls. If there is a diabolic infestation, the house must be blessed (and perhaps exorcized) by a Catholic priest in order to drive out the demons. Also, demons are attracted to people who live in mortal sin, so they will harass, annoy, and vex the household to cause as much damage and division as possible. This can continue until the entire household, beginning with the husband and wife, gets into a right relationship with God and live in a state of grace. In addition, sometimes people frequently move only to find that every house/apartment they move into is "haunted." In those instances, it is not the location but the individual who is afflicted and they should seek help from their local priest. While home blessings are good to do, recall the words of the famous exorcist Father Amorth: "One good confession is worth a hundred exorcisms."[4]

If a demon manifests, it is because God has forced it to the surface for some salvific purpose. When it happens in the home, this could be allowed by God so that the family will recognize the issue and rally around the individual through prayer. Think of it as a forced intervention by God. The demon is the instrument of salvation. For this reason, our prayer protocol is designed to get the whole family praying together for the liberation of the afflicted soul. Most often, the person is not in a state of grace, the couple is cohabiting, and/or there are cursed objects in the house. The salvific purpose of the

---

4 Amorth, *An Exorcist: More Stories*, 195.

extraordinary diabolic activity is a call to the entire household to return to Christ in all earnestness and begin to live seriously their Catholic faith. Going to confession, returning to Mass, and praying prayers of blessing and protection usually clears out the problem.

In His providence, however, God uses these situations to bring us to conversion and to bring more grace into the familial construct. It is important to always bear in mind that God is completely in control and if there is a manifestation of evil of some kind, it is for some greater purpose. Just as an enemy combatant does not want to be seen and potentially killed, neither does the demon. In like manner, if a demon plagues a place or object (or a soul), he will only manifest when God forces him to do so, usually so that the entire household will turn to God. The demon, in turn, will try to draw the attention away from God, striking fear and despair in the household by performing "parlor tricks" such as slamming doors, making strange noises, animal sounds, moving objects, and the like. One who is in a state of grace rarely experiences such diabolic attention. Maintaining a state of grace is the normal means to living in the freedom in Christ, so such people need first to "clean house"—both spiritually and the physically, beginning with the former.

3. What do I do when I awake at three o'clock in the morning with a sense of evil? Is that just a coincidence or is there more to that hour?

The devil tries to imitate God, and everything he does is a diabolic inversion of the truths of the Catholic faith. Three o'clock in the afternoon is the hour of mercy, the hour Our Lord died on the cross. Three in the morning is the exact opposite time on the clock, the time a tradition says that Jesus Christ was handed over to the Romans for crucifixion by Caiaphas (see Jn 19:34).[5] Hence, the enemy sees that hour as the hour of the triumph of evil and betrayal, the opposite of mercy, and sometimes afflicts souls at that hour. There are some who also hold that Jesus rose from the dead at three o'clock in the morning, so this hour commemorates Our Lord's resurrection. If you are awakened at that hour, or any hour for that matter, receive it as an invitation to prayer, specifically for the souls in purgatory. Ask your guardian angel to protect you and Our Lady to cover you with her mantle, then pray for souls (the Rosary or Divine Mercy chaplet are effective in this situation). Invoke Saint Michael's help, call on the names of Jesus and Mary, pray for souls, and you will find that the evil one will flee (and you will fall back to sleep, rosary in hand and with holy and pious thoughts).

4. I have dreams that often seem very symbolic. Is it wrong to interpret dreams?

Many people ask about dreams and potential meaning or messages from God that they may contain. Dreams can have three basic causes: natural (ourselves), preternatural (angel or demons), or supernatural (God). As to the first cause, Father Ripperger explains, "Prior intellectual and volitional acts can affect our dreams, because they can affect the imagination and the cognitive power."[6] During sleep, moreover, a person is in a supra-sensual state and vulnerable to the reactions of bodily functions and sensory stimulation, psychological projections, as well as demonic influence. Many have experienced,

---

5 See Lefebvre, "Timepiece of the Passion: Last Day in Our Lord's Life," in *Saint Andrew Missal*, 496.

6 Ripperger, *Science of Mental Health*, 612.

for example, nocturnal emissions, which can have either a psychological or spiritual source (or both). That is, what we experience in dreams can be the result of our experiences throughout the day, our daily actions, and even what we eat and drink. In a sense, the brain "reboots" itself through dreams. This means we may be influenced by a lack of custody of the eyes, movies or videos we witnessed, our conversations, etc.

The primary causes of dreams are natural, which can be biological, chemical/pharmacological (drugs or alcohol), or psychological. In the Wisdom literature, for example, Ben Sirach teaches how the daily, emotional struggles which include "wrath and envy, trouble and dread, terror of death, fury and strife" can continue in our dreams: "Even when one lies on his bed to rest, his cares disturb his sleep at night. So short is his rest it seems like none, till in his dreams he struggles as he did by day. Troubled by the visions of his mind, like a fugitive fleeing from the pursuer" (Sir 40:5). The majority of dreams, therefore, are largely "mental garbage" to which we should give little, if any, attention.[7]

A second cause of dreams can also be from good or bad angels, Father Ripperger explains; because they have "a limited influence over our bodies," they can cause an effect in the "appetites, the imagination, the cognitive power and the imagination."[8] Diabolic dreams are vivid, colorful, logical, and generally leave the individual waking up exhausted. When a dream is diabolic, moreover, it will be vivid and sequenced, as if watching a movie. Despite its impact on you at the time, the best advice is to ignore it and reject any disposition in you that may have arisen, such as the emotions of anger, lust, fear, confusion, etc.

---

7 Ripperger, *Science of Mental Health*, 615.

8 Ripperger, *Science of Mental Health*, 612.

The third cause of a dream, which is the least common, can be God. While God has indeed spoken supernaturally through the prophets in dreams, this is extremely rare in salvation history. When God does speak through a dream, moreover, it usually consisted of direct commands, such as when the angel told Joseph, "Rise, take the child and his mother, and flee" (Mt 2:13). Even rarer is dream interpretation. Sirach elsewhere is quite clear in cautioning against placing any stock in dreams:

> Empty and false are the hopes of the senseless, and dreams give wings to fools. Like one grasping at shadows or chasing the wind, so anyone who believes in dreams. What is seen in dreams is a reflection, the likeness of a face looking at itself. How can the unclean produce what is clean? How can the false produce what is true? Divination, omens, and dreams are unreal; what you already expect, the mind fantasizes. Unless they are specially sent by the Most High, do not fix your heart on them. For dreams have led many astray, and those who put their hope in them have perished. (Sir 34:1–7)

In the Old Testament, dream interpretation was largely a pagan phenomenon as seen in the schools of interpreters set up by their kings (see Dn 2:2; Gn 41:8). Dream interpretation was also cautioned against by the prophets: "For the teraphim speak nonsense, the diviners have false visions: deceitful dreams they tell, empty comfort they offer. This is why they wander like sheep, wretched, they have no shepherd" (Zec 10:2). This caution continued in the early Church, seen in the warnings by Saint Justin Martyr that Christians should

> be on your guard lest those demons whom we have been accusing should deceive you, and quite divert you from reading and understanding what we say. For they strive to hold you their slaves and servants; and sometimes by appearances

> in dreams, and sometimes by magical impositions, they subdue all who make no strong opposing effort for their own salvation. And thus do we also, since our persuasion by the Word, stand aloof from them [i.e., the demons] and follow the only unbegotten God through His Son.[9]

Thus, Father Ripperger advises that because "both good and bad angels can cause dreams, the Church has always cautioned people about interpreting dreams."[10] When we advise the rejection of all mystical phenomena, therefore, this includes dream interpretation.

God reveals Himself through the ordinary means of the Catholic faith: the sacraments, to include your vocational sacrament, and the discipline of mental prayer. Due to the demon's ability to project and distort images in the imagination from the "data storage" of your memory, we caution against giving any credence to dreams. At most, look at the general context of the dream—is it sexual, fear-based, centered around a person or place? This general context may show an area of psychological vulnerability (one which the demon may be exposing) that you need to shore up through the practice of virtue and penance. When you experience such a dream, bind in the name of Jesus any demon afflicting you, pray and give it no further thought. When you give credence to your dreams, the demon can exploit your curiosity and tease you down a dangerous path.

On a practical level, prayer or Scripture reading (not television) should be the last thing that enters your mind before falling asleep. Bless yourself and your room/home with holy water. Praying the Divine Praises, the Rosary, and Compline (to include ending with the seasonal Marian hymn) all help

---

9 Saint Justin Martyr, *First Apology*, 14.

10 Ripperger, *Science of Mental Health*, 563.

order the mind through God and wash the events of the day with the sacred. Also, the Punishing Prayer is helpful:

> *Lord Jesus Christ, I ask Thee that from now and until I fall asleep, while I sleep and during my dreams, that if any evil spirit tries to affect me that Thou wouldst punish him by making him focus on the thing that causes the most pain during the entire time he tries to affect me and for ten minutes more. I also ask Thee to not allow him to retaliate.*[11]

In addition, playing Gregorian chant at low level in the home helps to fight off spirits of the air. To combat night terrors, if needed, we recommend using blessed candles.

5. Is there such a thing as a Chucky doll?

Ever since the *Twilight Zone* episode called "Talking Tina" came out in 1963, people have been fascinated with the idea of evil talking baby dolls. The modern *Chucky* horror movies took Talking Tina to the next level of evil. In the field, we have encountered instances of a child's talking doll suddenly saying things off-script—that is, things not in its programmed repertoire of sentences ("Why did you leave me in the closet?" or "Why are you ignoring me?"). We have even seen talking Teddy Bears and the like. The demon can animate rational and irrational creatures, and even inanimate objects. Technically speaking, this phenomenon is known as the inanimate agency of preternatural power where the demons use various material objects in an inverted, but parallel, manner of Catholic sacramentals. We refer to these as parlor tricks, as they are meant to distract you by focusing instead on the signs and wonders of Jesus Christ.

---

[11] Ripperger, *Deliverance Prayers for the Laity*, 34.

6. What are "satanic" rosaries?

Cursed objects generally come in three forms. One, there is some intrinsic evil associated with the object, such as Freemasonic regalia, abortion tools, satanic altars, etc. Two, a neutral object can be cursed and used for evil purpose, such as barbie dolls, animal feathers, etc. Three, sometimes occultists will curse cursed religious objects, such as rosaries and medals. For a time, there were "satanic rosaries" made of plastic and string and shipped to parishes for free, many of which ended up in Catholic homes.

Glow-in-the-dark rosaries have been a favorite of Catholic children for decades, which perhaps is why these were once targeted as a way to get cursed objects into Catholic homes (and many shipped to parishes for free). When these cursed objects are inadvertently brought into a home, they act in an inverted manner to a blessed object. Instead of invoking God's blessing, they invoke the devil's curse. Many parents have reported that these cursed objects were accompanied by nightmares, sickness, bursts of anger and fighting, and other disruptions of family life. Notably, in nearly every case, this all ceased when the cursed objects were destroyed.

For example, a large box of "free" rosaries recently arrived at a local parish. One of the office ladies had heard about the so-called "satanic" rosaries and brought them to the pastor, who confirmed the symbols on the plastic rosaries were not Christian (occult-like sunbursts on the four corners with a large serpent wrapping around the body of Jesus). The well-intended church lady brought them home to burn them in her fireplace. The first handful smoked out her entire house and resulted in the fire department being dispatched. She returned them to her parish priest who gave them to the exorcist who had a team member dispose of them in a remote place according to the Liber Christo protocol. The team member tasked with destroying them went to a remote place in the desert to dispose of them when suddenly a pack of dogs burst out of the bushes and surrounded him. With the dogs circling him, he held up his shovel and prayed a binding prayer. At the moment, a woman in black robes then casually walked out of the bushes and, at the sight of her, the dogs immediately turned and followed her with no command. The cursed rosaries, simple plastic and string, took nearly an hour to completely burn.

See Appendix D for how to properly dispose of cursed objects.

7. How do I dispose of objects which I believe may be cursed? Can't I just throw them away?

It is not prudent to keep unholy or cursed objects in your home. Just getting rid of them is negligent because there might be a curse attached to the person who disposes of them, unless they have been decommissioned first. If you have any such objects in your possession, we recommend that you destroy them, specifically that they be "blessed, burned, and buried" by the head of the household, or the owner of the items. After sprinkling the objects with holy water, pray the following:

> *In the name of Jesus Christ and by the authority as head of household [or, as rightful owner of this object] given to me by God the Father Almighty through natural law, I ask Jesus Christ to bless this item and to decommission any evil from it.*[12]

Then destroy them and burn (and sprinkle ashes into running water) or bury the objects.

---

[12] Schneider, *The Liber Christo Method*, 85.

See Appendix D for how to properly dispose of cursed objects.

8. What is wrong with going to haunted houses?

There is no reason why Catholics should go to haunted houses, haunted theme parks and circuses, and other such events/places. Remember, curiosity can be an open door, and the demon always works in the objective. This means that even if your subjective intentions are neutral, this does not prevent you from acquiring a clinging spirit from visiting certain places. Like the (above) example of flashing gang symbols and colors in a bad neighborhood just for fun, while your *intention* was not to offend the gang members, you may well end up in the hospital anyway. Even though one's intentions might be neutral, there may be ramifications for entering unnecessarily into certain places.

The demons present will recognize the mark of Baptism and be attracted to it. That is, they would recognize that you are a Christian who has walked into their neighborhood, their territory, even if out of a seemingly innocent curiosity. Never contribute to the work of the enemy, financially or otherwise, by going to these places. You risk opening a door to a clinging spirit.

9. My father and grandfather were Freemasons. What prayers do I need to pray to break any curses? What do I do with his ring and apron?

A curse is an inversion of a blessing and a privation of the protection that blessing provides. When we speak of a generational spirit, we refer to the temporal effects of certain sins which can afflict families particularly when a family member abdicates his authority through grave sin. When that occurs, those under his authority now lack the provision and protection of blessing. One common such phenomena is Freemasonry. We recommend that you do the prayers of renunciations to break the effects of any curses associated with the rituals your father and grandfather performed. Notably, since the curse follows the bloodline, the person in the family line should do the renunciations, which sometimes means the mother. In those cases, the father, even if it is not in his line, should do it with the mother (see appendix).[13]

A general pattern seen in descendants of Freemasons is a broad rejection (often to the point of animosity) of Catholicism, same-sex ideation in males, and fertility issues in females (and sometimes gender confusion). Father Ripperger has noted that in the cases where childhood sexual abuse is present, in the majority of those cases there is Freemasonry in the family. The curses also tend to pattern with stomach and lung disorders of various kinds. The firstborn son is often the target, but other sons can be affected as well, especially if there is a potential priestly vocation. Often, things will shake up when the lodge member of the family dies, or when a child approaches a sacramental year. Again, these are general patterns and can vary from situation to situation.

You may notice an inner resistance to doing the renunciations, and also the freeing up of memories as you do them. Thus, we also recommend confessing weekly during the process. Discuss this with your pastor or confessor/spiritual director (in the confessional or by appointment) so he is informed. If anything should arise, he will be able to provide any pastoral care or refer you to a priest in the diocese who has experience in this. Our protocol is to have the person do the renunciations three times (usually, once a week for three

13 For more, see www.liberchristo.org.

weeks) in a church or parish hall (sacred ground) in front of a Christian witness. Sometimes the demon tries in many and varied ways to prevent the saying of the prayers, such as blurring vision, choking the person, causing the person to skip words or even whole lines, etc. If you were a member, then a priest should be present on the third day to pray severing prayers. For descendants, having a priest do severing prayers is good, but not necessary.[14] Having Masses said for any deceased family members involved (father, grandfather) is also good to do, as is confessing any participation with Freemasons or other anti-Catholic organizations.

Destroy all Freemasonic regalia you may have. The apron can be burned and then either sprinkled into running water or buried. The ring should be rendered unrecognizable and unusable with a hammer or table vice. If you can break it into several pieces, that is better. Then toss it into running water. If you do not have running water, then bury it.

Appendix E for the Liber Christo protocol for breaking the Freemasonic curse and how to destroy unholy or cursed objects.

10. What is a "demonic matrix?"

We refer to the patterned way of thinking of the fallen angels as the "demonic matrix," a logical coding that they instinctively follow according to their fallen nature. They act according to their natural inclinations, which means they are attracted to similar tendencies in fallen humans, and seek to drive us to habitual sin, to include a life of mortal sin, and the elevation of self (pride). The demonic matrix, then, is a set of rules; this is how the demon interacts with reality.

---

14 The renunciations can be found in Ripperger, *Deliverance Prayers for Use by the Laity*, 197–214.

Voluntary vicarious atonement (offering up your suffering in reparation for the sins another) breaks this diabolic logic. One fact of the fallen angel is that the essence of his fall is a rejection of suffering, specifically a higher creature serving a lower creature. What militates against that is when one offers up his sufferings in union with Christ (cf. Col 1:24), throwing a wrench into the matrix, breaking the pattern which attracts him to us. Offering one's suffering (such as with the Judo Prayer, above) means the demon now becomes an instrument of sanctification (not damnation). As Saint Augustine said of Job, his suffering was not in vain; rather, he was "turned over to the devil to be tempted so that, by withstanding the test, Job would become a torment to the devil."[15] Thus, enduring under trials and offering them up as a spiritual offering runs counter to the patterned and evil logic of the enemy and is the quickest way to break an attack. They will generally flee, as they do not want to cooperate with making someone holy. Pursuing holiness, forgiving those who have hurt you, making sacrifices for souls, and avoiding vice all break the demonic matrix.

11. What does Liber Christo mean when they say that a person has "fractured thoughts"?

Fractured thoughts describe the internal state of a person who has deep psychological wounds and cannot distinguish between his or her own thoughts from the demon's projections into his or her mind. This can be exacerbated through a high emotionality which attracts the demon. A fractured mind is compromised to the point where a person cannot distinguish between his own negative emotions and negative

---

[15] Cited in Thigpen, *Manual for Spiritual Warfare*, 144.

self-talk from demonic projections. Mental prayer and a media fast (part of the Liber Christo prayer protocol) helps a person to gain self-mastery and shut down diabolical projections because it helps a person to distinguish clean from unclean thoughts as they arise. Through spiritual discipline, a person can begin to identify any thoughts that are inconsistent with the thoughts of Christ. In so doing, we follow the words of Saint Paul:

> For, although we are in the flesh, we do not battle according to the flesh, for the weapons of our battle are not of flesh but are enormously powerful, capable of destroying fortresses. We destroy arguments and every pretension raising itself against the knowledge of God and take every thought captive in obedience to Christ. (2 Cor 10:3–5)

The battle takes place in the mind (or imagination) where memory and emotions can be used against us, and therefore, the discipline of mental prayer and various forms of self-denial assist greatly in helping a person "take every thought captive in obedience to Christ." The battle is in the mind as the demon tries to fracture our interiority so he can project unholy thoughts and drive us to sinful behavior.

12. Can a demon take on a physical body?

We know from Scripture that angels can take the appearance of a human being. Two angels went to Sodom to visit Lot and his family, and the men in Sodom had evil desires towards them because they appeared like two young men (see Gn 19:1–5). The Bible also warns us to treat strangers well because we could be interrelating with angels and be totally unaware (see Heb 13:1–2). Angels can also manipulate matter in the physical realm. Fallen angels retain that power. Saint

Padre Pio reported being physically beaten in altercations with demons. He reported that they left marks and bruises on him, which others in his community also verify. In his words: "Now, twenty-two days have passed since Jesus allowed the devils to vent their anger on me. My Father, my whole body is bruised from the beatings that I have received to the present time by our enemies. Several times, they have even torn off my shirt so that they could strike my exposed flesh."[16]

Elsewhere, he stated: "These devils don't stop striking me, even making me fall down from the bed. They even tear off my shirt to beat me! But now they do not frighten me anymore. Jesus loves me, He often lifts me and places me back on the bed."[17]

Saint Thomas Aquinas also states that angels can assume physical bodies. They do not take over an existing physical body, he states, but they can "manipulate matter so as to assume a physical appearance that is visible yet consistent with angelic character."[18] This suggests that demons can act upon material things directly by their wills so they do not have to take physical appearance, but also that they can take on a physical body, with God's permission, but that is extremely rare.

Demons can also manipulate the sense perceptions in our minds to distort the reality of the outer world. As Saint Thomas explains: "For just as he (the demon) can from the air form a body of any form and shape and assume it so as to appear in it visibly, so in the same way he can clothe any corporeal thing with any corporeal form, so as to appear therein."[19] This means that demons can mess with our minds by

---

16 Saint Pio of Pietrelcina, in Colacelli, ed., *100 Letters,* 74.
17 Saint Pio of Pietrelcina, in Colacelli, ed., *100 Letters,* 201.
18 Saint Thomas Aquinas, *ST* I, q. 51, art. 2.
19 Saint Thomas Aquinas, *ST* I, q. 51, art. 2.

altering our perceptions. A good reminder comes from Saint Paul, who exhorts us to "have the mind of Christ" (1 Cor 2:16) and to "be transformed by the renewal of your mind" (Rom 12:2). This only comes through prayer and cooperating with God's grace. Prayer for others helps to block the demon's ability to distort perceptions.

13. What makes the Rosary such a powerful weapon against Satan?

When the Virgin Mary gave the Rosary to Saint Dominic, she did not refer to it as fine spiritual jewelry or rose pedals going into the air. Rather, in her own words, the Blessed Mother called the Rosary a weapon to be used to reform the world: "Dear Dominic, do you know what weapon the Most Holy Trinity wants to use to reform the world? I want you to know that in this kind of warfare the 'battering ram' has always been the Angelic Psalter, which is the corner stone of the New Testament. So, if you want to reach these hardened souls and win them to God, preach my Psalter!"[20] A battering ram is used by police and soldiers to break doors down and take down bad guys.

In addition, as Saint John Paul II wrote, the Rosary is the "compendium of the Gospel" because it "conveys the depth of the Gospel message in its entirety," recalling the entire pascal mystery.[21] Thus, when we pray the Rosary, we invoke the salvific words and deeds of Jesus Christ while also training our mind in the ways of mental prayer, itself a battering ram where we "take every thought captive in obedience to Christ . . . ready to punish every disobedience" (1 Cor 10:5).

---

[20] Cited by Saint Louis de Montfort, *The Secret of the Rosary*, 18.

[21] Saint John Paul II, *Rosarium Virginum Mariae*, 19,1.

Chapter IV

BREAKING A VICE, GOD'S PROVIDENCE, AND EVIL

"WHILE PERFORMING THE exorcism over a woman, he ought always to have assisting him several women of good repute, who will hold on to the person when she is harassed by the evil spirit. These assistants ought, if possible, to be close relatives of the subject and for the sake of decency the exorcist will avoid saying or doing anything which might prove an occasion of evil thoughts to himself or to the others.

"During the exorcism he shall preferably employ words from Holy Writ, rather than forms of his own or of someone else. He shall, moreover, command the devil to tell whether he is detained in that body by necromancy, by evil signs or amulets; and if the one possessed has taken the latter by mouth, he should be made to vomit them; if he has them concealed on his person, he should expose them; and when discovered they must be burned. Moreover, the person should be exhorted to reveal all his temptations to the exorcist."

—*Praenotanda to the Rite of Exorcism*, nos. 19, 20

From the Field: "Leave."

Within your authority structure, power can be exercised without the demon being able to retaliate for the misuse of power or the misuse of authority. That being said, even if you have the requisite authority, the demon will be able to retaliate if you are not in a state of grace. You absolutely must be in a state of grace to engage in spiritual warfare. If you are not in a state of grace, then your sin is visible to the demon and unconfessed sin will be used as a weapon against you.

A parish priest once posted a Sunday homily on the internet where he stated that a person does not need to be in a state of grace to pray over others. That is, he said, the state of grace is not as important as using a spiritual charism of praying over someone in need. "If you are on your way to church to go to confession because of a mortal sin and someone calls and needs you to pray over someone who is dying in the hospital," the priest said, "then go straight to the hospital. God will protect you." If the person were in danger of death, however, the better response would have been to find a priest to administer Last Rites and give the Apostolic Pardon. What the priest advised, moreover, was not only false but also extremely dangerous.

The demon is known on occasion to call out the sins of the priest in session. Diversion is an effective tactic in battle. On rare occasions, however, the demon has been known to call out even the venial sins of even the lay participants, with such things as "There is lust in this room." Or "No one here is fasting." In one particular case, the lay associates were assisting in the Solemn Rite as intercessors for the exorcist. One of the intercessors had not come in a confessed state. He was not carrying any mortal sin but later admitted that on the way to the session, he had engaged in unholy speech and committed the sin of detraction. As the priest began the Rite, the demon manifested or came to the surface and began to scan the room. Normally, the lay assistants are largely invisible, and he focuses on the priest because the priest has the power and authority to command him, while the lay associates are of little consequence or threat.

The demon tracks, therefore, the hierarchy of authority in the room. The laity do have the power to command and to use Jesus's name, and the demon will respond. He may not comply, but he will respond. This is key. He is looking for who has the authority. An analogy to this is seen in law enforcement. A police officer's power is his weapon, the handgun on his belt. His authority is his badge. The demon is keenly aware of ranking, of a spiritual insignia, or spiritual significance. On several occasions, we have seen where there have been multiple exorcists present and the demon is only paying attention to the ranking clergy, the mandated exorcist. He will pay attention primarily to any bishop in attendance, even if the mandated exorcist is present. In fact, when forced to stare at the picture of the local bishop, the demon will also manifest in visible pain. Like a military combatant, he knows the ranking of authority of those present—who has the stripes on his sleeve or the brass insignia of the ranking officer.

He is also aware of who has unconfessed sin, especially mortal sin, because this represents a vulnerability. In this particular case, the priest began the formal session. The preliminary prayers were said, and as soon as the demon came up, or manifested, he scanned the room and locked eyes on one particular lay person. In that moment, the lay person began to choke, not just a little bit, but a lot. Within the rules of engagement, it is important to remember that, as articulated in the book of Job, God allows affliction but with the caveat "you may not kill him" (Job 2:6). This bears true. The demon may not kill us, but he can, because of our sin, exact punishment, or temporal consequences, if you will. The lay person began to choke, but the priest was not aware of what was happening behind him and continued with the prayer. The demon continued to stare at the assistant with a penetrating gaze, choking him all the while. The lay person obviously quit praying the Rosary, which was his assigned task, as he struggled for air. As he became both redder and bluer, someone alerted the priest and pointed to the person. The priest was a veteran and immediately knew what was going on. He bound the demon in the name of Jesus from affecting any of the assistants, particularly this assistant. Immediately, the breath returned to this assistant and the exorcist priest said to the man, "Leave." Just a simple word, leave.

This lay person gladly left the room, and the Rite continued. After the session was over, the priest very simply told him, "You have unconfessed sin. Would you like to go to confession?" This was pretty devastating to the person. He did not realize what could have happened, that he had shown up at this prayer session in an unconfessed state, and this resulted.

So, what does this have to do with authority? We see the proper use of power and authority clearly demonstrated by the priest who stopped the demon from choking the lay assistant. We also see the lay assistant who showed up with power to pray and to help, but also brought the vulnerability of sin. Therefore, even though this person was acting within the priest's instruction, praying as the exorcist priest would have him pray, the vulnerability here allowed the demon to exact a temporal consequence.

In this section, we discuss the topic of vices, obstacles to grace, and the vulnerabilities which attract the demon.

1. I need to work harder to stop being in mortal sin so much. My Achilles heel is lust. Any advice on what I can do to stay in a state of grace for longer periods and hopefully for good?

Perhaps nothing so blinds the intellect and weakens the will than sexual sin. Saint Alphonsus Liguori refers to impurity (sexual sins) as "hell's widest gate" because, he says, "it is by this gate that the greater number of the damned enter."[1] That being said, praise God that you recognize the sin in your life because it is the grace of God opening your eyes. As a reminder of the severity of this vice and how wide is this gate to hell, Saint Alphonsus gives stark counsel: "Beware, brother, if you do not be converted now, you may never be converted."[2] If you are married, know that while you are engaging in impure thoughts and acts, the enemy is using this to get his hoofs inside your family. He wants to neutralize you and then divide you and your spouse so that he can ultimately reach his main target, your children. So, if you will not fight this for your own soul, do it for your spouse and your children.

The primary and ordinary means of obtaining grace are the sacraments, which means you need go to confession weekly and attend Holy Mass daily if possible. This will strengthen you in developing the virtues requisite for this combat. Both virtues and vices are repeated acts. The enemy knows that we are creatures of habit by nature, and he seeks to habituate our behavior by projecting images into our imagination. Father Hardon breaks down sexual desire into three basic types:

> Normally they are directed to sexual union between men and women, and to the intimate acts that are the natural

---

1 Saint Alphonsus Liguori, *Six Discourses*, 33.
2 Saint Alphonsus Liguori, *Six Discourses*, 33.

> preliminaries to such union. Nevertheless, the impulses may also be directed elsewhere: to oneself for the solitary enjoyment of venereal pleasure which is commonly called masturbation; to another person of the same sex which is homosexuality; or to any of a multitude of approximations or combinations of the three prototypes.[3]

The *Catechism* refers to vices as "perverse inclinations" which "cloud conscience and corrupt the concrete judgment of good and evil" (CCC 457). The seven principal vices are pride, avarice, envy, anger, lust, gluttony, and sloth (or acedia). These must be militated against with corresponding virtues.

Vice	*Corresponding Virtue*
Pride	*Humility*
Avarice	*Charity*
Envy	*Compassion*
Anger	*Meekness*
Lust	*Purity*
Gluttony	*Temperance*
Sloth/Acedia	*Zeal*

This means you must eradicate a bad habit by replacing it with a good habit—specifically here, purity—while also avoiding the near occasion of sin. Perverse inclinations are also militated against through bodily fasting and a disciplined life.

Confessing the temptation is therefore necessary, with the caveat that temptation itself is not a sin but becomes sinful once the mind appropriates (or accepts) the temptation. This is a very fine line, so it is a good practice to confess these evil

3 Hardon, "Sex and Chastity" in *Moral Theology*, IX.

thoughts. In the case of habitual lust, there is a psychological obsession which can open the door to spiritual oppression. The bodily sensation combined with the emotional and neurological release in pornography embeds images into the imagination and creates a process addiction to the release of endorphins in the brain (not unlike a gambling addiction). Once the door to the soul's interiority is opened, the demon will be attracted in a symbiotic way to the wounded interiority. He now manipulates the person through a barrage of images and emotions.

Often, however, lust and the carnal sins are the most evident but not necessarily the most operant. For as Jesus warns us, "Whoever looks at a woman in lust has already committed adultery in his heart" (Mt 5:28). Note also the second example of interior sins that Jesus uses in the same section of Matthew (Mt 5:21–30) as it shows the other side of the lust coin: "Whoever is angry with his brother will be liable to judgment . . . whoever calls his brother, 'fool' . . . to fiery Gehenna." The person battling lust often reports also struggling with anger and the sin of detraction. Do not, therefore, focus only on lust, the carnal, but also look to the spiritual defects of anger or pride, which drive sinful speech.

Something seemingly unrelated to the carnal vice may be at work. Thus, we have found it also helpful to do a novena to Our Lady of Sorrows, asking her to reveal any sins, spirits, or vices that may be plaguing a person or family. Often, we focus on lust and anger, like the "whack-a-mole" game, to little effect because a much deeper vice is at root. Once that spirit is identified, the person(s) can begin militating against that spirit and the surface, carnal spirts begin to lose their strength. It is also good to do a general confession, going back as far as you can remember, so as to root out any unconfessed mortal sins and identify the root cause or wound which keeps feeding the demon of lust. An experienced confessor should be able to coach you through how to make this type of confession.

2. What does the battle with lust look like practically? What is "custody of the mind"?

Custody of the mind means having clean mental habits which begin with avoiding the near occasion of sin. For some people, this may mean starving out the imagery you let into your mind so the devil has less to work with. As in the above question, you must "take every thought captive in obedience to Christ" (1 Cor 10:5). Many people have reported that doing the Liber Christo prayer regimen has helped to free them from a life-long struggle with impurity. The discipline of the media fast and daily prayer regimen at set times helps to break unhealthy thought patterns.

On a practical level, you must first catch the movements of impurity before they grow in strength. In the monastic tradition of the Church, what is called the "imprecatory psalms" are seen as applied to the spiritual battle. Thus, when the psalmist prays that God would "seize the babies of my enemies and smash them against the rock" (Ps 137:9), the monks saw the "enemy" as the vices and their "babies" as the initial movements—that is, before they grow in strength. Christ is the Rock that we smash the vices against, and we do that through an act of the will and prayer. When assailed with the temptation to impurity, therefore, first take custody of your thoughts and snap your mind back into order with a simple binding prayer:

> *In the Name of Jesus Christ, I bind the spirit of impurity and command you to go to the foot of the cross to receive your judgement.*

Stopping the projection before it gains strength by willful appropriation will prevent the release of the endorphins which the enemy uses to burn into your memory through distorting your imagination. Crush it on the Rock before it gains strength.

Saint Alphonsus gives another sure remedy of devotion to the Blessed Mother. "In order to rid yourself of your evil habits," he says, "undertake some special devotion to Our Lady." The primary devotion to her is Marian Consecration, and then commit to saying the Rosary every day.[4] Saint Alphonsus also recommends that the person battling lust "fast in her honor upon Saturdays; contrive to visit her image every day and beg of her to obtain for you deliverance from that vice. Every morning immediately after rising, never omit saying three "Hail Marys" in honor of her purity and do the same when going to bed; and above all things, as I have said, when the temptation is most troublesome, call quickly upon Jesus and Mary."[5] At the root of this vice is a lack of both self-control and custody of the intellect. Remember Jesus's words to His disciples when they struggled with driving out a certain demon: "This kind can only come out through prayer [and fasting]" (Mark 9:29).

Mortify your body by doing a spiritual discipline like Exodus 90 or the Liber Christo Thirty Day Prayer Regimen. Pope Benedict XVI reminds us that "fasting means abstaining from food but includes other forms of self-denial to promote a more sober lifestyle. But that still is not the full meaning of fasting, which is the external sign of the internal reality of our

---

4 For Marian consecration, see Saint Louis De Montfort's *True Devotion to Mary*.

5 Saint Alphonsus Liguori, *Six Discourses*, 34.

commitment to abstain from evil with the help of God and to live the Gospel."[6]

Fast from meat on Fridays and do a media fast, which will help purify the imagination. The demon has access to the data set contained in your memory and imagination, so purify those images ("smash them" and "take them captive") with the words and deeds of Jesus Christ. This means you must battle back with mental prayer and mortification of the flesh, the fruit of which is custody of the mind, or imagination.

In addition to the daily Rosary, spend fifteen minutes a day slowly reading the Gospels, or the daily Mass readings. This means more than simple vocal prayer, like the above binding prayer, but also doing daily mental prayer where you will begin to gain control over your thoughts and imagination. This is where the battle takes place.

Monks know this. So be a monk—in the world but not of the world. This means taking on a monastic discipline and ordering your life to prayer. Pray the Angelus at 6 am, noon, and 6 pm and join with the communal prayer of the Church the Annunciation of the angel Gabriel and Mary's "yes" to the Incarnation. As Saint Isaiah the Hermit (488 AD) writes of the effects of meditation:

> Meditation melts our evil thoughts and withers the passions of the soul; it enlightens our mind, makes the understanding radiant, and fills the heart with joy. Meditation wounds demons and drives away thoughts of wickedness. Meditation is a mirror for the mind and light for the conscience; it tames lust, calms fury, dispels wrath, drives away bitterness, and puts irritability to flight. Meditation illuminates the mind and expels laziness. From it is born the tenderness that warms and melts the soul.[7]

---

[6] Pope Benedict XVI, *Message of His Holiness Benedict XVI for Lent 2009.*

[7] Cited in Peter John Cameron, "What is Meditation," *Magnificat* 16, no. 7 (September 2014), 5.

These words of this monk-saint are worth repeating: *meditation wounds demons.* Prayer is a weapon. When combined with acts of self-denial, it begins to transform you and strengthen you to overcome the temptation to impurity. Fasting trains you to master and control your passions, disconnecting you from this world. This opens your soul to deeper levels of prayer where you build your interior defenses.

Finally, the common experience of exorcists is that it is impossible to find someone who meditates regularly (speaking, of course, of Catholic meditation) who became either possessed or diabolically obsessed. The slow grind of freedom of this vice is the one-two combination of prayer and fasting.

3. I have heard you recommend that people who struggle with lust should gaze upon the crucified feet of Jesus. Will you give me instructions or ideas on how to proceed with this?

One tactic we recommend for combatting invasive, impure thoughts is to meditate upon the sacred wounds of Jesus, for as Isaiah prophesied about the Suffering Servant: "By his wounds we are healed" (Is 53:5). This is a simple and effective way to "smash the skulls of the babies of our enemy against the rock." In solemn exorcisms, moreover, we have discovered that one way an exorcist can discern the presence of a demon of a sexual impurity (and a potential entry and holding point) is by applying a blessed object—such as a crucifix, relic, rosary, or his priestly stole—to the possessed person's feet. When the demon of impurity is present, there is generally an acute sensitivity there. This may seem curious, but when that is the case, however, a second oddity seems to present itself: the demon of impurity also reacts in pain during the recitation of the Litany of Saints, specifically at the invocation of "All ye holy Virgins and Widows" and "Saint Mary Magdalene."

This field experience has led us to discover that meditating on the wounded feet of Jesus is a very effective counterpunch to lust. The feet of Jesus are the *locus* of discipleship, evoking the rabbinic imagery of the posture of the ancient rabbi who taught while seated with his disciples at his feet. Saint Mary Magdalene chose "the better part" and "the one thing necessary" when she sat at Jesus's feet while her sister Martha served (Lk 10:42). But was this the first and only time she was at the feet of Jesus? This tactic of meditating on the wounded feet of Jesus traces its roots to Saint Gregory the Great, who affirmed the ancient tradition that Saint Mary Magdalene is the sister of Martha and Lazarus and who anointed Jesus's feet at the house in Bethany (Jn 12:1–11; Mk 14:3–9; Mt 26:6–13) and was also the repentant sinner of Luke chapter seven. As Saint Gregory the Great said:

> She whom Luke calls the sinful woman, whom John calls Mary, we believe to be the Mary from whom seven devils were ejected according to Mark. And what did these seven devils signify, if not all the vices. It is clear, brothers, that the woman previously used the unguent to perfume her flesh in forbidden acts. What she therefore displayed more scandalously, she was now offering to God in a more praiseworthy manner.[8]

There, in a profound act of humility and repentance, she anointed the feet of Jesus, bathed them with her tears, and dried them with her hair (Lk 7:38), and immediately afterwards, Luke mentioned her as "from whom seven demons had gone out" (Lk 8:2).

[8] Gregory the Great, *Homily XXXIII*, no. 2.

Thus, meditating upon the wounded feet of Jesus does several things. It links the sin to the biblical icon of sexual sin and repentance (Saint Mary Magdalene), it gives the imagination a place to go when besieged with sexual temptation, and also helps to train the mind in self-mastery by the practice of the discipline of meditation. Custody of the intellect is key to liberation, as the demon has access to our own memories and can distort them to evoke certain emotions and thereby habituate our behavior. He acts by projecting images into the imagination, often those of previous sinful behavior or pornographic images. Meditation on the pierced feet of Jesus helps to purify those images embedded in the memory (and concomitant emotions) by a disciplined practice which washes the images with the Blood of Jesus and its redemptive power.

In addition, the Rosary also helps to develop in self-mastery so a person can reject (and not appropriate) the projected image. This is a classic example of "crushing the skulls of the babies of my enemies against the rock" by immediately and instinctively rejecting the temptations before they gain strength in the interior self. Once the mind appropriates the projection, however, the demon can now manipulate the mind with a flood of images and emotions. When not resisted, these, in turn, gain strength until the person finally surrenders to the temptation and acts out in some bodily way.

How do we do this practically? When you get that urge towards pornography, take your rosary in hand and look at an image of the pierced feet of Jesus—the more graphic and bloody the better. Counter the invasive thought of lust with short, thirty second bursts until the temptation dissipates. Think of it like the three-round burst of the M4 semi-automatic rifle used by American soldiers and Marines. When a sexual temptation arises, immediately draw your mind upon the bloody, wounded feet of Christ. Keep an image on hand of the pierced feet of Jesus; make it your screen saver on your phone. Always have a rosary in your pocket ready to pull out. Invoke the holy name of Mary and ask her to wrap her mantle around you, then look away, and cycle back, repeating as necessary until the image in the imagination dissipates. This projects into the cosmos the wounded feet of Jesus Christ, the feet that Mary Magdalene anointed and kissed in her repentance after being delivered from seven demons. Mediate on the same pierced feet she gazed upon at the foot of the cross as she stood next to the Blessed Mother. This works to push the pornographic images out of the imagination, and thereby lessens the fodder for the demon to work with, while training you to use Scripture as a weapon in prayer, "taking every thought captive" and "crushing them against the Rock."

4. What do you mean by "the demon enters through sin but holds through heresy"? How does that relate to removing obstacles to grace?

Father Amorth, who is said to have performed over fifty thousand exorcisms in his lifetime, warned, "There is always a strong temptation for charismatics, sensitives and exorcists . . . of finding the quickest way to heal, by going outside the common sacred means to obtain grace." We must remember that the primary means of obtaining grace is found in the sacraments of the Catholic Church. Other ordinary elements include ordering one's life to prayer, growing in virtue, and learning to offer one's suffering in union with Christ's for the reparation for sins. What happens when those in the exorcist community subvert or bypass these "common, sacred means" by praying too hastily over someone? Father Amorth says that those who do can "unwittingly fall into the trap of magic."[9] Many well-intended Catholics can fall into a kind of superstition when they step outside of the normal channels of grace. There, the devil waits to offer a quick fix.

Thus, one must first remove any deficiency in the sacramental construct. That is, if you are not married in the Church, or your children are not baptized, these must be remedied first so that sacramental grace may begin to flow. You can have your home blessed every day, but if you are living in sin, then the devil will eventually work his way in because you lack the protection of the sacraments. The goal is to lead the soul back to full assimilation into the Mystical Body. Other obstacles include persistence in sin and a failure to break both physical and spiritual ties to the past. This means removing all ties to evil in the home, such as horror movies, sex toys, unholy books, pornography, and the like. It also means reordering all relationships which are not holy, even ending certain friendships which are not leading you closer to God.

In addition, most who seek liberation generally have deep spiritual and psychological wounds and often unresolved trauma. *Trauma* is a "deeply subjective and volitional response to evil (whether physical, psychological, or spiritual)."[10] Replace the word *wound* with *opportunity* and begin to see your past traumas as an opportunity to do penance, make reparation, and grow in holiness. Your vices are holding points for the enemy, so the cleaner the soul, the less he has to work with.

A key point to understand is that a psychological obsession can open the door to a spiritual oppression, or even spiritual obsession. This can happen very quickly. We had a case where a very active parishioner at a parish in a small

9 Amorth, *An Exorcist Tells His Story*, 162.
10 Schneider, *The Liber Christo Method*, 26.

community found out that her husband had an affair. She had built her entire identity around being a good church lady and did so much at the parish that she neglected her home life, as is often the case. Because it was a small community, the rumor of the extramarital affair spread very quickly, and the wife immediately developed a psychological obsession in her shame response over the event, particularly in light of her self-identity as a good Catholic woman and active parishioner. Within a matter of weeks, moreover, she moved quickly from a psychological to spiritual obsession, refusing any help. Within two months, she left the church altogether and remained heavily afflicted. Any psychological obsession creates a vulnerability to the demon, but particularly those which involve deep traumas.

Finally, heresy and ignorance are always present in cases of diabolic affliction. Interestingly, we have found in most cases of diabolic possession that there is some Marian dogma that the person rejects, which is generally fueled by the demon who knows Our Lady's role in liberation. The energumen may have reached the point of accepting most of Catholic teachings as part of their conversion and movement towards liberation, but the demon will often project resistance to one of the doctrinal truths about the Virgin Mary. While he worked his way into the soul through some sin, he also holds where there is a rejection of the revealed truths of the Roman Catholic faith. We emphasize, therefore, the importance of living orthodoxy and orthopraxy—that is, right belief and right practice. Grace is occluded to the extent that doctrine and dogma are discarded.

5. What does it mean to live in a state of grace? How does that help in spiritual combat?

A simple definition of grace is the life of God, so being in a state of grace means that the life of God is alive in the soul. By *state of grace* is meant the restoration of divine friendship and, thus, the condition of a soul as pleasing to God because it is free from mortal sin. As the *Catechism* states, "Sanctifying grace is the gratuitous gift of his life that God makes to us; it is infused by the Holy Spirit into the soul to heal it of sin and to sanctify it" (CCC 2023). Elsewhere the *Catechism* further states:

> The grace of Christ is the gratuitous gift that God makes to us of his own life, infused by the Holy Spirit into our soul to heal it of sin and to sanctify it. It is the sanctifying or deifying grace received in Baptism. It is in us the source of the work of sanctification: Therefore, if anyone is in Christ, he is a new creation; the old has passed away, behold, the new has come. All this is from God, who through Christ reconciled us to himself. (CCC 1999)

This life of God infused in Baptism is destroyed through mortal sin. Father Hardon defines the state of grace as the "condition of a person who is free from mortal sin and pleasing to God. It is the state of being in God's friendship and the necessary condition of the soul at death in order to attain salvation."[11] If you are not in a state of grace, you are completely unarmed on the spiritual battlefield. For as Jesus said, "Truly, truly, I say to you, everyone who commits sin is the slave of sin" (Jn 8:34). The first layer of protection against demons, therefore, is living in a state of grace. This is your spiritual shield. Saint Thérèse of Lisieux said that "a soul in the state

[11] Hardon, *Modern Catholic Dictionary*, 519.

of grace has nothing to fear from demons, who are cowards capable of running away from the look of a child."[12]

Remember the definitions from the *Baltimore Catechism*:[13]

Q. 456. What do you mean by grace?

A. By grace I mean a supernatural gift of God bestowed on us, through the merits of Jesus Christ, for our salvation.

Q. 457. What does "supernatural" mean?

A. Supernatural means above or greater than nature. All gifts such as health, learning or the comforts of life, that affect our happiness chiefly in this world, are called natural gifts, and all gifts such as blessings that affect our happiness chiefly in the next world are called supernatural or spiritual gifts.

Q. 458. What do you mean by "merit"?

A. Merit means the quality of deserving well or ill for our actions. In the question above it means a right to reward for good deeds done.

Q. 459. How many kinds of grace are there?

A. There are two kinds of grace, sanctifying grace and actual grace.

Q. 460. What is the difference between sanctifying grace and actual grace?

A. Sanctifying grace remains with us as long as we are not guilty of mortal sin; and hence, it is often called habitual grace; but actual grace comes to us only when we need its help in doing or avoiding an action, and it remains with us only while we are doing or avoiding the action.

---

12 Saint Thérèse of Lisieux, *The Story of a Soul*, 28.

13 *Baltimore Catechism*, 137.

Q. 461. What is sanctifying grace?

A. Sanctifying grace is that grace which makes the soul holy and pleasing to God.

Remember, the ordinary means of receiving sanctifying grace is through the seven sacraments of the Catholic Church. Practically speaking, this means following the precepts of the Church:

1. Attendance at Mass on Sundays and Holy Days of Obligation
2. Confession of serious sin at least once a year
3. Reception of Holy Communion at least once a year during the Easter season
4. Observance of the days of fast and abstinence
5. Providing for the needs of the Church

If you are not in the state of grace, reconcile yourself with God through a good confession. Do this first, as this is the foundation of spiritual combat.

6. My son tries to practice his faith, but his speech is very vulgar. Is this dangerous for spiritual life, and what is the best way to break that habit?

In the Wisdom Literature of the Old Testament, we read: "The fear of the Lord is to hate evil. Pride, arrogance, the evil way, and the perverse mouth I hate" (Prv 8:13). As to the foolish man, Ecclesiastes states that "his lips consume him" and the "beginning of his words is folly, and the end of his talk is utter madness; yet the fool multiplies words" (Eccl 10:13–14). In a moral exhortation on that same wisdom tradition, Saint James reminds us of the dangers of wicked speech:

> The tongue is also a fire. It exists among our members as a world of malice, defiling the whole body and setting the entire course of our lives on fire, itself set on fire by Gehenna. For every kind of beast and bird, of reptile and sea creature, can be tamed and has been tamed by the human species, but no human being can tame the tongue. It is a restless evil, full of deadly poison. With it we bless the Lord and Father, and with it we curse human beings who are made in the likeness of God. From the same mouth come blessing and cursing. This need not be so, my brothers. (Jas 3:6–10)

Thus, the demon looks for the mouth that blesses and curses. By this is meant that he looks for inconsistencies in any speech or action which suggest a lack of integrity in thought, word, and deed. This is someone who blesses God with his mouth at Holy Mass and receives Him on his tongue in Holy Communion but then uses that same tongue to utter curses, slander, gossip, and detraction. These inconsistencies reveal our vulnerabilities and attract the demon to us.

Jesus was clear on the connection between profanity and holiness when He said, "It is not what enters one's mouth that defiles that person; but what comes out of the mouth is what defiles one" (Mt 15:11). Saint Paul is also very clear on using bad language: "Put to death, then, the parts of you that are earthly," he says, "immorality, impurity, passion, evil desire, and the greed that is idolatry" (Col 3:5). He warns the Ephesians, "No foul language should come out of your mouths, but only such as is good for needed edification, that it may impart grace to those who hear" (Eph 4:29).

A good examination of conscience to help stop sinful speech is found in the *Catechism*, paragraphs 2475–2487 (*Offenses Against Truth*). That section begins by reminding the Christian disciple of the words of Saint Paul that through Baptism, he has to "put on the new man, created after the likeness of God in true righteousness and holiness" and, therefore, the Christian should "put away falsehood . . . all malice and all guile and insincerity and envy and all slander" (CCC 2475). Being a Christian essentially means knowing the clean from the unclean in thought, word, and deed. Unclean speech includes tarnishing the reputation of others. The *Catechism* gives some definitions:

- *Rash judgment:* assuming as true, without sufficient foundation, the moral fault of a neighbor.
- *Detraction:* disclosing another's faults and failings (without objectively valid reason) to persons who did not know them.
- *Calumny*: remarks contrary to the truth, harming the reputation of others and giving occasion for false judgments concerning them.
- *Lying* is "speaking a falsehood with the intention of deceiving." Thus, the Lord denounces lying as the work of the devil: "You are of your father the devil, . . . there is no truth in him. When he lies, he speaks according to his own nature, for he is a liar and the father of lies."

Interestingly, in dealing with cases of spiritual oppression, we often see an oppression lift as a person grows in prayer, discipline, and the sacramental life. The oppression often returns, however, when the person returns to some familiar sin—such as masturbation, but also the seemingly harmless sin of giving into anger via sinful speech.

Thus, your son will need to confess the sin and militate against anger directly both in the sacraments and by the decision to change his behavior. To eliminate a habit, one must counter with another, the practice of the corresponding virtue. Anger is often the result of a fear of suffering, so small penances to quiet the flesh and emotions is always helpful.

Finally, the recitation of the Divine Praises is a good way to atone for unholy speech. You may suggest that as well. This is a good spiritual disciple and act of penance for anyone struggling with sins of the speech:

Blessed be God.
Blessed be his holy Name.
Blessed be Jesus Christ, true God and true Man.
Blessed be the name of Jesus.
Blessed be his most Sacred Heart.
Blessed be his most Precious Blood.
Blessed be Jesus in the most holy Sacrament of the altar.
Blessed be the Holy Spirit, the Paraclete.
Blessed be the great Mother of God, Mary most holy.
Blessed be her holy and Immaculate Conception.
Blessed be her glorious Assumption.
Blessed be the name of Mary, Virgin and Mother.
Blessed be Saint Joseph, her most chaste spouse.
Blessed be God in his angels and in his saints.

Pray this prayer as often as needed until the tongue is sufficiently "bridled."

7. I am a twenty-two-year-old that is on fire for my Catholic faith, but my parents are consulting a wizard and go to Mass as well. What can I do? I still live with them.

Out of filial piety for your parents, you must pray for them, but you cannot live there without opening yourself to spiritual problems. Sit down with your parents, have a heart-to-heart conversation with them, and tell them what they are doing is inconsistent with our Catholic faith. Express your desire for them to abandon their practice of the occult for the sake of their souls. This conversation may actually draw you closer. Whenever you think of your parents, project "The light of Christ Prayer" into the cosmos for your parents:

> *May the light of Christ be on (n.), so that they see themselves as the Heavenly Father sees them; and that I see them as the Heavenly Father sees them.*

Visualize your parents (in your mind or hold up a picture of them) when they were in a right relationship with God.

Think of prayer as a form of communication with God through projection. Angels communicate in this way—by projection (or illumination). By inviting the "Light of Christ" upon your loved ones, you evoke Our Lord, who prayed "Father, forgive them" from the cross. This saving light helps to uncover the demon's manipulation of the memory and emotions of the unconverted person. This also helps to cut off the demon's source of supply by shedding the healing light of Christ upon the mortal sin from which the demon both feeds and controls the person. This is the exact opposite of the darkness the demon projects into the cosmos when he accuses (Rv 12:10), deceives (1 Tm 2:11), and slanders (Ti 2:3).

You are doing more spiritual judo prayer by interceding to God in this way for the person in need of conversion. This, in turn, opens up a channel of communication between God and the soul, creating a pathway for grace and reconciliation with God. An additional effect is that God will let you see yourself as you pray this prayer, purifying your perception of the events and your parents. Thus, this prayer is a good model for intercessory prayer in general.

8. I keep hearing of the efficacy of the novena to Our Lady of Sorrows, but how exactly is this novena made? By praying the Rosary, by other special prayers?

The Devotion to Our Lady of Sorrows was given to us by Saint Bridget of Sweden (1303–1373). The Blessed Mother gave to Saint Bridget seven promises to console her sorrowful heart with this devotion:

1. I will grant peace to their families.
2. They will be enlightened about the divine Mysteries.
3. I will console them in their pains, and I will accompany them in their work.
4. I will give them as much as they ask for as long as it does not oppose the adorable will of My divine Son or the sanctification of their souls.
5. I will defend them in their spiritual battles with the infernal enemy and I will protect them at every instant of their lives.
6. I will visibly help them at the moment of their death — they will see the face of their Mother.
7. I have obtained this grace from My divine Son, that those who propagate this devotion to My tears and sorrows will be taken directly from this earthly life to eternal happiness, since all their sins will be forgiven, and My Son will be their eternal consolation and joy.

We need to recognize that we are powerless to protect ourselves in spiritual combat, and so should cling to her, and especially to her fifth promise listed above.

In addition, Saint Alphonsus de Liguori recounts that it was also revealed to Saint Elizabeth that Our Lord promised four principal graces to those devoted to her Sorrows:[14]

[14] Saint Alphonsus Liguori, *The Glories of Mary*, 419.

1. That those who before death invoke the divine Mother in the name of Her Sorrows will obtain true repentance of all their sins;
2. That He will protect all who have this devotion in their tribulations, and will protect them especially at the hour of death;
3. That He will impress on their minds the remembrance of His Passion;
4. That He will place such devout servants in Mother Mary's hands to do with them as She wishes and to obtain for them all the graces She desires.

For these reasons, Father Ripperger encourages "constant petitioning" and "perfect confidence in Our Lady" because she has "perfect coercive power over the demons." Devotion to her under the title Our Lady of Sorrows draws upon these realities, particularly for spiritual combat. He states that

> when Saint Joseph and Mary took Jesus to Saint Simeon, he said to our lady that her Heart would be pierced so that the thoughts of many would be revealed. Our Lady, by undergoing the Passion with Christ, would merit an intimacy with God that no creature had. As result, He reveals things to Her that He does not reveal to others. However, He will allow us to petition Her so that She may reveal hidden things relating to the spiritual life. This is true in relation to our own defects, but especially in matters of spiritual combat.[15]

Thus, devotion to her Sorrows taps into the special graces contained in the mystery of her unique union with her Son and superabundant merits.

On a practical level, Father Ripperger offers the following advice for those engaged in spiritual combat, particularly when facing great obstacles:

---

15 Ripperger, *Deliverance Prayers for the Laity*, 9.

> In spiritual warfare, precision is everything. In this respect, spiritual warfare is not any different than any other kind of warfare; the more accurate or specific the weapon the more effective it will be. For this reason, if we pray to Our Lady of Sorrows, She will reveal to us the nature of the demon we are dealing with, whether that is in our lives, or in the lives of those to whom we have obligations. This provides us a specific target to combat.[16]

The simplest way to achieve this is to pray the Chaplet of Our Lady of Sorrows (also called the Dolorosary) for nine days and ask her to reveal the evil spirit, spiritual defect, or whatever is blocking the flow of grace in this or that situation so that you can then begin to militate against it in prayer. This is like using night vision goggles in combat, as it allows Our Lady to illuminate the darkness that surrounds us so that we can uncover and, therefore, more directly engage the enemy.

9. I am under spiritual attack. What should I do?

First of all, replace the phrase "spiritual attack" with "spiritual formation" because everything the demon does is controlled by God, who is allowing the demon to afflict you to help you grow in holiness. According to Saint Bonaventure, God allows the demon to afflict us (and, therefore, train us in holiness) for four main reasons: to reveal God's glory, to punish sin, to rebuke a sinner, or to educate a person.[17] That is, God allows all demonic activity (whether ordinary or extraordinary) for a greater good.[18]

---

16 Ripperger, *Deliverance Prayers for the Laity*, 9–10.

17 Cited in Smit, *De Demoniacis*, 79.

18 "People have to understand that it is not unfair for God to allow this because He is actually giving them something greater." Ripperger, *Dominion*, 214.

Remember that the demon has no rights over a soul; that is, the baptized soul belongs, *by right*, to Jesus Christ. The demon can, however, claim *permissions* which were granted to him though our sinful behaviors. God's mercy is perfect, but His justice is as well, requiring satisfaction to be made for the offense of sin. The *Catechism* reminds us that "sin has a double consequence" (CCC 1472). That is, because in man the spiritual and the bodily form a single nature, what he does in the body impacts him both spiritually and bodily. Thus, "every sin, even venial, entails an unhealthy attachment to creatures, which must be purified either here on earth, or after death in the state called Purgatory. This purification frees one from what is called the 'temporal punishment' of sin" and flows "from the very nature of sin;" this purification leads souls to conversion (CCC 1472). Thus, diabolic affliction is the cause of both sanctification and satisfaction for the effects of past sins. In this sense, then, the demon becomes an instrument of God's perfect mercy and justice.

Father Ripperger affirms that the principle reason God allows demons to tempt and afflict us is "for the sanctification of those who engage in the spiritual battle."[19] He further breaks down Saint Bonaventure and expands several ways in which "attack" is "formation" for the Christian:[20]

1. Satan is an instrument of purification;
2. Temptations coming from demons serve as a corrective to the individual;
3. Fighting the diabolic increases one's virtue;
4. It detaches the person from this life and things of the world;
5. Diabolic attacks turn our eyes toward heaven so that we desire eternal attitude and eternal salvation;

[19] Ripperger, *Dominion*, 214.

[20] Ripperger, *Dominion*, 214–16.

6. The spiritual battle is a manifestation of God by meting out justice on the demons, as well as increasing God's glory in this world via advancing a virtue of those who fight the battle;
7. Those who fight the spiritual battle are instruments of God's justice itself;
8. Those who fight the spiritual battle are an instrument of God's charity;
9. Sometimes God allows demons into the life of an individual in order to punish him;
10. By battling the diabolic and undergoing the suffering that is involved in spiritual warfare, if properly offered up, one can use the diabolic battle and subsequent suffering as a valuable means of reparation to God;
11. A means of education;
12. So that the individual learns the mercy and love of God;
13. So that the person is drawn closer to God;
14. So that the individual develops greater confidence, hope, and trust in God;
15. Spiritual attacks are means of sanctification, or more specifically, a means of merit;
16. Sometimes God allows the demons to attack in order to give the person an indication that he is doing the good;
17. One of the most apparent is to make sensible the existence of the invisible world and the reality of future life; to render more apparent, by the power of exorcisms, the divinity of the Church, the power of the sacraments and the prerogative of his ministers and saints;
18. So that the demons in our lives and in the lives of others are weakened by effectively and victoriously combating them;
19. So that one gains a healthy distrust of oneself;
20. So that one develops a strong virtue of humility;
21. In some cases, to break the generational spirit within the generational line, where the spirits' activities are observed.

Father Ripperger notes the importance of discerning the will of God for the person under attack, suggesting prayers to Our Lady of Sorrows to "ask Her what it is that Her Son wants him to gain from this attack." The "formation" one undergoes is a cross, and the temptation is temporary "until God's will has been served in the process."[21] If your family struggles with a spirit of impurity or anger, for example, God allows it so that you can drive it from your family line. This is because "by fighting demons and vanquishing them, the demons become weaker, not only in the lives of the individual who fights them, but in the lives of others, as well."[22]

10. What are "generational spirits"? Is this the same as "healing the family tree" and "generational sin"?

The concept of a generational spirit or curse as part of the temporal punishment due to sin within the familial/authority structure is decidedly not the same as the modern, charismatic notion and praxis of "healing the family tree" due to "intergenerational sin." The Conference of Catholic Bishops in Spain has recently addressed the issue and cites Father John Hampsch and Robert Degrandis as popularizing the practice, although there are others.[23] Often, those who propose a system of a sin that is "transgenerational" or "intergenerational" (these words appear to be used interchangeably) fail to give proper theological distinctions in putting forth this novel idea (by novel, I mean not grounded in Tradition).

---

21 Ripperger, *Dominion*, 213–16.

22 Ripperger, *Dominion*, 214.

23 Hampsch, *Healing the Family Tree*. Degrandis, *Intergenerational Healing: A Journey to the Depth of Forgiveness*. For the Spanish Bishops' statement, see Conferencia Episcopal Española, *Su misericordia se extiende de generación en generación (Lc 1,50)*.

The lack of precise language, moreover, betrays a Protestant and modernist influence in asserting that there is an intergenerational transmission of personal sin. If by "generational" is meant a personal sin that is committed by an ancestor that then transmits down the family line, then this is contrary to Catholic teaching. In the Catholic tradition, only original sin is generated in this sense, and proponents of this concept reflect an ancient error called Traducianism (from the Latin *traducere*, which means "to hand down, transmit, deliver").[24] As the Spanish bishops note, moreover, the subtle error in the assertion that a sin is transmitted intergenerationally implies that a child's soul is created (*viz.*, generated) not by God but by the parents. As Father Hardon teaches, "the theory [Traducianism] is in contradiction with Catholic doctrine that each person's soul is individually and separately created by God at the time of conception."[25] This also suggests that if a sin is intergenerational, then healing can also be intergenerational, which has resulted in Holy Mass being used outside of its proper theological, ecclesial, and liturgical context in some circles. In addition, this has led some proponents to blame their ancestors for their problems too readily rather than take personal responsibility for their own sinful behavior.

The first distinction to be made is that you cannot heal the family tree, only family members. That is, through your prayers, sacrifices, and voluntary penances, you can help your family members, both living and deceased. When the merits of our suffering are applied, in union with the suffering of

[24] Whether or not modern proponents intentionally adhere to some form of Traducianist belief is beyond the scope here. That those who put forth this concept appeal more to field experience than theological discourse does highlight the dangers of uncritically accepting Protestant beliefs and practices and the need to stay grounded in the Tradition of the Church when participating in apostolic works.

[25] Hardon, *Modern Catholic Dictionary*, 544.

Christ (see Col 1:24), in reparation for the sins of another, this is referred to theologically as voluntary vicarious atonement. The basis of this understanding is what the *Catechism* speaks of as the dual nature of sin itself, containing both spiritual and temporal effects, both of which need to be remedied (see CCC 1471–72). The application of the merits of your prayers and sacrifices help to make satisfaction for sin, your own or even those of others. As for deceased ancestors, Masses for them and for the souls in purgatory, not intergenerational healing Masses, is the proper use of the liturgy to help our departed loved ones.

The second distinction is that while personal sins of parents are not inherited, the Church teaches what is repeatedly affirmed in Tradition that the *effects* of the personal sins of parents can be inherited—that is, carried down to their children as part of the temporal punishment due to sin.[26] As the *Catechism* states, due to the nature of evil and its offense against God's holiness, all sin requires satisfaction be made. This includes what the *Catechism* refers to as "the temporal punishment due to sins" which remains even for those "whose guilt has already been forgiven" (CCC 1471).[27]

Saint Thomas addresses the issue in the context of God's words to Isreal at Sinai: "For I, the Lord, your God, am a jealous God, inflicting punishment for their father's wickedness on the children of those who hate me, down to the third

---

26 Saint Augustine actually used Exodus 20:5 and the punishment due sin as an inherited guilt in his argument for original sin against Julian of Eclanum, who both rejected an original sin and fervently denied that God punishes sin. In particular, Julian, the spokesman of the Pelagians, argued against Saint Augustine and held that God does not punish a father's sin in the children but rather asserted incorrectly that all sin is imitated, and no guilt is inherited. See Saint Augustine of Hippo, *Against Julian*. Also, Augustine of Hippo, *Answer to the Pelagians III*.

27 "For all lives are mine: the life of the father is like the life of the son, both are mine; only the one who sins shall die" (Ez 18.3).

and fourth generation" (Ex 20:5). He discusses how the sins of a father, due to the nature of the authority structure, can have a temporal effect upon the children, according to God's providence:

> Therefore, it should be known that there are two punishments that follow on sin. One is the *essential* punishment, which pertains to the soul, both in the present—such as the loss of grace, a troubled conscience, and things of this sort—and in the future—such as the punishment of hell. And a child is never punished with this kind of punishment for his father's sin, since this punishment does not regard him insofar as he is something of his father's. The other punishment follows on sin, as it were, *incidentally*, such as bodily infirmities and other temporal punishments. Hence it is also not the case that such punishments are always inflicted on those who sin. Rather, this takes place in accord with the direction of divine providence, which governs all things. And a child is sometimes punished with this kind of punishment for his father's sin, unless there is an impediment on the child's part, such as being contrary to the father's sin by way of a good life. For this punishment befalls him as being something of his father's.[28]

Elsewhere he further distinguishes between the "punitive" (spiritual) and the "medicinal" (temporal) effects of sin and further expounds the general theological concept of inherited guilt within the familial structure. Punishment of sin, he says, is salutary (that is, producing good results) because of its beneficial effect of both healing and preventing further evil in individuals, families, and communities.[29]

That is to say, if a person has the sin of anger (or infidelity, or gossip, or alcoholism, etc.), that sin does not pass down like

[28] Saint Thomas Aquinas, *II Sentences*, d. 33, q. 2.
[29] Saint Thomas Aquinas, *ST* I-II, q. 87, art. 3.

the sin of Adam and Eve passed down through natural generation. The punishment for sin, however, can pass down along the family line because the sins of the father. That breach of the protection which comes through blessing makes the child "more prone to sin," says Saint Thomas, due to the privation of the protection which comes with blessing and the poor example of the father. This, in turn, means a greater propensity to imitation because of a disordering in the child's socialization. Notably, however, this is not deterministic. Saint Thomas says that when the child offers "impediments" to th effects of his parents' sins by living a life of holiness and the state of grace, he is freed from the effects.[30]

Accordingly, original sin sets a pattern for all sin in that there are twofold consequences and twofold punishments, the spiritual and temporal. With regard to the former, the developed tradition is clear that each person has a personal responsibility for his own sins. Nonetheless, with regard to the latter, the temporal effect of the sins of a father can be experienced by the children, according to divine providence. Both Saint Augustine and Saint Thomas are clear on that. This is quite different than an intergenerational sin and healing the family tree by using the Mass in a superstitious way.

Perhaps the problems lie in the fact that many of us live as if semi-habituated by modernism, which tells us that there are no effects of sins if we do not intend them. As mentioned in an earlier answer, however, Saint Bonaventure gives four specific reasons as to why God allows demons to afflict us, two of which are seen acutely here: to punish sin and rebuke a sinner. Saint Thomas likewise affirms that such punishments are not God being cruel but rather "are directed by Divine

---

30 Saint Thomas Aquinas, *II Sentences*, d. 33, q. 2. For more on the concept of generational spirits, see Ripperger, *Dominion* 174–86. Also, Schneider, *The Liber Christo Method*, 53–66.

providence, to the salvation of men, either of those who suffer, or of others who are admonished by their means—and also to the glory of God."[31]

To that end, Saint Augustine likewise acknowledges that sins of parents have effects which must be recognized. Among the list of the evils that infants suffer due to the effects of the sins of their parents, he lists "the attacks of demons."[32] Demons attack children, he argues, as punishment for the sins of their parents. He further notes: "By divine, not human, justice children are also punished for the sins of their parents." This is because, "God, after all, knows when and how to do this with perfect justice, but human beings do not know this and must pass judgment in accord with their knowledge."[33]

With regard to punishment for familial sin, he highlights God's providence and how His merciful love is still at work: "By God's secret and just judgment the children receive for the sins of these parents a punishment that is far different and far less. For he arranges all things in measure and number and weight, and he truthfully says, 'I shall punish the children for the sins of their parents' (Ex 20:5)."[34] Here he affirms the reality of a temporal punishment as generational, but notably, the effects are weighed and measured "by God's secret and just judgment" such that "the children receive for the sins of these

---

31 Saint Thomas Aquinas, *ST* I-II, q. 87, art. 7.

32 Augustine, *Answer to the Pelagians III*, 309. Physical sickness, like mortal sickness, is a privation of the good, a defect in nature as the result of the first sin. Augustine continues: "But you wise heretics, you are ready to fill paradise with such flowers to avoid admitting original sin. For if you say that these evils were not going to exist there, I ask you why they exist in little ones who have, as you claim, absolutely no sin. But if you are not ashamed to say that they were going to exist there, what need is there for us to say what sort of Christians you are?"

33 Augustine, *Answer to the Pelagians III*, 317.

34 Augustine, *Answer to the Pelagians III*, 317.

parents a punishment that is far different and far less" than the parents receive.[35]

In this sense, we can rightly speak of the *effects* of sin as *generational* not because the sin is "generated" but due to both the nature of sin (CCC 1471) and the *familial* construct of authority whereby God Himself states: "For I, the Lord, your God, I am a jealous God, inflicting punishment for their fathers, wickedness on the children of those who hate me, down to the third and fourth generation" (Ex 20:5).

The Church Fathers, then, provide the correct theological context for the phenomena of familial spirits. God honors our free will and withdraws His blessing when we commit grave sins, such as idolatry. A curse is the privation of that blessing, just as darkness is the privation of light, and He uses the evil spirits as the instrument of reparation (to restore balance) and satisfaction (temporal debt due to sin). Accordingly, the phenomenon may be correctly termed "generational" only if one is clear in distinguishing what is passed down—not the sin but its effects, which requires satisfaction to be made for the temporal debt.

11. I know IVF (in vitro-fertilization) is a grave sin, but is it a satanic ritual?

IVF may be a satanic act in the sense that all mortal sin is "satanic" by that definition. Unless a para-liturgical ritual was performed, then it would simply be a grave mortal sin.[36] As the *Catechism* states, "Since it must be treated from conception as a person, the embryo must be defended in its integrity, cared for, and healed, as far as possible, like any other human being" (CCC 2274).

[35] Augustine, *Answer to the Pelagians III*, 317.
[36] CCC 2273.

That being said, our experience is that the act of IVF is one that the demon quickly moves to exploit, especially when one considers the number of fertilized embryos frozen and eventually destroyed. Some of the worse cases of possession we have seen involves IVF as the entry point. This presents an open door to the diabolic to enter both the mother and the familial construct.

12. What is the most effective protocol for decommissioning tattoos, especially those in which the ink might have been cursed, or the image itself might be evil?

As actions which violate bodily integrity, tattoos are very difficult to separate from their ancient connection to slavery and paganism. As such, these constitute a form of self-mutilation, which is forbidden by the fifth commandment (see CCC 2297). In addition, because tattooing can be performed in a ritualistic manner, they can enable the demon to be physically present to the individual. As it applies here:

> *Tattoos* are occultic in as much as the person who gets a tattoo becomes part of a confraternity of others who wear the same image, or who went to the same tattoo artist. The person's flesh has been marked with an unnatural and foreign (and sometimes Satanic) object and image. Often, sigils of demons may be hidden in the imagery of the tattoo, which acts as a calling card for the demon.[37]

In addition, Father Amorth notes:

> Tattooing and piercing, like non-satanic rock, do not necessarily have an evil objective. Man from time immemorial

[37] Liber Christo, "Companion Guide," 162.

> has adorned his body. But I ask myself: Does adorning with indelible images on the skin embellish or disfigure the body, God's creation and therefore already beautiful in itself? In our view (as exorcists) it is always necessary to look at the intentions. Some of the symbolism and the designs on the body can make explicit or implicit referral to monsters or demons, nearly evoking them. At times one can associate these forms of expression as signs of belonging to the devil: in this case, they are connected to the satanic rites of initiation. Other times, more simply, it is done to impress friends. Still other times, it can be done with explicit sexual references or to scorn one's own body. All these examples do nothing good for the soul.[38]

To aid in removing any occult connection, tattoos and ritualistic scarring can be decommissioned by a priest.[39]

See Appendix F for the suggested ritual for decommissioning tattoos.

13. Is all magic evil? Didn't Saint John Bosco do magic tricks?

There are no such things as "white" or "black" magic. As Father Amorth reminds us, "Every form of magic is practiced with recourse to Satan."[40] "Magick" is a term coined by satanist Alastair Crowley and is ritualistic, drawing upon and manipulating preternatural powers. This is different than the stage performance of Saint John Bosco who entertained the young men in his home for boys. For example, when St. John Bosco performed roped tricks (tying three ropes together to explain the Trinity) or performed other tricks to promote Christian

---

38 Amorth, *Exorcist Explains the Demonic*, 57.
39 For the full ritual, see www.liberchristo.org.
40 Amorth, *An Exorcist Tells His Story*, 60.

values, this was not witchcraft. This is quite different than what the *Catechism* states about magic:

> All practices of magic or sorcery, by which one attempts to tame occult powers, so as to place them at one's service and have a supernatural power over others—even if this were for the sake of restoring their health—are gravely contrary to the virtue of religion. These practices are even more to be condemned when accompanied by the intention of harming someone, or when they have recourse to the intervention of demons. Wearing charms is also reprehensible. Spiritism often implies divination or magical practices; the Church for her part warns the faithful against it. Recourse to so-called traditional cures does not justify either the invocation of evil powers or the exploitation of another's credulity. (CCC 2117)

Note that it alludes to both white magic (such as "for the sake of restoring their health" and "so-called traditional cures") and black magic ("the intention of harming someone, or when they have recourse to the intervention of demons"). Both types of magic "are gravely contrary to true religion" and must be strictly avoided by Catholics. If you have participated in any such activities, go to confession for this violation against the first commandment.

14. Megan Fox recently said that she and her boyfriend drink each other's blood. Is that satanic? Vampirism?

Here is an example of how the demon militates against human behavior to the point of absurdity. Megan Fox has said publicly that she and her fiancé drink each other's blood for ritual purposes. Vampirism is a false eucharistic system that militates against (and is a mockery of) Our Lord's Bread of Life discourse and the need to eat His body and drink His blood to attain eternal life (Jn 6:53–56). This is an offense against the first commandment, as well as the sin of self-mutilation.

The Israelites were prohibited from drinking the blood from any living creature, as the life-force was seen in the blood: "Since the life of every living body is its blood, I have told the Israelites: You shall not partake of the blood of any meat. Since the life of every living body is its blood, anyone who partakes of it shall be cut off" (Lv 17:14). As Catholics (the new Israel), we believe that the only Life that we want in us is the life of Jesus Christ, who is the Way, the Truth, and the Life (Jn 14:6). We receive that life most profoundly through Holy Communion. Drinking human blood is a satanic parody and an insult, a diabolic imitation of what Catholics do at Mass.

This practice is also an example of what is referred to as *pelican witchcraft*. In antiquity, the pelican was thought to pull the flesh and blood from her own breast to feed her young. This was perhaps due to the reddish tip of the pelican's beak and the manner in which she feeds her young from beneath her wing. Thus, "pelican witchcraft" is a classification of occult practices mocking this ancient symbol of Christ, the Great Pelican, who offered His Body and Blood both to save us and to feed us in the Holy Eucharist. The image became a common symbol of Christ through the Middle Ages and is seen in iconography adorning both tabernacles and crucifixes.

This third-century anonymous Christian work allegorized various animals of the day as symbols of Christ:

> If the pelican brings forth young and the little ones grow, they take to striking their parents in the face. The parents, however, hitting back kill their young ones and then, moved by compassion, they weep over them for three days,

> lamenting over those whom they killed. On the third day, their mother strikes her side and spills her own blood over their dead bodies and the blood itself awakens them from death. This is what our Lord did. . . . The Maker of every creature brought us forth and we struck him when we served the creatures [i.e., in idolatry] and not the Creator. The Lord ascended the height of the cross and the impious ones struck his side and opened it, and blood and water came forth for eternal life.[41]

The blood and water that flowed from the side of Christ (Jn 19:34), the author states, are symbols of Baptism and the Eucharist. The occultists mock and invert this primitive Christian symbol. In this type of witchcraft, for example, the practitioner (a witch, *santero,* etc.) uses part of his/her own flesh or blood in the ritual. They may also use part of the body of petitioner in the curse, or that of animals, etc. Thus, these types of practices are also called *ex carne* curses. Through the shedding of blood and using certain incantations and rituals, a diabolic entity is invoked and conscripted.

15. If you renounce God and Our Lady and even sign a pact with the devil, can you ever come back?

Yes, a sixth-century Catholic bishop named Theophilus of Andala reportedly sold his soul before renouncing his pact and retuning to God (through the intercession of the Blessed Mother and after much penance). Blessed Bartolo Longo (1841–1926) was an Italian Catholic who rejected his faith and became a satanist for many years. He also repented

[41] Anonymous, *Physiologus,* 9–10. Excerpted from Schneider, *The Liber Christo Method,* 69.

through Our Lady's intercession and spent his remaining years in penance and promoting the holy Rosary.

16. My adult son does not go to Mass anymore. Where do I begin?

You cannot force someone to convert or live out their baptismal dignity, but only encourage and pray. As Jesus told the disciples after He delivered a possessed boy, "This kind can only come out through prayer and fasting" (Mk 9:29). This one-two combination takes many forms. Since he is an adult, your husband's (and your) authority over him has shifted, but the most important thing is to pray together and make little sacrifices for your son.

Offer your suffering to Our Lady of Sorrows and ask her to reveal to you whatever is blocking the graces of conversion so that you can better pray for him. Ask her to bind any demons who are blocking the graces of conversion, and then consecrate his conversion to the Blessed Mother daily.[42] Another simple prayer to begin with is the Light of Christ Prayer:

> *May the light of Christ be on (n.), so that they see themselves as the Heavenly Father sees them; and that I see them as the Heavenly Father sees them.*

By inviting the purifying light of the One who is "the way, the truth and the light" (Jn 14:6), you are projecting the love of Christ upon your son and militating against the evil that may be working against him. This prayer also increases your loving trust in God while opening him to reconciliation with the Father. Jesus is the way to the Father: "No one knows who the Son is except the Father, and who the Father is except the

---

[42] Ripperger, *Deliverance Prayers for the Laity*, 44.

Son and anyone to whom the Son wishes to reveal him" (Lk 10:22). Our Lady is Mediatrix of all Grace, so go to her with confidence and ask her to take your son to her Son.

Also, do not underestimate the power of penance and prayers of reparation. Make small sacrifices for him. Storm heaven with your maternal prayers, tears, and sorrows and Our Lady will help you through this.

17. I think my husband is possessed. Can you help me?

Speak to your parish priest. If he cannot help, make an appointment with your diocesan chancellor. In addition, your husband needs to be on a spiritual workout plan. He needs to become a practicing Catholic so he can defeat this diabolical affliction. He should:

1. Attend Mass every week.
2. Attend Mass on Holy Days of obligation.
3. Go to confession at least once a year, minimum.[43] I would recommend once a week for your husband.
4. Believe with all his heart in the Real Presence (Body, Blood, Soul, and Divinity of Our Lord Jesus Christ in the Holy Eucharist).[44] Go to visit the Blessed Sacrament during the week and pray the Divine Mercy chaplet.
5. Not receive Holy Communion if he knows he has a mortal sin on his soul. That would be yet another and worse mortal sin called a sacrilege. An examination of conscience is suggested each day and especially before confession. It is necessary to be in a state of grace[45] and in full communion with the Church in order to receive Holy Communion.[46]

---

[43] CCC 1457–58.
[44] CCC 1396.
[45] CCC 1415.
[46] CCC 1395.

6. Obey the teaching of the Holy Father, the pope, and the teaching of the Magisterium (Lk 10:16; Mt 28:18–20; Jn 14:16, 26).
7. Have a loving devotion for Our Blessed Mother. See Luke 1:26–28, 42, 48. She leads us to Jesus (cf. Jn 2:5).
8. Pray the Rosary every day. See 1 Thessalonians 5:17.
9. Do the Liber Christo prayer regimen.
10. Say his prayers three times a day (Dn 6:10–11). Say the Act of Contrition each night before he goes to bed.

God put us in the world to know, to love, and to serve him and so to come to paradise (CCC 1721). If he does all of these things, he can liberate himself from demonic harassment. The greatest weapon we have is to live in a state of grace. If you are not in state of grace, you will fall prey to the devil.

18. Should a Catholic use "healing rocks" for physical, spiritual, or emotional healing of self? Did St. Hildegard of Bingen use healing rocks or stones?

Like Saint Walburga, Saint Hildegard of Bingen has been somewhat usurped by the New Age movement and even witchcraft. Saint Hildegard explored the use of natural remedies for healing, combined with prayer and the liturgical calendar, which is quite different than seeing "magical" power in crystals, stones, herbs, etc. The key difference is the source of healing or "energy" as they often speak of today. If a material thing is used to draw out the body's natural healing power, then the source is natural and perfectly fine. If, however, the source of the energy invoked is from outside the body, then the source is other than natural and should be avoided. Avoid also any practitioner (such as with reiki or reflexology) who purports to channel energy along chakras, so called, in your body. It is one thing to drink a certain type of tea because it is known for helping gastrointestinal issues, for example, and another to use a tea as a love potion or for "spiritual healing." One draws on the body's natural powers and the other on a source foreign to the body (and usually diabolic).

Crystals in and of themselves are not intrinsically evil. One of the main reasons crystals are used for healing, however, is because of a "spiritual connection" between crystals and the "energy field" that surrounds a human person. This is the sin of superstition. As the *Catechism* states:

> Superstition is the deviation of religious feeling and of the practices this feeling imposes. It can even affect the worship we offer the true God, e.g., when one attributes an importance in some way magical to certain practices otherwise lawful or necessary. To attribute the efficacy of prayers or of sacramental signs to their mere external performance, apart from the interior dispositions that they demand, is to fall into superstition. (CCC 2111)

Jesus Christ—not stones, rocks, or crystals—is our Rock and the One who heals us. Healing crystals or healing rocks, as they are called, are considered by many as helpful in curing or providing healing to various conditions, but you risk falling into the sin of superstition, or worse, opening the door to evil.

19. Is burning sage in your home OK with the Catholic Church?

Burning sage is thought by some to remove negative energies, and it is usually dispersed in a place or over an afflicted person who stands still while another person lights the sage and walks around him. Various incantations may be used during the ceremony. The use of sage, like healing stones and crystals, is superstition because it draws upon energies or powers to bring about healing or spiritual cleansing and, accordingly, is an offense against the first commandment and a mockery of Catholic sacramentals. Stick to Catholic sacramentals, such as holy water, exorcised salt, or blessed incense.

20. What is the role of sacramentals in spiritual warfare?

The above questions on crystals and sage shows that we instinctively recognize the ability to use material things to convey the immaterial. Sacramentals convey the blessing of the Church, and accordingly, they become instruments of divine grace. Demons traffic in the senses and react to holy water, exorcised salt, or incense. Thus, we should use such sacramentals in our homes to repulse the demons and diminish their nefarious activity. In a similar way, demons are also repulsed by blessed medals and other sacramentals such as the Saint Benedict Medal (which has prayers of exorcism engraved into it), the brown scapular, the Miraculous Medal, and the rosary. Such blessed items have an efficacy of their own accord but also to the degree the person using them has faith and is living in a state of grace. Sacramentals are powerful weapons, but we must use them with faith and trust in God (not superstitiously).

Here is part of the prayer by a priest who exorcises salt. Notice how the prayer evokes biblical imagery, as well as the words of spiritual warfare:[47]

> P: O salt, creature of God, I exorcise you by the living (+) God, by the true (+) God, by the holy (+) God, by the God who ordered you to be poured into the water by Elisha the prophet, so that its life-giving powers might be restored. I

[47] Weller, *Roman Ritual*, 212.

exorcise you so that you may become a means of salvation for believers, that you may bring health of soul and body to all who make use of you, and that you may put to flight and drive away from the places where you are sprinkled; every apparition, villainy, turn of devilish deceit, and every unclean spirit; adjured by him who will come to judge the living and the dead and the world by fire.

R: Amen.

P: Let us pray. Almighty and everlasting God, we humbly implore you, in your immeasurable kindness and love, to bless (+) this salt which you created and gave to the use of mankind, so that it may become a source of health for the minds and bodies of all who make use of it. May it rid whatever it touches or sprinkles of all uncleanness and protect it from every assault of evil spirits. Through Christ our Lord.

And holy water has a similar blessing:

P: O water, creature of God, I exorcise you in the name of God the Father (+) Almighty, and in the name of Jesus (+) Christ His Son, our Lord, and in the power of the Holy (+) Spirit. I exorcise you so that you may put to flight all the power of the enemy and be able to root out and supplant that enemy with his apostate angels, through the power of our Lord Jesus Christ, who will come to judge the living and the dead and the world by fire.

P: Let us pray. O God, for the salvation of mankind, you built your greatest mysteries on this substance, water. In your kindness, hear our prayers and pour down the power of your blessing (+) into this element, made ready for many kinds of purifications. May this, your creature, become an agent of divine grace in the service of your mysteries, to drive away evil spirits and dispel sickness, so that everything in the homes and other buildings of the faithful that is sprinkled

> with this water, may be rid of all uncleanness and freed from every harm. Let no breath of infection and no disease-bearing air remain in these places. May the wiles of the lurking enemy prove of no avail. Let whatever might menace the safety and peace of those who live here be put to flight by the sprinkling of this water, so that the health obtained by calling upon your holy name, may be made secure against all attack. Through Christ our Lord.

You can hear in these blessings the principle that prayer begets what it signifies, based on the words of Jesus, "Ask, and it will be given to you; seek, and you will find; knock and the door will be open to you" (Mt 7:7).

One field test we have utilized with cases is to place two cups of water in front of a possessed person—one blessed and one regular tap water. Inevitably, the possessed person can tell which one is blessed when touched. We have seen a blessed crucifix burn an imprint on the flesh of the possessed, where an unblessed one has no effect. This is because the blessing of Christ, through the Church, conveys on the object. When sacramentals are used with faith, they are powerful weapons.

Chapter V

QUESTIONS FROM PRIESTS—GENERAL

"If it can be done conveniently the possessed person should be led to church or to some other sacred and worthy place, where the exorcism will be held, away from the crowd. But if the person is ill, or for any valid reason, the exorcism may take place in a private home.

"He ought to have a crucifix at hand or somewhere in sight. If relics of the saints are available, they are to be applied in a reverent way to the breast or the head of the person possessed (the relics must be properly and securely encased and covered). One will see to it that these sacred objects are not treated improperly or that no injury is done them by the evil spirit. However, one should not hold the holy Eucharist over the head of the person or in any way apply it to his body, owing to the danger of desecration.

"He will pay attention as to what words in particular cause the evil spirits to tremble, repeating them the more frequently. And when he comes to a threatening expression, he recurs to it again and again, always increasing the punishment. If he perceives that he is making progress, let him persist for two, three, four hours, and longer if he can, until victory is attained."

—*Praenotanda to the Rite of Exorcism, nos. 11, 13, 17*

From the Field: "What is your name?"

A story similar o that from Chapter One comes from a priest visiting the United States from Africa. He was working in a diocese with the permission of the local bishop but was not yet incardinated.[1] Like the priest above, he did not have permission to pray Chapter Three. An afflicted woman had asked for help and the visiting priest took her straight to prayer, as they do in his country. He gave no consideration as to whether the woman was in a state of grace, did not include her husband in the session, or even speak to her pastor.

The young priest also did not know the woman was possessed by a demon as the result of years of kundalini yoga. Kundalini means "serpent," and this type of yoga focuses on awakening (or "uncoiling") dormant energies within the body. Specifically, this practice of Kundalini Shakti is meant to release "serpent power" by seeking to connect the base of the skull (where cognition meets motor movement) to the generative principle and reproductive organs. The kundalini spirit is symbolized as a double-headed snake uncoiling along the spine as the person progresses though the awakening process. Since she and her husband had problems conceiving, this woman had done this type of yoga at the advice of her gynecologist for several years. This practice, combined with other grave sins, eventually led to her possession.

---

1 "The canonical attachment of a cleric to a particular diocese, with correlative rights and duties under the local ordinary." Hardon, *Modern Catholic Dictionary*, 272. See also *Code of Canon Law*, nos. 265–72.

As soon as the priest began the prayer session, the kundalini spirit manifested, contorting the woman's body to move in serpentine fashion, wisping her tongue like that of a snake. At the sight, the priest then began to use ejaculatory deliverance prayers, commanding the demon to leave. Meanwhile, the demon contorted the woman's entire body to move like a huge, angry, coiling snake. The priest then imposed hands on the woman and commanded the demon to leave, but to no avail. He then invoked the power of his priesthood.

"I am a priest of the living God, and I command you to leave her."

Amidst the serpentine movements, and in a snake-like voice, the demon coolly and quietly asked the priest:

"What is your name?"

"I am a priest of God, and I command you to leave this woman."

"Yes, but what is your name?" the demon wisps.

The priest does not hesitate:

"My name is Father (he gives his name), and I command you to leave in the name of Jesus."

The demon stopped movement for a moment while the priest continued his adjuration. Finally, the demon again spoke, as a silence came over the room. In a snake-like voice, he calmly replied:

"You have no authority here."

Realizing that the demon was right, the priest stopped the prayer session and sent the woman home.

In this chapter, we discuss the authority structure and the *tria munera* unique to the priesthood by answering questions from priests who want to know how to engage in spiritual warfare at the parish level.

1. How does the ministry of exorcism relate to me as a parish priest? What does it have to do with the *tria munera*?

The *Catechism* states: "The ministerial priesthood differs in essence from the common priesthood of the faithful because it confers a sacred power for the service of the faithful. The ordained ministers exercise their service for the People of God by teaching (*munus docendi*), divine worship (*munus liturgicum*) and pastoral governance (*munus regendi*)" (CCC 1592).

Munus is the Latin word for *office*, but in the sense of service, post, gift, employment, function, or duty. As explained above, authority is based on office which, in turn, is derived from natural or divine positive law (which is an additional layering of law given to the Church which builds upon natural law, such as the priesthood). According to Ludwig Ott, "The hierarchical magisterial powers of the Church embrace the teaching power, the pastoral power (i.e., legislative, juridical and punitive power), and the sacerdotal power. They correspond to the threefold office, laid on Christ as man for the purpose of the redemption of mankind: the office of prophet or the teaching office, the pastoral or royal office, and the priestly office."[2]

As William Arndt explains, as used in the New Testament, "power" is "the ability to do a certain thing" and "authority" is "the *right* to perform an act."[3] When Jesus used the words "power and authority" as to what He bestowed upon the apostles when He sent them out (Lk 9:1), the deeper meaning is often lost to the modern reader. According to Werner Foerster, the meaning of *authority* is an ancient concept which means "the right over something" and is based upon one's office according to natural law relationships. This means, he says,

2 Ott, *Fundamentals of Catholic Dogma*, 276.
3 Arndt, *St. Luke*, 250

"the rights of parents in relation to children, of masters, in relations to slaves, of owners in relation and of individuals in respect to personal liberty."[4] This carries over into Scriptural usage, and means the right to command. Sometimes translated into English as "power," it is interrelated with but distinct from power. Where *power* is an extrinsic, often physical, "possibility of action," authority is an intrinsic, a lawful *right of disposition* over person, place, or object. Ultimately, all authority derives from God's supreme authority. This distinction is key for understanding the priest's jurisdictional authority over the demon. Where the layman has the right to command according to his office as head of household, property owner, etc., the priest shares in the universal jurisdictional authority of his bishop.

When Jesus sent the apostles (notably, apostles, not lay people) with "power and authority" (Lk 9:1; cf. Mk 6:7), He empowered them specifically to do three actions: to preach, to heal, and to govern. In Luke, we read: "He summoned the Twelve and gave them power and authority over all demons and to cure diseases, and he sent them to proclaim the kingdom of God and to heal the sick" (Lk 9:1–2). In Mark, we read: "So they went off and preached repentance. They drove out many demons, and they anointed with oil men who were sick and cured them" (Mk 6:13).

These three correspond to the *tria munera* unique to the ordained, which are called the *munus docendi* (office/responsibility to teach), the *munus sanctificandi* (office/responsibility to heal by the administration of the sacraments, thus also called *munus liturgicum*, the pastoral ministry), and the *munus regendi* (the office/responsibility to govern or rule). A priest uniquely shares in the threefold office of priest, prophet, and

---

4 Foerster, ἐξουσία ("Authority") in Kittel, ed. *Theological Dictionary of the New Testament*, 562.

king. The *munus regendi* is where every priest—notably, not just the diocesan exorcist—have the office, duty, and responsibility to assert his authority over the demons who afflict his flock. Whether you know it or not, the demon keenly knows this fact and does all he can to get you to not engage.

What does this all mean? In the strict sense, juridical authority is given to the apostles and their successors. In a wide sense, all of the baptized have power over demons, but the authority to wield that power stems from the office one holds within the Body of Christ. By definition, a *munus* is the responsibility to discharge an office. When you are frustrated because the men in your parish are not engaging as spiritual leaders in their homes, remind them that they, like you, have the responsibility and duty to engage their office.

2. What is "exhausting the pastoral response"? Phase zero?

When a difficult situation presents itself, particularly someone claiming to have diabolic affliction, a very busy pastor often too readily calls the diocesan exorcist and passes the person off. Recall that a generation ago, however, the word *pastoral* meant *the administration of the sacraments*. Today, it has come to mean whatever the priest thinks in his prudential judgment is best for the person, or (worse) a consideration of the subjective feelings of the parishioner, some vague "accompaniment," or some other subjective response. By "exhausting the pastoral response" is meant doing all the sacramental and basic spiritual work for the petitioner. This, in turn, will allow the ordinary means of grace to begin to flow. The words of Father Amorth are worth repeating: "One good confession is worth one-hundred exorcisms."[5] Thus, before handing off this difficult parishioner, do the pastoral spade work necessary to

5 Amorth, *An Exorcist: More Stories*, 195.

get the entire family into a state of grace by addressing the areas where sacramental grace is being occluded. How long has it been since they went to confession? What are their sacraments? Are they married in Church? In light of Father Amorth's observations, a general confession and disciplined prayer life can be quite effective in clearing out spiritual oppression.

We utilize a four-phase protocol, with the first phase being a thirty-day prayer regimen designed to help reorder a person's life to prayer. Many people have reported being freed of lifelong addictions to pornography or substance abuse simply through the basic prayer regimen, media fast, and weekly/regular confession. You could prescribe the phase one prayers as a spiritual discipline. Any priest who has done *Exodus 90* with the men of his parish will know that short bursts of ascesis can be very helpful in the spiritual life. We have found, however, that many individuals seeking help lack even a very basic catechetical and prayer life of rudimentary Catholicism. They also lack requisite virtue to sustain liberation, should it be attained. Many who come to the parish who want their home blessed because it is "haunted" or a child is afflicted, moreover, are often in irregular marriages, do not regularly attend Mass, allow contraception in the home, practice some syncretism with paganism (using sage cleansings or dream catchers in the home, for example), and do not live in a state of grace. Sadly, many Catholics do not even know what a state of grace means.

The goal of phase zero, therefore, is to get your parishioner's spiritual life in order by focusing on three specific areas. First, look at the sacramental life and state of grace. Here, the pastoral remedy is addressing primary, habitual sins and removing the obstacles to grace. Demons attach to sin, so you must clear that out first if you hope to drive the demon out. Typically, you will find that the person will want the demon gone but has little or no desire to change his life of sin. That is, most want spiritual pain management, or to be "demon free," but have little or no desire for conversion. You may have, for example, an obsession case where the husband is addicted to pornography, but the wife is the one afflicted, or they call because the house is infested (so they think). You need to clear the husband's addiction first before addressing the diabolic affliction. If you bless the house and they are still living a life of sin, you can actually open a bigger door to the demon. The demon is not leaving until the spiritual house is clean.

Second, address the need for prayer and mortification. Are they doing basic penance and elementary levels of self-denial? Are they praying? Doing any acts of self-denial? Most who have problems with the diabolic lack even an elementary level of discipline. Typically, there is not found a single place in their life where they practice any self-denial at a basic level. Instituting a prayer discipline often clears it up.

Third, you will need to get people to follow the right authority structure. If the household is out of order, such as the wife assuming headship, this can cause problems. In cases where they come to you because of a child with spiritual problems, you will often see the wife resisting the husband's authority. Notably, yielding to authority is not a groveling obsequiousness but utilizing her right role as helpmate. Quite common as well is the husband who fails to engage as spiritual leader. When combined with the above, helping that family dynamic back into right order will often clear out spiritual oppression, even some low-level obsessions. Rightly order the authority structure in the home and teach the husband to engage in battle on behalf of his family. Thus, you must probe: Where is the father? What is going on in the home? Is the father engaged and the household rightly ordered? Is everyone in a state of grace? Are they united in faith in both belief and practice?

In addition, a common problem in the field of exorcism and deliverance is aftercare. What do you do with the individual post-liberation? The importance of exhausting the pastoral response not only cuts down the case load of the diocesan exorcist but also saves time along the long process of liberation. In addition, this also keeps the petitioner connected with his pastor. By using all of the remedies at the local level first, you keep them connected to the parish priest throughout the process, which, in turn, facilitates the individual's integration with the Mystical Body. Exhausting the pastoral response, then, means fully engaging the *munus sanctificandi* before turning to the *munus regendi*.

3. I had a good formation in the seminary, especially regarding sacramental theology, but we never learned anything about praying deliverance prayers after sacramental absolution. Wouldn't it be best for the diocesan exorcist to pray these types of prayers?

Here is how Father Ripperger summarizes the duty of the priest vis-à-vis spiritual warfare:

> Saint Alphonsus Liguori and other saints have always held that each priest is required to do exorcisms and deliverance, depending on his state in life. This does not necessarily mean that he will do exorcisms as directed by his bishop, but it does mean that, as the saint says, in every parish and diocese there are people who are under attack from the fallen angels who need the assistance of the priest to whom their care and protection has been entrusted.[6]

6 Ripperger, *Minor Exorcisms*, "Instruction."

Notice here two things. One, implied in the writings of Saint Alphonsus (along with other saints) is what was answered above—namely, that a *munus* is not just an office or task but a responsibility, a duty to engage. You have the obligation to engage if you have been given an office. Two, implied as well are the twofold ends of authority structure to provide and protect. Pope Benedict XVI linked these two ends to the command of Jesus to Peter at the Sea of Tiberias (Jn 21:15–17): "Feed my lambs" (provide) and "Tend my sheep" (protect).[7] Many priests lament that the men in their parish let the women do everything and do not engage as spiritual leaders in the home, but they themselves fail to do the same in their parishes. Just as a priest has the obligation to engage in "the care and protection" (*viz.*, the two ends of the authority structure are provision and protection), so also the husband and head of household. If you want men to come alive in your parish, engage in your own *munus regendi* and teach the men to do the same. The failure to do so is negligence for which you will be held accountable.

4. I was told by a priest-mentor not to pray deliverance prayers/minor exorcisms, since only the diocesan exorcist has the authority of the Church behind him, and therefore I would be spiritually vulnerable engaging the demons on my own. How do I respond to him?

In the same instruction as the previous question, Father Ripperger invokes apostolic succession as how Christ, in conferring Holy Orders, has "put in the different Orders certain

[7] Pope Benedict XVI, "Munus Regendi," General Audience (26 May 2010).

powers necessary to provide for the faithful as well as to protect them and free them from the adversary."[8] While solemn exorcism and the use of Chapter Three is restricted to the order of exorcist, there are many prayers contained in the Church's treasury and patrimony which every priest can and should be utilizing to fight off the enemy's attacks against his parishioners. It is completely licit for you to pray minor exorcism—and even simple binding prayers over your parishioners—in the faithful execution of your office as pastor, guide, and guardian of the souls entrusted to you.

If a priest does not have permission to pray **restricted** prayers like those of Solemn Rite of Exorcism or Chapter Three,[9] then he does not have the protection of the Church. With regard to all **unrestricted** minor exorcisms and deliverance prayers, however, he can and should swing away, and he does so with the full protection of the authority of the Church. This is part of his ordained ministry, and he has the right (and duty) to engage this powerful weapon in defense of his flock.

5. When do you recommend that I use exorcised oil in deliverance ministry?

We have seen blessed oils used for the protection of the senses, particularly for team members who assist the priest in prayer at exorcisms or deliverance sessions. Remember, the demon traffics in the senses and generally will hold in that part of the body where he entered into the person or where he is using as a holding point, which is generally connected to the sin. When

8 Ripperger, *Minor Exorcisms*, "Instruction."

9 Any priest can pray Chapter Three as a private devotion but requires his bishop's permission for public use. A lay person cannot use this prayer, as it is a reserved prayer for priests only.

you encounter sins of pornography, for example, anoint the back of each eyelid with the sign of the cross. When a particular body part heats up or becomes numb or pained during deliverance (you will often see the throat become constricted), use blessed oils there as well.

6. I see many priests and exorcists being taken down in this ministry by women. Why is this seemingly more common among those who engage in spiritual warfare?

The demon can alter our perceptions and feelings towards other people. As Father Ripperger notes:

> Exorcists have noticed that demons can cause amorous feelings, emotions, or sentiments in people in relationship to anyone that God permits. It is entirely possible for a demon who is obsessing someone to make them have feelings for the wrong kinds of individuals, which could cause them harm or not be good for them spiritually. They can also give one a psychological perspective and amorous feelings for someone . . . contrary to our own dispositions of emotional patterns.[10]

For example, we had a case where a possessed woman was sexually abused as a child by a stepfather. She later became possessed, and this was a holding point for the demon. At the moment when she was making good progress in the weekly exorcism sessions, a much older man who looked exactly like her abuser (or so she reported) suddenly knocked on her door and invited her to dinner. She unexplainably agreed, and a sexual relationship immediately ensued, completely undermining the progress she had made; previously, she was not

---

[10] Ripperger, *Dominion*, 271–72.

in mortal sin, but she was psychologically obsessed. She was a successful and well-educated woman who was trying to live her Catholic faith and sought liberation. He was a transient, at least twenty-five years older than her, and lived in a van which he had parked along the river. Despite the obvious disparity, she felt an irresistible, sexual drive towards him, and every day after solemn session, she would drive down to the river for a sexual tryst (markedly disordered and violent, and eerily parallel to the manner of her abuse thirty years ago), thereby effectively undoing the work of the exorcist.

Thus, the demon can create feelings of being loved in a manner beyond the natural in order to maintain control over a person. He does so by manipulating an afflicted person's perceptions of others. He can also cycle someone into a person's life who meets the exact specifications, so to speak, of what he thinks will trap his prey. This is a repeated tactic used against priests. Saint Alphonsus Liguori says that the devil is always trying to get a priest to fall because "if he succeeds . . . he obtains a greater prey . . . [because the priest] drags down many others with him."[11] The demon is an apex predator who knows the value of a priest and also his weaknesses. Father Ripperger states:

> Exorcists have noticed that demons can cause amorous feelings, emotions, or sentiments in people in relationship to anyone that God permits. This is a key in understanding for the exorcist, because any feelings he might have for those he works with (and amorous feelings experienced by those he works with) must be immediately aired out, severed, or bound and immediately dealt with per the principle of St. Ignatius. They cannot be allowed to be hidden or fester, as

---

11 Saint Alphonsus Liguori, *Dignity and Duties of the Priest*, 356.

> that will continue to allow the demon to work silently in the background to amplify and perpetuate those feelings.[12]

The demon is the world's greatest actuary because he knows statistically what our predictable behavior is and exploits our vulnerabilities.[13] That means the priest who struggles with chastity hits his radar, and he can send someone your way to probe that vulnerability.

An evil spirit can also give an afflicted woman the impression that the priest loves her very deeply, fulfilling a deep, psychological void in her. They can manipulate any bodily organ (remember, demons traffic in the senses) and thus change the way the woman perceives a man, and vice versa, such as the case above.[14] They do this in two ways. One, by directly manipulating the exterior sense so that what they see or hear is distorted. Secondly, they can manipulate the cogitative power and thus put a perspective on the image. They can cause the afflicted woman to fall madly in love with a priest. At the same time, the demon appeals to impurity or a similar wound in a priest which desires feminine (or masculine) affirmation. We have seen good, faithful priests get taken down this way. While you may think that by leaving the priesthood and getting married you will live happily ever after, this is not the case. After he takes a priest down, the demon generally flips the switch and removes those feelings, turning the woman against you, even causing repulsive and angry feelings towards you. He has done his job, however, and moves on.

So, keep good boundaries, stay humble, and have a good confessor or spiritual director with whom you can be brutally honest when temptations come.

---

12 Ripperger, *Diabolic Influence*, 269–70.

13 Liber Christo, "Companion Guide," 150. Schneider, *The Liber Christo Method*, 180.

14 Saint Thomas Aquinas, *De Malo*, q. 16, a. 12, ad 2.

7. Some of my brother priests think that when it comes to deliverance, we should just leave well enough alone, or at least let the diocesan exorcist deal with it. What should I say to that?

The office of priesthood means a responsibility to engage, to include the *munus regendi*. There are no conscientious objectors in this battle. You have been issued weapons, so use them. Many priests do not want to engage because they say they do not "want a target on my back." Do not think that the demon only targets exorcist priests and that if you start to engage in spiritual warfare, you will be retaliated against, or somehow suddenly show up on the radar. He will whisper lies to you like, "if you stand down, I will stand down" or, "if you start doing spiritual warfare, I will make your life miserable." I have news for you: he is lying and fully intends never to stand down and never cease trying to make your life miserable. He hates you more than he hates your flock because you are a priest of the living God, a priest forever, and are *in persona Christi*. As stated above, a *munus* is not just a function, nor is a priest a mere functionary or figurehead. The devil knows sacerdotal theology better than any of your seminary professors.

Do not give in to this fear. Also, do not give up because the last time you tried this or that prayer you got some pushback. This is war, and you are a field officer in the Church Militant. You are targeted anyway, so take to heart the words of Saint Paul to Timothy: "Bear your share of hardship along with me like a good soldier of Jesus Christ" (2 Tm 2:3). Recall in the old Rite of Confirmation where the bishop gave a symbolic blow to the cheek called the *colée* slap, a reminder that the confirmed Christian is now a soldier for Christ. A civilian can flee battle, but not a soldier. How much more must an officer stand his ground? This is part of being a *cura animarum*, a guardian of souls. You cannot abrogate this responsibility to the exorcist.

You put a target on your back when you prostrated yourself before your bishop and were ordained a priest of the living God, a priest forever. That is when you told the devil "game on," and he will do everything he can to get you to not engage. Meanwhile, he is circling the flock. If you are baptizing, hearing confessions, and preaching, then you are already engaging in spiritual warfare. So now is a time to fully engage your sacerdotal dignity. Live your priesthood, daily consecrate your priesthood and your reputation to the Blessed Mother. Pray, fast, and become a saint. And keep your head on a swivel.

8. I am hesitant to engage in deliverance ministry because of fear of transference. Am I as a priest vulnerable to this, especially if I pray with my hand on the person's head?

As stated above, the twofold end of the authority structure is provision and protection. This also applies to you as a priest. If you are working under the authority of your local bishop, then you will be afforded protection. A priest always operates within proper spiritual authority of the divine positive law as spiritual father, and so possesses a universal authority. The authority of the office of priesthood means that the posture of imposition of hands—your hands are anointed for a reason, after all—is the correct posture of blessing and you should have no fear of clinging spirits whatsoever. This is so long as you are in a state of grace, of course. Remove that protection, and you are fair game. This applies, moreover, even if you are preaching, hearing confessions, and in the course of the normal duties of the *munus liturgicum*.

9. Doesn't the Bible show us that lay people can impose hands as well?

Yes, but not in the manner that is commonly believed today by some in the Church. In the Old Testament, the imposition of hands was largely a priestly gesture, but also patriarchal, part of the blessing of a father over his children. From the *Revised Book of Blessings,* we read: "The God from whom all blessings flow favored many persons—particularly the patriarchs, kings, priests, Levites, and parents—by allowing them to offer blessings in praise of his name, and to invoke his name, so that other persons or works of creation, could be showered with divine blessings."[15] Note who offer blessings—namely, patriarchs, kings, priests, Levites, and parents. That is, the right to bless flows from office, not a charism.

This twofold usage of imposing hands as priestly and patriarchal carries from the Old to New Testament. Imposition of hands is used by Jesus for the healing of the sick (Mt 9:18; Mk 5:23, 6:5, 8:23; Lk 13:11) and for blessing (Mt 19:15). The power of healing of the sick by the laying of hands is given to the apostles ("the Eleven") at the Great Commissioning (Mk 16:18). In Acts of the Apostles, the gesture is expanded to more than healing to include ordination, as in ordaining the first deacons (Acts 6:6). Peter and John lay hands on the Samaritans to receive the Holy Spirit in a post-baptismal anointing/Confirmation (Acts 8:17). Ananias (one of the seventy-two in Luke chapter 9 and first bishop of Damascus) lays hands on Paul so that "you regain your sight and be filled with the Holy Spirit" (Acts 9:12). In Acts 13:1–3, Symeon Niger (one of the seventy-two), Lucius of Cyrene (one of the seventy-two, bishop of Laodicea in Syria), and Manaen

---

15 USCCB, *Book of Blessings,* no. 6.

(elder/*presbuteroi* of the Church at Antioch) were instructed by the Holy Spirit to impose hands on Barnabas and Saul who were "set apart for me . . . for I have called them" (Acts 13:3). Paul baptizes and lays hands on some believers in Ephesus so that they also receive the Holy Spirit (Acts 19:6). The imposition of hands is used three times in the Pauline letters, and once in Hebrews, all in reference to the priesthood or post-baptismal anointing/Confirmation (1 Tm 5:22; 1 Tm 4:14; 2 Tm 1:6; Heb 6:2).

Three points here may help to clarify. One, the imposition of hands is a sacred gesture imbued with theological meaning that is based on the office of the one who imparts the blessing. Two, the imposition of hands has distinct meaning that carries from the Old and into the New Testament, and nowhere is that gesture used for driving out demons. Three, the right to bless flows from office, which means there are rules which govern this gesture.

Your priestly hands are sacred. In the Rite of Ordination, moreover, the priest's hands are anointed, such that when a priest receives last rites, it is customary that the back of this hands (not the palms) be anointed since the palms have already been anointed. When God initiated the first priesthood, he gave the command to Moses to ordain Aaron and his sons. He not only specified sacred vestments but also a consecration to include the anointing of their hands. The Vulgate reads: "and you will consecrate the hands and sanctify them so that they may serve as a priesthood for me" (Ex 28:41). The NAB reads "you shall ordain them," but the Greek and Latin read "fill/anoint their hands." Because they offer sacrifice and touch sacred vessels, a priest's hands are sacred, set aside for sacred purposes.

Under laying on of hands in *Strong's Bible Concordance*, you will never find a lay person laying hands upon another lay person of equal rank. Moreover, those who do impose hands in both Testaments in prayer are those in spiritual authority either by being directly appointed by God or by delegation from those who have God's authority (such as the prophets or apostles). This is affirmed also in biblical encyclopedias and dictionaries.[16] In Scripture are found religious leaders in both the Old and New Testament, along with fathers of a family, praying over someone under their authority as they raise their right hand in prayer. Again, this is exercised by office, not charism.

This custom from Scripture carries into tradition and the practice of the Church. According to Father Hardon, the imposition of hands is defined:

> **In both the Old and New Testaments, [the imposition of hands is] a significant symbolic action, denoting various meanings.** Examples: **Israel giving his parental blessing** to Ephraim and Manasseh (Genesis 48:18); **Moses passing his authority to his successor** (Numbers 27:18); Joshua receiving the spirit of wisdom to lead the people (Deuteronomy 34:9); **Aaron, preparing the ram for sacrifice** (Exodus 29:10).
>
> In the New Testament [its] symbolism took on a further and deeper meaning: **Jesus blessing the children** (Matthew 19:15); **Jesus bringing the official's daughter back to life.** (Matthew 9:18); **Peter and John, calling down the Holy Spirit on the Samaritans** (Acts 8:17). **After Pentecost, the laying on of hands especially denoted the conferral of the powers and authority of the episcopacy,** which Christ had given to the Apostles. In the Catholic Church, the **sacrament of orders**: the diaconate, priesthood, the episcopate [are] administered through a bishop through the laying on of hands.[17]

16 See Hahn, *Catholic Bible Dictionary*, 22.

17 Hardon, *Modern Catholic Dictionary*, 270.

Thus, and significantly, nowhere in the Old or New Testaments is the imposition of hands used in connection with the driving out of demons. Not a single reference. In the 1962 Rite of Exorcism, moreover, there is an adjuration by the priest whereby he places his stole (not his anointed hand) upon the neck/base of the skull (in reference to Gn 3:15) as well as place his other hand upon the head of the energumen. Notably, the rubrics state that when the priest places his hands upon the head, he should do so "with a sacramental, such as a relic or crucifix." At the end of the Rite, he does impose hands, not in adjuration but in blessing.[18]

In addition, in the healing of the crippled woman in Luke 13:10–17, we do see how the demon can sometimes mask behind physical sickness, or even cause (or exacerbate) physical illness. A woman was "crippled by a spirit" and "bound by Satan" (Lk 13:11, 16) and Jesus "laid hands on her" in healing (Lk 13:13–14). The question remains: If a mandated exorcist himself commands the demon in adjuration but does not impose hands but rather uses his stole or a crucifix or a relic, then why would we presume it in conformity to liturgical norms for a "lay deliverance team" to drive out demons through the imposition of hands and direct adjuration of the demon? And, more specifically, why do we think that there is no risk of transference of clinging spirits to those lay people,

[18] In the revised Rite of Exorcism, the new rubric removes the barrier of sacramentals used by the priest (stole, relic, or crucifix) and does call for the imposition of hands by the priest. Notably, however, there was not a single exorcist on the committee who wrote the revised Ritual, but rather it was composed by liturgists. In their attempt to move the emphasis away from the Christological to the Pneumatological and Ecclesial, as well as the focus on healing, the authors (in my theological opinion) made a significant break from the received tradition of the Rite. Nonetheless, the laying of hands used in liberation is done by the priest and used in the revised Ritual only by a priest with permission from his ordinary.

as if the retaliation upon the sons of Sceva (Acts 19:16) is not relevant?

We have seen many well-intended lay people, who were asked by exorcists to act as handlers to hold down the possessed, retaliated against for just the skin-to-skin contact with the manifesting demon. Some were minor, but others have suffered health and other problems over time. One young team member had night terrors after every session for months after holding the head of a possessed woman during sessions. Another team member would come home after assisting at a session where he held the possessed person down and his wife (not he) would have nightmares.[19] These were individuals working under an exorcist, not commanding the demon—how much more vulnerable is a well-intended lay woman imposing hands for healing or in adjuration over strangers with no discernment whatsoever as to what demons may be present.

10. Someone showed up at my parish and said he is possessed. What should I do?

While not always the case, you will generally find that when someone demands to see an exorcist, or any priest for that matter, it is a telltale sign that he is not possessed. The last thing a demon wants is a showdown with the diocesan exorcist. This is probably psychological, and the demon likes to send mentally ill people to disrupt parish life and distract you from your mission. Exhaust the pastoral response (see

[19] For the protection of the team members, exorcist, and diocese, our protocol does not use handlers. By the time the person works through the protocol and comes to prayer session, we have found the demon sufficiently weakened and the individual strengthened in the will, such that the manifestations are generally controlled by word of command by the exorcist.

the question on "phase zero" above) and all natural remedies (to include mental health counselling, etc.) before assuming the diabolic. You can put them on the Liber Christo prayer regimen, and you will know in thirty days. That first phase serves as a diagnostic to determine the level of diabolic activity and helps to determine whether the principal affliction is spiritual or psychological (or which is primary). After exhausting these remedies, consult with the diocesan exorcist. In our system, phase two is a catechesis (using *The Liber Christo Method: A Manual for Spiritual Warfare*), and phase three is minor exorcism done by the local pastor (often in consultation with the diocesan exorcist) which is well within your bounds of authority and part of the *tria munera*. You are quipped not only for the pastoral response of phase zero but the next three phases.

11. I have a deacon at my parish. What can deacons do in deliverance ministry? Can they lay hands? Can they pray imprecatory prayers?

As ordained ministers, deacons share in the *tria munera*, but in a unique way. While the priest serves *in persona Christi capitis* (in the Person of Christ the Head), the deacon serves *in persona Christi servi* (in the Person of Christ the Servant). The deacon baptizes (which includes exorcisms within the ritual) and preaches, but his authority is also bound by the unique diaconal charism.

While there is some confusion today over the limits of this office, the Congregation for the Doctrine of the Faith in 2015 offered a point of clarity on the diaconal ministry. Because there was no clear answer on what deacons can and cannot pray, for example, the Pope Leo Institute reserved judgement to the local level on the use of Chapter Three by deacons. The matter appears now to have been answered in the negative. When asked "Can a deacon validly confect blessings, which are not *expresse jure* permitted to him in the 1956 *Rituale Romanum*," the Congregation for the Doctrine of the Faith (CDF, now called the DDF) stated:

> It is clear from Can 1169 para. 3 that the faculty granted to a deacon to confect a blessing must be expressly conceded. Now, it does not appear that any faculty has been granted to deacons by Church authority as regard to the use of blessing rights contained in the 1952 *Rituale*. Such concessions indeed exist in the 1984 *De Benedictionibus* but these are given on a rite-by-rite basis, and therefore only pertain to those particular rights referred to and laid out, and that liturgical book, without any influence on the rights to use the blessings of the 1952 *Rituale*.[20]

Notably, and adding to the complexity of the issue, there was no such thing as the permanent diaconate in 1952, so the delimiting of what a deacon can or cannot pray in the years after its re-institution has been slow in its evolution. This document, however, gives a clear principle. Just as at Mass, a deacon can only pray those prayers specifically granted in the liturgical book, so when blessing, he can only pray those blessings which are specifically proscribed to him in the 1985 *Book of Blessings* (*De Benedictionibus*). This means he should not pray other blessings, such as exorcism, found in other books of blessings.[21]

---

[20] Rorate Caeli, "Dubia Answered: Warning for priests treating afflicted souls, guidance on blessings by deacons."

[21] *Code of Canon Law*, no. 1169 §1: "Those marked with the episcopal character and presbyters permitted by law or legitimate grant can perform consecrations and dedications validly. §2: Any presbyter can impart blessings except those reserved to the Roman Pontiff or bishops. §3: A deacon can impart only those blessings expressly permitted by law."

As to the imposition of hands, deacons should again follow the rubrics directly granted to him in the appropriate liturgical books (such as the rite of Baptism) but otherwise not perform blessings or other actions proper to the priesthood. He works safely and effectively when he remains *in persona Christi servi* and resists the temptation to priestly functions. The hands of the priest, not the deacon, are anointed. In deliverance ministry, the additional ecclesial layering of Holy Orders provides a layer of protection exceeding that of the laity, as we have found deacons to be very effective as case managers, program facilitators, catechists, and liturgical assistants to the exorcist. We have also seen deacons (and their wives) be severely retaliated against for not following this norm—namely, when praying Chapter Three or minor exorcism prayers over people, even with "permission" of their local bishop or exorcist. Authority flows from office, not charism. Even a bishop cannot give "permission" for someone to perform a duty proper to an office that person does not hold. He cannot give permission, for example, to a layman to say Mass because the layman speaks Latin better than the priest. The demon will probe these boundaries.

12. Some parishioners want to set up a deliverance team at my parish. Is that safe?

Let us first distinguish between "praying over" someone and "praying with" someone. All Christians should pray *with* each other, but to pray *over* someone implies a position of authority. In addition, we prefer not touching, as we have seen demonic transference take place via skin-to-skin contact if the person is diabolically afflicted. As for lay prayer meetings, it is better to lead someone to use the imprecatory form of prayer for themselves or use the deprecatory form when praying with one another. Also, teach them to do severing of spirits prayers and renunciations for themselves. In addition, there is a serious problem when a diocese or parish, in effect, outsources to laypeople what is proper to the *tria munera* of the ordained. This is like a father paying someone to go to his children's baseball games because he is too busy. Man up, fathers; this is your sacred duty.

Consider the above 2015 CDF clarification on deacons when discerning whether to allow lay deliverance teams at your parish. The *Catechism* gives further principles: "Sacramentals derive from the baptismal priesthood: every baptized person is called to be a 'blessing,' and to bless. Hence lay people may preside at certain blessings; the more a blessing concerns ecclesial and sacramental life, the more is its administration reserved to the ordained ministry (bishops, priests, or deacons)" (CCC 1669). The permanent deacon has "a place and office within the People of God" (using the language of the *Revised Book of Blessings*) which is higher than and distinct from the lay person. His office means when he blesses as an ordained minister, it is distinctly different than a lay person and confects blessings "reserved to the ordained ministry" (CCC 1669).

In the *Revised Book of Blessings*, moreover, when a deacon celebrates a blessing, the rubric prescribes that the deacon should pray "with hands outstretched" while the lay person is instructed to pray "with hands folded."[22] In the few instances

[22] Note, for example, in the Order for Blessing of a New Home, the rubrics states: "A minister who is a priest or deacon, says the prayer of blessing with hands outstretched; a lay minister says the prayer with hands joined." USCCB, *Book of Blessings*, no. 673. In that same blessing, the ordained minister prays "Peace be with this house and all who live here." If there is no ordained minister, however, the homeowner can lead the prayer, but the formula changes to a deprecatory form: "May the God whom we glorify with one heart and voice enable us, through the Spirit, to live in harmony as followers of Jesus Christ, now and forever." USCCB, *Book of Blessings*, no. 666.

when a lay person can bless, the ritual states that "whenever a priest, or deacon is present, the office of presiding should be left to him." With respect to the laity, in every instance (and there are very few) where a lay person can preside over a blessing—it assumes a priest or deacon is not present—the formula for blessing is changed from imprecatory to deprecatory. That is, the lay presider is instructed to pray with folded hands, not outstretched, as when a priest or deacon presides.

This begs the question: If a deacon is bound by liturgical rubrics, to include being strictly limited in his bodily gestures and blessings, why would it be acceptable for lay people to lay hands and drive out demons at your parish? Simply stated, you are opening them (and you) up to diabolic retaliation when you permit this at your parish. You have a duty to protect your sheep, even if they want to hunt the wolf for you.

13. What do modern exorcists say about the imposition of hands by the laity? Don't sponsors impose hands during the Rite of Confirmation?

With regard to the laying of hands, Father Amorth criticized its use by the laity because he saw this gesture as having a specifically liturgical function reserved for the clergy. He says that laymen who lay hands on other lay people are "exalting themselves." At most, he says, they should "raise a hand but nothing more."[23] Remember, there is a difference between praying with someone and praying over someone (see above). To pray *over* someone, you must have requisite authority by virtue of an office.[24]

[23] Rossetti, *The Pope's Exorcist*, 19–20.

[24] Saint Thomas, for example, delimits the proper use of the divine Name in adjuration in *ST* II-II, q. 90.

Modern exorcists agree with Father Amorth. The International Association of Exorcists, for example, cautions that, "the lay faithful, in particular, may not lay hands or make gestures normally reserved for sacred ministers."[25] Notably, in addition to the IAE, other experienced exorcists have recently stated that lay people should not lay hands on other lay people to drive out demons. Father Winston Cabading, chief exorcist in the Philippines, addresses the question directly:

> *Is it licit for laypeople to lay their hands as a gesture of healing or sending of the Holy Spirit like what priests do?* In the practice of the Catholic Church, the "Laying of Hands" symbolize and formally manifests the invocation of the Holy Spirit. It has been primarily used in the sacraments of baptism, confirmation, anointing of the sick, and the ordination of deacons, priests, and bishops. Likewise, the imparting of specific blessings to persons and the blessing of sacramentals, and during exorcisms, the gesture is used. It is primarily an epiclectic (invocation of the Holy Spirit) gesture and is priestly. In many healing services led by laypeople in the charismatic renewal, this has also become relatively common such that laypeople begin to make the gesture even when a priest is present doing the blessing or prayer of healing or exorcism. Although the practice is not reprobated (forbidden) formally by the Church, the praxis of laypeople laying their hands over priests or bishops, or over others is not theologically sound. Moreover, it generates confusion both doctrinally and liturgically—doctrinally because the laying of hands over a person signifies spiritual authority and power. The ordination of bishops, priests, and deacons give them explicitly and with divine assurance this spiritual authority and power over those under their charge. Laypeople do not have this even if they are the leader of a group. The lay faithful's spiritual authority is limited only to those within their

[25] IAE, *Guidelines for the Ministry of Exorcism*, 90.

> family and proprietary circle. Hence, parents can bless their children even if their child is a cleric. They explicitly give their parental blessing but not anything else. Liturgically it is also confusing because a priestly blessing is different from lay blessing. So, a priest laying hands over people or things and then simultaneously laypeople extending their hands over them give a confusing sign.[26]

In addition to Father Amorth and Father Cabading, other exorcists who agree include Father Ripperger, Father Dan Reehil, Monsignor Rosetti, and Monsignor Charles Pope.[27] Monsignor Pope, for example, states that lay people should indeed pray for and with one another, affirming that "the charism to bring physical or spiritual healing and consolation to others is not exclusive to the clergy." Nonetheless, he states, "the laity should not use priestly gestures such as the laying of hands upon a person's head or making the sign of the cross over them similar to the gesture of priests when giving a blessing."[28]

The advice from the IAE and modern exorcists, however, is directly contradicted by some Protestant-type models of liberation. For example, in *Unbound*, Neal Lozano instructs lay people to "say firmly, with authority, while placing your hand on the persons head, 'In the name of Jesus I break the power of every spirit that *n.* has renounced and I command it to leave right now.'"[29] Accordingly, Monsignor Rossetti rightly cautions that lay people should "tread lightly in regard to Key #4/Authority and the 'word of command'" found in *Unbound*, where lay people impose hands on other lay people and

[26] Cabading, et.al., "Frequently Asked Questions," no. 77.

[27] See Rossetti, "Guidelines for Laity." Also, Ripperger, *Deliverance Prayers for Laity*, 9.

[28] Pope, *Our Sunday Visitor* (April 18, 2022), "Can laypeople lay hands on others during prayer?"

[29] Lozano, *Unbound*, 54.

command demons.[30] He further states, "Many Catholic exorcists agree that pastoral prudence is called for when suggesting that lay Christians directly command demons to be cast out. While theologically it is true that every baptized believer has authority to serve in Jesus' name, laity with the intent to directly command demons to be cast out can be inviting trouble."[31] In addition, Monsignor Rossetti affirms what is found in Scripture, namely that the "gesture of imposition of hands . . . is a priestly gesture and a gesture for fathers to bless their children. In fact, this gesture in the Bible is generally done in blessing and a priestly blessing to confer the Holy Spirit sacramentally."[32] Biblical theologian Brant Pitre likewise affirms Monsignor Rossetti's explanation of the biblical meaning of the gesture.[33]

That Lozano, author of *Unbound,* holds a position contrary to the common teaching of the above-named experienced exorcists and theologians is seen in his comment: "Some teach that you should not touch the person. I believe this is a deception based on fear and a focus on demons. If you have authority to pray for a person, you can touch them without fear."[34] The former is conjecture, and while the latter may be true, it depends upon on how one determines the "authority over" another person. Lozano defines authority, moreover, in a manner inconsistent with Scripture and Tradition when he suggests that authority is eaned through merit.[35]

---

30 See Lozano, *Unbound,* 57, 98–109.

31 Rossetti, "Frequently Asked Questions." He refers here to Key #4, where a lay leader is instructed: "I place my hand on his head and say, 'In the name of Jesus I break the power of every spirit that (name) has renounced and any related spirit, and I command them to leave in the name of Jesus." Lozano, *Unbound,* 202.

32 See Rossetti, "Frequently Asked Questions."

33 Pitre, *Catholic Productions,* "The Laying on of Hands."

34 Lozano, *Unbound,* 250.

35 Saint Thomas, for example, distinguishes the right either "to beseech" or "to command" as based upon one's intrinsic relationship towards a

For example, Lozano asserts that authority depends upon the merit of the petitioner: "We gain more authority as we bring more areas of our lives under [the Lord's] authority."[36] Elsewhere, he notes that the right to execute what he calls a "word of command" over another is based on charism: "The greater the anointing, and the more authority the person praying has received, the faster the power of the enemy is exposed and broken."[37] Who or what determines that "anointing" and, therefore, authority over another is not explained. As I critiqued elsewhere, one cannot "grow" in authority. To wit, "Your prayers may grow in merit as you grow in holiness, but your authority over a person, place, or object is tethered to your office as in relation to the same. You do not 'take' authority; rather, you claim what is yours by right given through natural or divine law by God the Father."[38]

Lozano appears, moreover, to confuse authority (the right to command) with power (the ability to effect change) and supernatural merit (reward for good works and the efficacy of prayer as the result of habitual virtue and depth of holiness). These, however, are three interrelated but distinct theological concepts. Authority cannot be gained, taken, or earned, but rather simply *is*—that is, according to one's office in relationship with the person, place, or object.

In addition, as Father Reehil and Father Ripperger have noted, physical contact with a manifesting person, particularly

---

person, place, or object. He also distinguishes between *solemn adjuration* (in the name of the Church and by her ministers) and *simple imperative adjuration* (lawfully made by anyone depending upon one's office vis-à-vis the other). The key distinction is what he identifies as a relationship of either "superiority" or "inferiority" with regard to whether one can either command with the imprecatory formula or beseech by means of the deprecatory form. That relationship, Saint Thomas says, carries also into the right to adjure demons. See *ST* II-II, q. 90.

[36] Lozano, *Unbound*, 103.

[37] Lozano, *Unbound*, 99.

[38] Schneider, *The Liber Christo Method*, 230.

in such a charged religious setting of a minor exorcism (deliverance session), can result in a transfer of demonic spirits, called "clinging" spirits. This is precisely why Monsignor Rosetti cautions that well-intended laity can be "inviting trouble"—that is, diabolic retaliation—when driving out demons without requisite authority. This is not, therefore, "a deception based on fear and a focus on demons," but rather the exercising of pastoral prudence.

Perhaps these experienced exorcists, priests, and theologians know the sacredness of both the anointed hands of the priest as well as the rich symbolism of this gesture. When praying, therefore, the laity should not use priestly gestures such as the imposition of hands upon a person's head or making the sign of the cross over them similar to the gesture of priests when giving a blessing. If hands are imposed when praying with someone, it is better to place them upon the shoulder while having a sacramental in hand, or better, placed in the folded position as indicated in the *Revised Book of Blessings* as the proper posture for laity.[39]

Conversely, the gesture at Confirmation is not the imposition of hands as seen in the biblical references above, nor is it a priestly or patriarchal gesture. At the Holy Saturday Mass, for example, the sponsors put their right hand on the shoulder (notably, not the head) of the candidate as the sponsor stands behind their candidate, as per in the rubrics. The ritual states: "The one who presented the candidate places his right hand on the latter's shoulder and gives the candidates name to the bishop."[40] This occurs at the Novus Ordo Mass as well as

---

39 USCCB, *Book of Blessings*, no. 673.

40 Weller, *Roman Ritual*, 76. In the new *Rite of Confirmation* #26: "The deacon brings the chrism to the bishop. Each candidate goes to the bishop, or the bishop may go to the individual candidates. The one who presented the candidate places his right hand on the latter's shoulder and gives the candidate's name to the bishop; or the candidate may give his own name."

the Traditional Latin Mass. The sponsors are to lay their right hands on the shoulder which is their oath-swearing hand. This indicates that the sponsor is making a commitment to provide spiritual guidance to the confirmed. The purpose of this gesture during the liturgy is not to bless or drive out demons, but to show solidarity and fraternity with the Christian community.

14. A group from our diocese wants to lead a retreat doing "impartation" at my parish. I have never heard of it. What is impartation?

Impartation is a Protestant Pentecostal phenomenon that they define as "reproducing in others what, by God's grace, we have sought to cultivate and develop within ourselves,"[41] and "the giving and receiving of spiritual gifts, blessings, healing, baptism in the Holy Spirit, etc. for the work of the ministry."[42] In Protestant parlance, this means "the transference of these 'gifts' from one man or woman of God to another, especially through the laying on of hands." Their proponents conclude that "when we impart to others, we are not merely giving them knowledge or information; we are actually pouring ourselves into them." The ability to impart is also a spiritual gift in and of itself: "It is not enough for Christian to be anointed by God . . . such an anointed person must also have the gift or ability of impartation" and this "cannot even be done by the person when he/she wants but has to be initiated by the Holy Spirit."[43]

---

41 Phipps, "The Principle of Impartation."
42 Budiselić, "The Impartation of the Gifts of the Spirit," 247.
43 Budiselić, "The Impartation of the Gifts of the Spirit," 247.

This phenomenon has made its way into Catholicism, and many parishes, by means of the charismatic renewal, which employs a similar definition:

> The term "impartation" as it is often used today is a way of speaking about how a grace of the Holy Spirit can be passed on from one person to another. The grace may be a specific charism or manifestation of the Spirit, or a fresh infilling with the Spirit, or baptism in the Spirit. Those who have a particular anointing are often the very people whom God uses as instruments to impart that same anointing to others in the Body of Christ. Impartation in this sense is not to be confused with the full gift of the Holy Spirit that is given through the sacraments of Baptism and Confirmation, nor with the gift of ordained ministry that is conferred through the sacrament of Holy Orders. The fact that the Holy Spirit can overflow from one ordinary believer to another is a sign of the interconnectedness of the body of Christ, in which all the members are joined and knit together in love (Eph 4:16).[44]

Functionally, what this looks like is a group of lay people will invite others to your parish and then give presentations on the various charismatic gifts such as healing, discernment of spirits, teaching, praying in tongues, driving out demons, etc. Then they will ask who wants this or that gift, and someone who already has that "particular anointing" will come forth and lay hands on the person's head and impart the gift to them. While their literature attempts to distinguish this from the sacraments of Baptism and Confirmation, it is, in effect, a total collapse of the two priesthoods—the universal priesthood of the baptized and the unique, sacerdotal priesthood of the ordained.

---

[44] Encounter Ministries, "Is it legitimate to speak of 'impartation' of the Holy Spirit?"

There are several reasons not to allow this at your parish, primary being that impartation is a Protestant practice based upon a Protestant interpretation of Scripture devoid of any standing in Tradition. Further, there is no evidence of this practice anywhere throughout the centuries of the lived tradition of the Church. That is, nowhere do we find "impartation" in the reception of Scripture in monuments of councils, papal decrees, and the writings of the Fathers, saints, and doctors of the Church. On the contrary, this practice has been uncritically received from Protestantism into many parishes in recent times, with no cautionary glance, no theological rigor, and no critical discernment.

As a pastor, you have an obligation to protect your sheep. While potentially syncretistic (and even gnostic, to wit, those with a "particular anointing" who are "actually pouring ourselves into" other lay people), this practice is, in fact, imprudent and spiritually dangerous to your parishioners. Other—namely, unholy—spirits can also be inadvertently "imparted" in the process. As Father Aumann notes, habitual sin and first commandment violations are not the only way a demon can gain access to a person. He states that, "A person may also come under the power of the devil by reason of the habitual practice of evil or the uncontrolled desire to experience extraordinary, mystical phenomena or receive charismatic graces." For this reason, he says, "it is necessary to exercise discernment of spirits when the person claims to have received some special grace or favor from God."[45]

You do not have to practice witchcraft or fall into habitual sin, moreover, to come under the power of the devil. His words bear repeating: "A person may also come under the power of the devil by . . . the uncontrolled desire to experience extraordinary, mystical phenomena or receive charismatic

---

[45] Aumann, *Spiritual Theology*, 411.

graces." This unholy desire (often fueled by the sins of presumption and curiosity) for charismatic gifts and extraordinary, mystical phenomena can open a door to the diabolic. This is problematic first because charisms by their nature are gratuitous (charism means "gift") and should not be asked for. Second, one must also be concerned what else may be transferred. Besides the fact that this can easily fall into superstition or a Christian version of spirit channeling, there is a risk of transference of other spiritual baggage someone may be carrying (whether the giver or the receiver). Remember, authority flows from office, and office provides someone spiritual protection. You are protected from clinging spirits in the ordinary practice of your priestly ministry by virtue of your office, but a layman outside of his office as head of household does not have that protection. Thus, the retaliation often patterns with the demon entering the family and moves laterally, whittling away at the marriage first and then the children.

Accordingly, this is why it is important to discern any spiritual gifts to determine if they are natural, preternatural, or supernatural. That is, one must determine whether they are beyond what is normal due to some unique human ability, psychological state, or diabolic influence; or, whether they are truly supernatural—God's direct action for the building up of the Body. Father Aumann makes two points worth noting along these lines. First, he states, "It would be temerarious in the normal course of events to desire or to ask God for graces *gratis datae* or charisms. They are not necessary for salvation nor for sanctification, and they require the direct intervention of God. Far more precious is an act of love than a charismatic gift." He thus affirms the age-old teaching of the saints is to not desire extraordinary gifts but conformity to Christ and the will of God. It is, in fact, "temerarious" (which means reckless or rash) to do so. Second, he states that in his priestly experience, "those who have authentic charismatic graces often do not want them known by others and do not actually want the graces themselves since they often involve suffering, undue attention, etc."[46] Here Father Aumann suggests that it is not only "temerarious" to ask for gifts but also presumptuous. Those who have authentic gifts seek to hide them, as authentic gifts are crosses to bear. The witness of the saints is not to desire extraordinary gifts but rather conformity to the will of God.

Father Amorth also echoes Father Aumann with regard to true charismatic gifts. "When the sensitives are persons of prayer and truly humble," he says, "they try to remain hidden; these are the positive signs. But if a person says, 'I am a charismatic,' then he has no charism. The charismatic is humble and has hidden gifts that God gives him."[47] When the saints exhibited some charism, especially an extraordinary one, they did not set up shop but rather focused on prayer, penance, charity, and self-sacrifice.

Often found in these lay ministries, however, is a disordered attachment to emotional states which inevitably confuse emotional experiences (which can be manipulated) with authentically spiritual ones. Thus, Saint Bonaventure cautions:

> If you wish to know yourself better, you must . . . reflect and see if in you there thrives or has thrived a *disordered desire (concupiscentia) for pleasure, curiosity, or vanity* . . . surely the disordered desire of curiosity thrives in the servant of God when she *desires to know the occult, when she yearns to see the beautiful, and when she wants to possess what is rare*. Obviously, the disordered desire of vanity thrives in the spouse of Christ (the soul) when she seeks the favor of others, when

46 Aumann, *Spiritual Theology*, 423.
47 Rossetti, *Pope's Exorcist*, 19.

she yearns for their praise, and desires to be honored by them. The spouse of Christ must flee like poison all of these things because they are the roots of evil.[48]

The same can be said of this Protestant phenomena of impartation, which is fueled by a subtle presumption. For this reason, regarding the charismatic gifts, the *Catechism* states that all charisms must be submitted to the local bishop: "It is in this sense that discernment of charisms is always necessary. No charism is exempt from being referred and submitted to the Church's shepherds. 'Their office [is] not indeed to extinguish the Spirit, but to test all things and hold fast to what is good,' so that all the diverse and complementary charisms work together 'for the common good'" (CCC 801). With regard to the asking for gifts, the Church's teaching on *grata gratis data* (graces gratuitously given) is based on centuries of reflection upon the Scriptures, particularly Saint Paul's letters, and the reception in the writings of the Fathers and Doctors, and lives of the saints. Any discernment or reception of the Protestant practices associated with charisms should be subject to the Church's precedence, with focus on virtue, prayer, and the teachings of the Church.

15. What about Vatican II's "active participation" of the laity in deliverance ministry? Isn't that part of the rights of their universal priesthood as baptized Christians?

Bear in mind two distinctions from *Lumen Gentium*. One, according to the Second Vatican Council, the universal priesthood of the baptized differs both in *essence* and *degree* from the

---

[48] Saint Bonaventure, *De Perfectione Vitae Ad Sorores*, 14. Emphasis mine.

sacerdotal priesthood of the ordained.[49] Two, the same conciliar document further distinguishes by affirming that "the lay charism is secular in nature," or *indoles secularis*—that is, oriented towards the world and secular matters. By contrast, the council affirms that the priestly charism is "sacred" and, therefore, "ordered to sacrifice."[50] Pope Saint Leo X, moreover, condemned the beliefs of Martin Luther, which held that "in the sacrament of penance and the remission of guilt, the pope or bishop does no more than the lowliest priest; in fact, where there is no priest, any Christian can do as much, even a woman or a child."[51] Accordingly, to understand each properly, we must hold these two priesthoods in tension, and not collapse the two. Perhaps nowhere is the blurring of this distinction and this collapse of the two priesthoods found more today than in deliverance ministry.

The post-conciliar Church has placed great emphasis on the priesthood of the laity. Some dioceses even issue financial grants to groups of lay deliverance teams to drive out demons for them, as if to fill the pastoral gap with spiritual mercenaries. This is a complete collapse of the two priesthoods. Some wrongly claim that this right comes through baptism. The CDF under Pope Saint Paul VI, however, affirmed that "baptism does not confer any personal title to public ministry in the Church. There is a universal vocation of all the baptized to the exercise of the royal priesthood by offering their lives to God and by giving witness for his praise."[52] Thus, an equality of dignity based upon a common baptismal integration into Trinitarian life does not mean that there does not exist what Father Aumann calls "varying degrees of incorporation"

---

[49] Pope Paul VI, *Lumen Gentium,* no. 10.
[50] Pope Paul VI, *Lumen Gentium*, no. 31.
[51] Pope Saint Leo X, *Exsurge Domine,* 13.
[52] CDF, *Inter Insigniores: On the Question of Admission of Women to the Ministerial Priesthood,* 6.

in the Church. The fervent Christian who lives a life of holiness, states Father Aumann, has a deeper incorporation into the People of God than, say, the lukewarm soul in a state of grace or the "dead branch" attached to the Vine yet in state of mortal sin. While all of the baptized do indeed share in the priestly, prophetic, and kingly office of Christ, as Father Aumann rightly states, nonetheless, they "exercise these functions according to their condition and state of life."[53]

The *Catechism* echoes this in affirming the differences between the laity and the ordained. Both vocations, the *Catechism* states, have "their own assignment in the mission of the whole people of God" (CCC 873). The laity serve "in the world" and to the priesthood is "entrusted the office of teaching, sanctifying, and governing in his name and by his power" (CCC 873). This language is also heard in Canon Law, which likewise uses the language of "according to their condition" or "in their own manner" in describing the role (and authority) of the laity.[54] Thus, Father Aumann concludes, "What this means is that although the faithful of Christ share in the priestly, prophetic and kingly functions of Christ by sanctifying, teaching and governing, they do not all perform those functions to the same degree. This necessarily calls for a diversity of ministries, as well as a differentiation of classes or groups of the members of the Church. Moreover, not all of the faithful have the same rights and duties in the Church."[55] To consider the sacred goods of the ministerial priesthood as a human right would be to completely misjudge the nature of the priesthood. The *tria munera* are proper to the ordained, not the laity.

---

[53] *Apostolicam Actuositatem*, no. 2. Aumann, *On the Front Lines: The Lay Person in the Church After Vatican II*, 31.

[54] *Code of Canon Law*, no. 209 §1.

[55] Aumann, *On the Front Lines: The Lay Person in the Church After Vatican II*, 31.

16. I recently preached on the priesthood and cautioned lay people against imposing hands. A woman accosted me after Mass and accused me of clericalism. How is that clericalism?

Father Hardon defines clericalism as "the advocacy of exaggerated claims on the part of the clergy, especially in matters that belong to the jurisdiction of the state. More commonly it is used as a term of reproach by secularists and unfriendly critics of the Catholic Church, who aim to banish all religious influence from public life."[56]

In some Catholic dioceses (particularly in Europe), we have found a total collapse of the two priesthoods which effects how we approach the right to bless, heal, to command demons, and even to confect the sacraments. This is seen in the 4th Key of *Unbound* (see above) where lay people confess their sins to other lay people (a parallel confession),[57] the phenomenon of "baptism in the Holy Spirit" (a parallel baptism), and now the novelty of "impartation" (a parallel confirmation) are all officiated by the laity. In some dioceses in Germany, for example, lay people are baptizing, preaching, laying hands for healing, and performing interments rites. That leaves only the confection of the Holy Eucharist for the priest. Unfortunately, one priest reported that a charismatic priest claims to be able to "impart" the ability to pray the prayers of consecration to lay people. This, notably, is in a country where exorcism is outlawed. Even Martin Luther would shake his head at such a low ecclesiology.

---

56 Hardon, *Modern Catholic Dictionary*, 109.

57 Lozano instructs his lay prayer team leaders, for example, that before they impose hands upon another layman during a deliverance session, "when someone comes to you for prayer, telling you secrets, you are invited in as a representative of Christ, an instrument of the love and mercy of God." Lozano, *Unbound*, 103.

What you are accused of is not clericalism but rather Catholicism.

17. I did not learn anything about spiritual warfare in the seminary. How can I use it to help my parishioners and protect my parish?

Do not be afraid to be unpopular. Speak the truth. Stand in the breach. Regularly pray binding prayers for your parishioners. Simple binding prayers can be very effective in your priestly ministry. One way is to pray binding prayers before hearing confessions, binding any demon who would try to block any penitent from making a holy confession, or any demon causing confusion or blocking the memories of those who will confess today. Priests who do this have reported the quantity and quality of confessions at their parish have increased exponentially.

A simple binding prayer can also be used before you celebrate Holy Mass. Here, bind any demon preventing your parishioners from coming to Mass and any demon blocking those who attend this Mass from receiving all of the graces God would have them receive. Priests who do this before Mass have recounted how Mass attendance has gone up, and many of their parishioners begin to tell them how much they are getting out of the homily (i.e., his preaching is suddenly "on fire"). Nothing has changed, mind you, but the binding prayer now prevents the demon from blocking or diminishing the graces available through the Holy Mass.

One of the titles of the devil in the old Rite of Exorcism (sadly, removed in the revised Rite) is the "fomenter of discord." You will find this spirit active in many parishes, causing discord, division, and strife. When you encounter such resistance, bind the spirit of the fomenter of discord and you will find many of these situations will clear out peacefully.

Finally, consecrate your priesthood and your parish to the Blessed Mother. As Saint Bernard of Clairvaux said, *de Maria numquam satis*! No words are sufficient to describe her holiness, purity, and the glories of her unique privileges which give her total coercive power over the devil. As a priest, you are her special son. Here is a word of wisdom from Saint Alphonsus Liguori: "Woe to those, says St. Anselm, who despise the light of the sun, who despise devotion to Mary! St. Francis Borgia used to fear for the perseverance of those in whom he found no devotion to Mary. He warns the novice master to keep an eye on such unfortunate novices. It happened that every one of those eventually lost his vocation and left the Order."[58]

The demon will use detraction, gossip, and slander to undermine your ministry, so consecrate your reputation to Our Lady as part of your prayer life. Here is a prayer of consecration you should pray daily and is particularly useful for breaking various forms of oppression.

Consecration of One's Exterior Goods to the Blessed Virgin Mary[59]

I, (Name), a faithless sinner, renew and ratify today in thy hands the vows of my Baptism; I renounce forever Satan, his pomps and works; and I give myself entirely to Jesus Christ, the Incarnate Wisdom, to carry my cross after Him all the days of my life, and to be more faithful to Him than I have ever been before. In the presence of all the heavenly court, I choose thee, O Mary, this day for my Mother and Mistress. Knowing that I have received rights over all my exterior goods by the promulgation of the Natural Law by the Divine Author, I deliver and consecrate to thee, as thy slave, all of my exterior goods, past, present and future; I

[58] Saint Alphonsus Liguori, *Glories of Mary*, 83.
[59] Ripperger, *Deliverance Prayers for the Laity*, 44.

relinquish into thy hands, my Heavenly Mother, all rights over my exterior goods, including my health, finances, relationships, possessions, property, my job and my earthly success (add any exterior good being oppressed) and I retain for myself no right of disposing the goods that come to me but leave to thee the entire and full right of disposing of all that belongs to me, without exception, according to thy good pleasure, for the greater glory of God in time and in eternity. As I now interiorly relinquish what belongs to me exteriorly into thy hands, I entrust to thee the protection of those exterior goods against the evil one, so that, knowing that they now belong to thee, he cannot touch them. Receive, O good and pious Virgin, this little offering of what little is, in honor of, and in union with, that subjection which the Eternal Wisdom deigned to have to thy maternity; in homage to the power which both of you have over this poor sinner, and in thanksgiving for the privileges with which the Holy Trinity has favored thee. Trusting in the providential care of God the Father and thy maternal care, I have full confidence that thou wilst take care of me as to the necessities of this life and will not leave me forsaken. God the Father, increase my trust in Thy Son's Mother. Our Lady of Fair Love, give me perfect confidence in the providence of Thy Son. Amen.

Chapter VI

QUESTIONS FROM PRIESTS—SPECIFIC

"In order to understand these matters better, let him inquire of the person possessed, following one or the other act of exorcism, what the latter experienced in his body or soul while the exorcism was being performed, and to learn also what particular words in the form had a more intimidating effect upon the devil, so that hereafter these words may be employed with greater stress and frequency.

"Sometimes the devil will leave the possessed person in peace and even allow him to receive the Holy Eucharist, to make it appear that he has departed. In fact, the arts and frauds of the evil one for deceiving a man are innumerable. For this reason, the exorcist must be on his guard not to fall into this trap.

"Let the priest pronounce the exorcism in a commanding and authoritative voice, and at the same time with great confidence, humility, and fervor; and when he sees that the spirit is sorely vexed, then he oppresses and threatens all the more. If he notices that the person afflicted is experiencing a disturbance in some part of his body or an acute pain or a swelling appears in some part, he traces the sign of the cross over that place and sprinkles it with holy water, which he must have at hand for this purpose.

"The exorcist should guard against giving or recommending any medicine to the patient but should leave this care to physicians."

—*Praenotanda to the Rite of Exorcism, nos. 4, 9, 16, 18*

From the Field: "Look at the Anointed Hands of a Priest of the Living God."

A priest had finished his exorcist training at the Pope Leo Institute and had his first case of probable possession in his home diocese. The energumen was a single mother of several small children, and the demon afflicting her was resistant to come to the surface. Demons, or fallen angels, are personal beings; that is, they are individual persons (see CCC 328). In fact, according to Saint Thomas Aquinas, each angel (glorified or fallen) is his own species.[1] As such, they have unique personalities, but like humans, some are more open and others more closed.

This particular demon was not quick to come to the surface, as is sometimes the case. A lay instructor had been called in to transition the priest from classroom knowledge to his first real case in real time. In that role, the experienced lay assistant was instructing the young priest on which prayers to pray, walking him through the Rite of Exorcism. After receiving each brief explanation, the priest would then pray the various prayers. Little by little, the demon's defenses began to wear down at the barrage of prayers, and the priest's prayers began to hit their target. The priest, however, was largely focused on the minor exorcism and other prayers, paying little

[1] Saint Thomas Aquinas, *ST* I-II, q. 50, art. 4.

attention to the young woman. At some point, as the prayers finally wore down the demon's resistance, the demon manifested and appropriated the woman's senses.

The lay associates on the team had noticed the change, but the priest continued the minor exorcism prayers, head downward, unaware. The demon was growing in anger, with his primary focus on the lay assistant who had been guiding the young priest throughout the prayer session. The priest would pray a prayer, and the demon would feel its effects, exhibiting bodily pain as he appropriated the senses of the woman. With a chilling growl, the demon began to wildly and angrily curse the lay assistant and command him to be silent with the most colorful language. At that, the priest stopped and pulled his head up just as a string of profanities issued forth from the demon. All eyes were on the demon who was becoming increasingly aggressive, perched as if to strike. The priest stopped, fixed on the demon, and was unsure of what to do. The lay assistant then held up a Saint Benedict crucifix and recited the words to himself:

"Ecce Crucem Domini. Vade retro Satana!"[2]

At the sight of the crucifix, the demon stopped and snapped back as if punched. The lay assistant then walked over to the priest, who was at a loss and didn't know what to do.

"Can I see your hand, Father? Hold up your hand . . . your right hand. I want him to say that again to you."

The demon was still visibly angry, fuming actually, but would not look at the priest. He folded his arms defiantly and looked to the side.

"Hold out your hand, Father," the assistant instructed.

[2] The Latin inscription on the Saint Benedict medal which reads: *Behold the cross of the Lord! Get behind me, Satan!*

The instructor then gently helped the priest to extend his right arm fully towards the demon, who looked away deliberately. The priest's hand was shaking.

"Command the demon, Father. Command him to stare at your anointed hands. You have the authority. Make him obey."

The priest hesitated, then spoke:

"I command you to look at my hand."

"Your anointed hand, Father."

"My anointed hand."

The demon complied with a skirting glance but then immediately looked away.

"Father," the instructor said, "you are a priest of the living God. A priest forever. Your hands are anointed. Make the demon fix his eyes on your anointed hands."

The demon now defiantly looked away but was no longer speaking and his body language was like a schoolboy called into the principal's office. A quiet confidence then came over the priest as he saw the demon backing down.

"I am a priest of the living God," the priest barked, hand no longer wavering. "And I command you in the name of Jesus Christ to be silent and to obey! In the name of Jesus Christ, fix her eyes on my anointed hand!"

At that command, the demon complied, immediately snapping the woman's head to the front and eyes fixed, unblinking, on the hand of the priest in complete obedience to the command.

"It is not I who commands you; it is Christ who commands you!"

The demon's rage now left, and a fear came over him as he shrunk into the chair. As the priest held his hand out, no longer shaking, and repeated the command with greater confidence, the demon began to visibly tremble and shake. The lay assistant stepped aside and henceforth the priest had total command of the session.

In this section, we field questions from priests who inquired on specific tactics of spiritual warfare and the dignity of the sacerdotal office.

1. Who can pray Chapter Three? How often should I pray it over my parish property?

In the above question on deacons, we cited a *dubia* (Latin for "questions") sent to the CDF in 2015 to clarify what deacons can pray. The first *dubia* in the same document asked whether "a priest [is] allowed to publicly and/or privately use the *Exorcismus in satanam et angelos apostolicos* (the so-called exorcism of Leo XIII) found in Title XII of the 1956 *Rituale Romanum* without expressed permission of the Ordinary." The CDF affirmed that this prayer of minor exorcism is a restricted prayer, meaning for a priest to pray it over persons, he must acquire "special and express permission of the local Ordinary." With regard to public use, "such as over places, objects, or in other circumstances, this is also subject to the authorization of the Ordinary." It cites the rubric itself and also the 1985 CDF document *Inde ab aliquot annis*, which clarified that only priests with express permission from his bishop can pray this prayer. It also affirms that lay people are not to pray exorcism over others.[3] By "public use" by priests, the CDF says, "one should understand any use made by a priest in the name and with the authority of the Church for the benefit of the faithful." Any priest can pray this prayer privately—namely,

---

[3] Rorate Caeli, "Dubia Answered: Warning for priests treating afflicted souls, guidance on blessings by deacons."

"outside of any pastoral context and/or request by the faithful, and simply as a *pia oratio*" (a private devotion).[4]

Why such restrictions? In her wisdom and two thousand years of experience and deepening understanding, the Church has recognized that this is a high-flash weapon. When it goes off, it lights up the cosmic battlefield and the preternatural world takes note. Sometimes a priest will pray this at an abortion clinic because he knows that this is a powerful weapon, but he should get permission from his bishop first. When someone prays it without requisite authority, the demons can, and often do, retaliate. That being said, a priest should regularly pray this prayer as part of his private devotions. You have that authority, and this prayer is quite effective even when prayed privately.

2. I am an exorcist, and I noticed that when possessed people see me, they get fidgety and struggle to make eye contact. Why is that?

The demon is an apex predator and wants to avoid you at all costs. This is not because you are smart or handsome, or that being an exorcist makes you holier than other priests, but because the authority of the mandate that you possess. This is why when a person shows up at the diocese and demands to see you because she is possessed, it is probably a good sign that she is not. You and the bishop, whose authority you wield, are the last people a demon wants a chance encounter with.

The word *apostle* is from the Greek word *apostello,* meaning "to send." Thus, an apostle is "one sent." You can order a pizza, and the delivery driver is *sent* to give you your food and to collect payment. When Jesus calls and sends the twelve and

[4] CDF, *Letter to Ordinaries Regarding Norms on Exorcism.*

later the seventy, this is decidedly *not* what is meant because it is not what *apostello* means in the Greek (or its Hebrew equivalent). That is, the apostles are not mere delivery men who collect the bill for another. In the New Testament, the meaning of *apostle* as being one sent is based upon an Old Testament, Hebrew concept of *šālîah*. In the ancient Jewish tradition, a *šālîah* was sent on behalf of another to act in juridical agency, as representative. This is seen in the Mishnah (a collection of Jewish sayings contained in the oral tradition) which states that "a person's šālîa*h* is the person himself." The *šālîah* acts as legal agent, and in matters of religion, according to Ceslas Spicq, "when the *šālîah* acts on God's orders, it is God himself who acts" as seen in such figures as Abraham, Elijah, and Elisha.[5] Thus, "this person is not a mere envoy but a *chargé d'affaires*, a person's authorized representative," whose actions are binding upon both the person to whom he has been sent and also to the sender.[6] This is summarized in this ancient rabbinic statement: "the messenger of a man is as the man himself." Therefore, the apostles "stand in the place of Jesus, and are as He is . . . and continue His work."[7]

This pertains not only to the apostles and their successors but also to exorcists and every priest. In the Blessing of Fields or Mountain-Meadows in the old Rite, the priest invokes this reality:

> God of mercy and of strength, **Who didst confer on thy priests above all others so great grace, that whatever they**

---

5 Cited in Spicq, *Theological Lectionary*, 189. The legal agent is referred to by the terms שָׁלִיחַ (*shaliach*) and שָׁלוּחַ (*shaluach*), both of which mean "one who is sent." The first *shaliah* inferred in the Bible is the servant in Genesis 24 who was sent by Abraham to find a wife for Isaac. The "emissary" or "messenger" is a legal agent.

6 Spicq, *Theological Lectionary*, 189.

7 Grundmann, δύναμις ("Power") in Kittel, ed. *Theological Dictionary of the New Testament*, 310.

> **do worthily and perfectly in thy name is, as it were, done by thee,** we beseech thy boundless goodness, that **whatever we presume to visit, maybe visited by thee, and whatever we presume to bless, may be blessed by thee. Stretch out thy hand of might over what we are about to do,** and at our lowly coming, through the merits and prayers of the saints, [expell] the devil and let thine angels preside. Through Christ our Lord. Amen.[8]

The demon is acutely reminded of this fact during the Rite of Exorcism when an exorcist invokes this ancient idea that the unworthy priest stands *in persona Christi*. The exorcist prays:

> I cast you out, unclean spirit, along with every Satanic power of the enemy, every spectre from hell, and all your fell companions, in the name of our Lord Jesus Christ. Begone and stay far from this creature of God. **For it is He who commands you,** He who flung you headlong from the heights of heaven into the depths of hell. **It is He who commands you,** He who once stilled the sea and the wind and the storm.
>
> Hearken, therefore, and tremble in fear, Satan, you enemy of the faith, you foe of the human race, you begetter of death, you robber of life, you corrupter of justice, you root of all evil and vice, seducer of men, betrayer of the nations, instigator of envy, font of avarice, fomenter of discord, author of pain and sorrow. Why, then, do you stand and resist, knowing as you must that Christ the Lord brings your plans to nothing? Fear Him, who in Isaac was offered in sacrifice, in Joseph sold into bondage, slain as the paschal lamb, crucified as man, yet triumphed over the powers of hell.[9]

What a priest commands, therefore, is not done by his own merits but by the merits of Jesus Christ and through the apostolic authority in which he shares through office. An

---

8 Weller, *Roman Ritual*, 357. Emphasis mine.
9 Weller, *Roman Ritual*, 185. Emphasis mine.

exorcist is the legal agent of the bishop who is a prince of the Church in that diocese. He can echo with authority the words of his Sender: *For it is He (not I) who commands you.* The demon has been defeated by priests like you long before you came along and will continue to be defeated long after you take your final breath. The demon knows both this biblical theology and your ontological reality very clearly.

3. Is it true that deliverance prayers are most effective following the words of the absolution in the sacrament of confession, and if so, why?

As part of the preparation for solemn session, we have the energumen go to confession (to their parish priest or other local priest) as close to the day of exorcism as possible. Sacramental absolution brings forgiveness, reconciliation, healing, and "the recovery of the grace of justification" (CCC 1477), while also reestablishing communion with God and the Church (CCC 1488, 1462).

If you are preaching, baptizing, and hearing confessions, you are engaging in spiritual warfare. Confession is hand-to-hand combat. As Father Amorth states clearly: "Satan is more enraged when we take souls away from him through confession than when we take away bodies through exorcism."[10] This is because, he says, sacramental confession "is the most direct means to fight Satan because it is the sacrament that tears souls from the demon's grasp, strengthens against sin, unites us more closely to God, and helps to conform our souls increasingly to the divine will. I advise frequent confession, possibly weekly, to all victims of evil activities."[11] Thus,

10 Amorth, *An Exorcist Tells His Story*, 67.
11 Amorth, *An Exorcist: More Stories*, 195.

"one good confession is worth a hundred exorcisms" and "the best exorcism is confession" and "confession is stronger than exorcism!"[12]

Sacramental confession and exorcism, however, are not mutually exclusive. As Father Aumann explains with regards to spiritual remedies for diabolic affliction, when someone has "come under the power of the devil by reason of the habitual practice of evil," he counsels, one method for the priest is to "apply an abbreviated form of exorcism when giving absolution to habitual sinners."[13] You will find that praying certain prayers after absolution is quite effective because the penitent has just been "torn from the demon's grasp" and the demon now is vulnerable, with hands down, so to speak. Praying a binding and severing prayer silently or quietly is sufficient, as the effectiveness of the prayer is not dependent on whether the penitent hears or understands you. The demon, whose claims to the soul have been severed by sacramental absolution, always hears and understands when a priest of the living God commands him with authority.

As explained earlier, doing binding prayers before hearing confessions will greatly enhance the quality and quantity of your confessions. It helps to free up the penitents' memories so they can make better confessions. Sacramental absolution frees the soul from the demon's grip. His nefarious activity has been halted and his momentum thwarted. Like a boxer on the ropes whose legs are wobbly, his hold on the penitent has now been released. Thus, this is the time to go for the knockout—first the sacrament, then the sacramentals of deliverance prayers/minor exorcisms. Sacrament followed by sacramentals like old-school deliverance prayers (binding, severing, etc.) can be very effective.

---

12 Amorth, *An Exorcist Tells His Story*, 86.
13 Aumann, *Spiritual Theology*, 411.

4. If I pray deliverance prayers in the sacrament of confession, am I protected by that sacrament from demonic retaliation?

In the exercising of his pastor ministry (and recall that by definition, *pastoral* means the administrations of the sacraments), the priest is protected because he is working within the bounds of his office. Office, recall, is the duty or responsibility to engage on behalf of those under one's authority. If the priest is not in a state of grace, however, his sins are exposed to the enemy, and he is fair game.

5. I have been considering praying deliverance prayers in the confessional following sacramental absolution, but what prayers should I begin with?

As stated above, before you begin hearing confessions, do the perimeter prayer around yourself and parish, prayers against retaliation, and then do simple binding prayers to stop any diabolic interference, to include any demon who would attempt to block the memories of the penitents or prevent them from making good confessions. Once you have given absolution, a simple binding prayer can be quietly prayed for the penitent, with a focus on specific sins, vices, or spirits.

> *Spirit of (n.), I bind you in the Name of Jesus, by the power of the Holy Cross, by the power of the most Precious Blood of Our Lord Jesus Christ, by the authority of my priesthood and by the intercession of the Blessed Virgin Mary, St. Michael the Archangel, the blessed Apostles, Peter and Paul and all of the saints, and I command you to leave (n.) (Name of person or object) and go to the foot of the Holy Cross to receive your sentence, in the Name of the Father, the Son and the Holy Spirit. Amen.*

If somebody is struggling with sixth commandment sins, then insert "spirits of lust, impurity, pornography, masturbation, fornication, contraception, etc."

See Appendix G for more suggested prayers before saying Mass or hearing confessions.

6. If a penitent manifests in the confessional, then the demons try to attack the priest physically, but it goes away after the priest does binding prayers, what is the demon's end game in attempting to attack? (e.g., panicking, retaliation, affirming the priest that he's getting them angry because you're about to absolve, etc.?)

All the above. A word of caution, however. The demon will often try to bully you and make you stand down. He will also make you think you are a superhero, have a special gift, that he fears you, etc. What he reacts to (and fears) is not you but the indelible mark and sacramental seal of Holy Priesthood. Cling to that and militate from that reality (not your own strength). Ask the Blessed Mother to cloak you in her mantle, and consecrate your priesthood and parish to her daily.

7. I was recently ordained, and after one of my first Masses, a woman manifested right outside the sacristy right after Mass. A group of lay people jumped in to help, but it seemed to make things worse. When I raised my hands in prayer, the demon seemed to be in pain. Why did this happen and how do I shut it down?

Well-intended lay people can cause more harm than good when they raise their hands like a priest and try to bind a demon. What they fail to realize is that they may find themselves retaliated against. The Latin *manifestare* means "to be made clear, plain, apparent, palpable." As stated above, whenever a demon manifests, it is because God is forcing it out for some salvific reason. Remember that Saint Bonaventure gives four reasons why God allows the demons to afflict a soul—to glorify God, to punish sin, to chastise the sinner, and to educate us. This happened for your education. One initial reason on the part of the demon may have been to scare you or challenge you, like a stray dog jumping out behind a garage as you walk by. Always remember, however, that this is God's house and not the demon's. Thus, God forced the demon out for your benefit as well as that of your parishioner—to stir up priestly courage in you to do battle, to put you on alert, and to prompt her to seek proper help (or perhaps one of the other reasons of Saint Bonaventure).

One salvific purpose served is that the Lord educated you on the existential experience of the demon. You saw the horror and contempt towards you when you approached. You also saw him cringe in pain when you raised your anointed hand and began to pray. The priest's hands—not the layman's—are anointed and, therefore, sacred. When you raise them in either blessing or command, the very cosmos is placed on alert. You may have been taught that in seminary, but you needed to see that ontological reality in real time, especially now as you begin to live your priestly vocation. Not only do you now know that this sheep has an acute spiritual sickness, which you may not have known before, but you also now know the position from which to operate the *munus regendi*. You need not be afraid.

The immediate goal here is to shut down the manifestation. Even praying the Rosary can exacerbate the situation. Remember, when Our Lady gave the Rosary to Saint Dominic, she called it a "weapon" and specifically a "battering ram." The Rosary is an offensive weapon that lights up the demon. On our teams, the lay associates generally pray the Rosary in session to intensify the prayer of the priest and to protect themselves. The foyer of a church after a crowded Sunday Mass, however, is not the place or time for battle, so if you command the demon to leave, he will generally dig in. In this scenario, shut it down quickly. You can always pick the fight another day, but on your terms.

The best way to shut down a manifestation is to stop the Rosary and have the lay people present kneel and pray quietly in the *orans* position (not extended hands, which is a priestly gesture and also signals battle). Have those present sing Marian hymns while the priest (and ONLY the priest) commands the demon *to recede* and then calls forth the person ("In the name of Jesus Christ, I command you to recede from n. and I command n. to come forth"). Place your stole on the person's head, if needed, while commanding the demon to recede. The Marian hymns invoke the Blessed Mother and her presence, combined with the priest's command to recede, will quickly cause the demon to comply.

8. A parishioner says she is hearing voices. How can you tell if this is demonic?

Look first to whether there is a familial history of mental illness or past substance abuse. The use of psychotropic drugs can cause auditory hallucinations. The context of the voices—i.e., the devil telling her this or that—is not necessarily a positive indicator. We have had cases where someone with a high religiosity had auto-locutions that seemed to be diabolic in nature but there was no indication of anything spiritual at its root. Religiosity can carry over from the person's mental state with no diabolical source. At other times, we have seen hallucinogenics used for PTSD and a demon manifests. Since the demon is generally attracted to wounded human nature, you must be aware of the vulnerability but also look for larger causality to determine which is the primary vector (that is, whether the psychological or spiritual is the primary defect which drives the disordered thoughts). Also, ask if the person is taking any kind of prescribed psychological medicine, or even other non-psych medicines which may have drug-to-drug interactions, as these can sometimes have auditory hallucinations as a side effect. Thus, look first at family history, personal history, past psychotropic drug use, and any medicines she may be taking and rule out all natural causalities before moving to the preternatural.

If you move too quickly to pray over her, you risk doing more harm than good. It is always prudent to exhaust all natural (physical, psychological, emotional) and pastoral (sacramental) remedies before praying over someone. The devil is an opportunist and apex predator and always circles around when he senses human woundedness and vulnerability. When prayers of liberation have no effect because the root cause is psychological, he then moves in quickly to exploit the situation with, "See, even Jesus can't help you. You need to give up. You're doomed" or "It must be really bad if exorcism didn't work" or other lies. A psychological obsession can expose the person to a spiritual oppression or even obsession, so proceed methodically and cautiously to determine causality. Grace builds on nature, so sometimes you must first shore up the wounded nature (by natural and pastoral means) so that grace has more to build upon. When you exhaust those remedies, our phase one protocol works as a diagnostic to determine causality (psychological or spiritual), so place the household on the protocol and see the results.

9. I started doing some deliverance prayers and now things are lighting up. I hear that a priest will get his toughest case up front. Why is that?

In our prudential experience, the first case a priest gets is often his toughest and designed to probe what the demon thinks is one of the priest's weaknesses. In Father Amorth's very first exorcism, for example, the energumen began to levitate in the middle of the exorcism but floated softly to the ground when Father Amorth continued the ritual and placed his stole on the man's shoulder as per the rubrics. In all his subsequent years, he never saw that phenomenon again. He tells how he was at first tempted to pride until his mentor Father Candido Amantini gave him good counsel. When Father Amorth wondered why his first case was such a success and shared all the thoughts running around in his head, what God was trying to tell him, etc., Father Candido frankly told him: "It is not God who was speaking to you, but Satan. Never ask yourself if God is behind an exorcism. Certainly, it is God who defeats Satan. He is victorious through the exorcism.

But do not ask yourself things that no one can answer. Do not commit the sin of pride. Do what you must and do not ask too many questions. Don't you know that we are merely useless servants?"[14]

In addition, the first manifestation in any case is often quite telling, as if the demon throws puzzle pieces in the air which the team is meant to figure out (sensitivity to certain saints or Scripture passages, bodily pain, etc.). You do not build your theology around these things, but they are helpful in being more precise in your prayers, as well as how to direct the energumen in their prayer life and devotions, as well as what spiritual defects to militate against.

That being said, if things are lighting up, that is likely a good sign. As Saint Josemaría Escriva says, "a task which presents no difficulties lacks human appeal—and supernatural appeal too. If you find no resistance when hammering a nail into a wall, what can you expect to hang on it?"[15]

10. I am doing minor exorcisms, and another priest told me I needed to find a "sensitive" to help me. What is that?

A "sensitive" refers to one who shows a propensity for discernment of spirits. One of our teams had a blind man who saw things in the spiritual realm that no one else could. Father Amorth had a very holy woman who worked closely with him, which led many to think every team needs someone with charismatic gifts to help. On multiple occasions, we have seen the team "sensitive" become a case or become enmeshed with the case. Too often this person lacks the humility, spiritual

[14] Agasso, *Rome's Exorcist,* 123.

[15] Saint Josemaría Escriva, *The Forge,* 86.

maturity, and marital stability properly to differentiate the good from the bad spirit and, as a result, is often used by the demon to distract and destabilize the priest and team.

Bearing in mind the words of Our Lord that "the devil is a liar and the father of lies" (Jn 8:44), a priest should be cautious lest the demon run him down a rabbit hole of pseudo-mystical phenomena. This can often come obliquely, through someone on his team. For example, the original exorcist assigned to clean out the infestation of the house on famous Brownsville Road in Pennsylvania had a "sensitive" who directed where and how to pray, even to the point of eventually convincing the priest that, based on her mystical insights, he should not go into the house. This only unnecessarily prolonged the case, which was not resolved until an exorcist was brought in from another diocese who performed the *Roman Ritual* according to the rubrics. After years of being led down a rabbit hole, the house was cleaned up in a short period of time.

While we have seen true spiritual gifts, the more common experience is the team sensitive subtly manipulating the exorcist. One priest who started engaging the enemy with a minor exorcism also felt the need to have a sensitive. Before sessions, the priest would sprinkle holy water in the room only to have the woman tell him, "Father, you missed one. There's a demon over here." So, the priest would immediately sprinkle holy water in that spot. As he continued his preparations, she would say, "Oh Father, you missed another one. He's in this corner. Put some holy water there." Surprisingly, this very educated and spiritual priest interrupted his preparation and obeyed. This sensitive was also said to be able to "see the sins" of everyone in the room, so the participants—including the priest himself—would rush to confession before session so that she did not see and reveal their sins. This type of manipulation and complete disorder is more common on teams than one might think. In this case, she was being used by the demon to distract the priest and undermine his authority, thereby weakening him from the outset.

Father Amorth himself cautioned against using charismatic gifts as a diagnostic tool (what he referred to as a "medical model"); that is, do not rely on private revelations when dealing with the demonic. Exorcism is, after all, a sacramental and the means by which Church has long battled Satan. *Rubric,* recall, comes from the Latin word for the color red. This may sound oversimplistic, but when it comes to the Church's liturgy, "Do the red, read the black."

11. I serve in an area where the charismatic movement and also laying on of the hands has been widespread for decades. It is expected that eventually a charismatic, usually a woman, will come back into the sacristy and say something like, "Father, I have gifts. Can I pray over you?" I'm not sure how to respond to her.

In the final blessing at Holy Mass, the priest instructs the faithful to "bow your heads and pray for God's blessing"—not the other way around. In the traditional Mass, the lay faithful still kneel to receive the priest's blessing. While not uncommon, when lay people seek to pray over a priest, they usurp the authority of his office. Recently, Rainer Maria Cardinal Woelki of Cologne, Germany, addressed a youth leader's conference in Germany. At the end of his presentation, the emcee wanted to show her gratitude for his talk and mistakenly started to lead the young adults in the crowd to extend their hands over the cardinal to bless him. The cardinal corrected the error by rightly telling those present, "I am your spiritual father. You do not bless me, I bless you." He then instructed the crowd to bow their heads so they could receive his blessing.

As the *Revised Book of Blessings* teaches, "the ministry of blessing involves a particular exercise of the priest of Christ and, in keeping with the place and office within the people of God belong into each person."[16] The *Book of Blessings* then lists the hierarchy beginning from bishop down to layman. Notably, the former (priests) takes precedence whenever he is present, and the latter (laity) only in two specific circumstances—namely, in their own homes and with family members. In fact, nowhere does the revised *Book of Blessings* instruct a layman to extend his hands; rather, it instructs the *orans* (hands folded) as proper posture.

The demon takes note of such disorders in the authority structure. When you bow to another, you are yielding to them (and to any demon present to them). When the charismatic lady in the parish wants to lay hands on you, take it as an opportunity to help her formation. She would be better served if you use those moments to redirect her zeal with proper catechesis, as did Cardinal Woelki. And do so always with her husband present.

12. What is "saturation prayer"? Some people want to teach this at my parish.

Saturation prayer is another Protestant phenomena that has made its way into the Catholic Church. It is an attempt to be "thoroughly saturated" by the presence of God in a continuous, expectant way. Rather than introduce a form of prayer that centers on the emotions, however, it's better to teach your

[16] USCCB, *Book of Blessings*, no. 18.

parishioners the ways of mental prayer, as taught by Saint Teresa of Avila and other saints. Hold public Rosaries and Eucharistic processions. Teach them the Benedictine tradition of *lectio divina* and how to meditate on Holy Scripture. Guide them to the Blessed Sacrament, do a Forty Hour's Devotion, and even set up perpetual adoration at your parish. These traditional devotions and Catholic mental prayer, including, silent adoration of our Eucharistic Lord, is Catholic "saturation" prayer.

13. I had always had the impression that a general confession should not be made because it would foster scrupulosity. Why then is a general confession especially recommended before deliverance prayers are prayed?

A general confession is good way to uncover past sins which have not been confessed, especially mortal sins which may have been omitted. Many Catholics have made bad or sacrilegious confessions in the past, especially during their teenage and young adult years, sometimes purposely omitting at least one mortal sin. General confession will clear out these defects. On a practical level, the humility and vulnerability of the deep uncovering often bears the fruit of self-knowledge, fear of the Lord, and hatred of sin.

This is perhaps why a general confession is made during the first week of the Ignatian spiritual exercises. The purpose of this discipline is to uncover what one's sins are symptomatic of—that is, the root causes of these sins. Specifically, in this preparation, the penitent meditates upon hell with a crucifix in hand. In this way, a general confession will expose any unresolved psychological trauma and deeper spiritual defects which are not only symptomatic of the sin but also where the demon may be hiding.

In a discussion of diabolic possession, therefore, Father Aumann states: "Whatever will weaken the power of the devil over a person can be utilized as a remedy against diabolical possession." He cites several "certain principal remedies" from the Roman Ritual. These remedies include first and foremost sacramental confession, but also fasting and prayer, sacramentals, the cross, relics of the saints, and the holy names of Jesus and Mary. Notably, Father Aumann states that not only sacramental confession is efficacious in weakening the power of the devil, but specifically: "It will have a special efficacy if it is a general confession of one's whole life, because of the humiliation and renewal of soul it presupposes."[17]

Again, this weakens the demon's grip and exposes his flank, if you will, by providing specific intel for subsequent deliverance and specific binding prayers. It also gives the penitent a clearer focus on the root causes of their sins, to include any areas of psychological trauma which creates a psychological compatibility and unholy symbiotic relationship with the demon.

14. In my pastoral experience, breaking soul ties is very effective with regard to sexual sins and even sins of abortion, but some priests think breaking soul ties is not in Catholic tradition and has Protestant or New Age origins and therefore is a suspicious pastoral practice at best. How do I respond?

You have undoubtedly noticed that many of your penitents or directees are plagued by certain memories associated with

[17] Aumann, *Spiritual Theology*, 410.

past sins.[18] In modern times, the concept of "soul ties" has been popularized by Christian psychologist James Dobson and not often presented from a traditional Catholic point of view. One modern psychologist defines a soul tie as an "emotional or spiritual cording . . . an inexplicable, powerful emotional bond to another person."[19] The broad appeal of the idea of soul ties suggests that they are part of the human experience.

Alliances can be either holy or unholy. Holy alliances are created between married couples, holy friendships, and the like. Even your parishioners who meet to pray, or to work in evangelization or other good works, create holy bonds with each other. Conversely, unholy alliances are created when sinful acts are performed together. Our understanding of holy and unholy bonds which unite souls traces its roots to both Saint Paul and Pope Saint Leo the Great. Saint Leo alluded to holy alliances when he wrote of "that peace of soul that the most intimate bonds of friendship and the closest affinity of minds cannot truly lay claim to . . . if they are not in agreement with the will of God." These, Pope Saint Leo writes, "are bound together in holy harmony and are rightly given the heavenly title of sons of God, co-heirs with Christ."[20] These holy bonds are formed between parents and children, spouses, friends, teachers and students, etc. and lead souls closer to God.

The opposite, however, appears also to be true. Unholy alliance describes the psychological and emotional ligatures that enmesh individuals who committed certain bodily acts together. Man is a hylomorphic being, a body-soul composite, and those intermingle when we sin together. As Saint Paul reminds us, "do you not know that anyone who joined

---

18 This section is an adaptation from Schneider, *The Liber Christo Method*, 49–57. Used with permission.

19 Manly, "Pros and Cons," 4.

20 Pope Saint Leo, *Sermon* 95, 8–9.

himself to a prostitute becomes one body with her? For 'the two,' it says, 'will become one flesh'" (1 Cor 6:16). Elsewhere, the Apostle writes, "Do not be deceived, bad company corrupts good morals" (1 Cor 15:33). This means that "we adapt the attributes of those with whom we associate with, particularly the effect that immoral people can have on those who are moving closer to God."[21] Certain acts bind people together in an unholy way and, consequently, away from God because they are "formed in practices and associations which are a perversion and corruption of the above [and] are forged in the transgressions of the commandments."[22]

Thus, Father Ripperger defines a soul tie as "a spiritual bond between two individuals, normally as a result of a mutual sin committed together or the sin of one committed against the other."[23] In our prudential experience, certain acts are so gravely evil that they have diabolic accompaniment. That is, the demons present to the act both co-animate and accompany the sinful behavior. The most common sins which create unholy soul ties include incest and rape, homosexual acts, physical and emotional abuse, unholy sex acts (even within marriage), vows and pacts in the occult such as Freemasonry and other witchcraft, tattoos, criminal acts, pornography, abortion, and participation in satanic rock music.

As Saint Leo affirms: "Alliances based on evil desires, covenants of crime and pacts of vice all lie outside the scope of this peace [the fruit of most intimate bonds]."[24] Thus, while holy alliances bring peace, unholy ligatures bind those who commit grave sins together, creating unrest. The very word

---

21 Liber Christo, "Companion Guide," 157.
22 Liber Christo, "Companion Guide," 78.
23 Ripperger, *Dominion*, 555.
24 Pope Saint Leo, *Sermon* 95, 8–9.

conspire means to "breathe together," and when two people conspire and commit evil, a spiritual bond is created.

After giving absolution, have your penitent go into the church and pray this prayer to break any unholy alliances:

> *Lord Jesus Christ, I recognize that an unholy soul tie was created between me and (n.), whenever we (n.). In the name of Jesus Christ, I give back any spiritual thing of the interior self that I took from (n.), and I take back anything of my interior self that I gave to (n.) and hereby break any and all unholy soul tie(s) with (n.).*

Encourage them also that when the memory arises again, to be assured of their forgiveness, but also to take it as an invitation to pray for that person with whom they sinned in the past, as part of reparation and satisfaction for past sin.

Chapter VII

CONCLUSION—SMASHMOUTH CATHOLICISM

"He will be on his guard against the arts and subterfuges which the evil spirits are wont to use in deceiving the exorcist. For oft times they give deceptive answers and make it difficult to understand them, so that the exorcist might tire and give up, or so it might appear that the afflicted one is in no wise possessed by the devil.

"Once in a while, after they are already recognized, they conceal themselves and leave the body practically free from every molestation, so that the victim believes himself completely delivered. Yet the exorcist may not desist until he sees the signs of deliverance.

"The exorcist must not digress into senseless prattle nor ask superfluous questions such as those prompted by curiosity, particularly if they pertain to future and hidden matters, all of which have nothing to do with his office. Instead, he will bid the unclean spirit keep silence and answer only when asked. Neither ought he to give any credence to the devil if the latter maintains that he is the spirit of some saint or of a deceased party, or even claims to be a good angel."

—*Praenotanda to the Rite of Exorcism, nos. 5, 6, 14*

From the Field: Prayer begets what it signifies

The demon traffics in the sense and reacts to sacramentals. Some have more auditory sensitivity to the sacred, while others olfactory (incense), or tactile (holy water, blessed oils, and exorcized salt), or visual (sacred art, blessed candles), or taste (Holy Eucharist, holy water). Just as a demon is repelled by Gregorian chant, so also by blessed bells. Thus, some exorcists use bells during exorcisms as an aid in casting out demons and also to punish the demon (i.e., using the bell to force the demon to be quiet, or stop harming the energumen).

A priest was working with a parishioner who was possessed. One day while speaking with her, he noticed that when the church bells rang, the woman immediately reacted with a deep, cavernous yawn, which the priest knew can sometimes be a mild manifestation, or reaction, by the demon.

"Do you always yawn when the church bells ring?"

"Yes."

Thinking, he then asked her if she also yawns when the bells are rung during the consecration.

"Never," she replied.

He later inquired with his pastor whether the consecration bells used at Mass had even been blessed. They both concluded, after some investigation, that they had not. The pastor then blessed the consecration bells using the prescribed ritual.

When the exorcist next met with the possessed woman, without telling her that the consecration bells had now been blessed, he asked her about her experience at Mass that previous Sunday.

"How was Mass this past Sunday?"

Terrible," she answered.

"Why terrible?

She told him that at the ringing of the bells during the consecration at Mass that she began to uncontrollably yawn and then was flooded with fatigue and feelings of anxiety and nausea. She had never had this happen before but now whenever she goes to Mass, she said, that same dread and anxiety come over her when the bells are rung at the consecration.

This final story from a parish priest is very telling because it reveals the power of the priestly blessing as well as how the sacramentals, which are extensions of the liturgical and prayer life of the Church, are effective in spiritual combat. That demons respond to blessed sacramentals suggests a key principle at work—that is, prayer begets what it signifies. Our Lord commanded to "ask and you shall receive" (Mt 7:7). Notably, the abovementioned priests blessed the bells according to the traditional ritual, which reads, in part:

> Let the people's faith and piety wax stronger whenever they hear its melodious peals. At its sound let all evil spirits be driven afar; let thunder and lightning, hail and storm be banished; let the power of Your hand put down the evil powers of the air, causing them to tremble at the sound of this bell, and to flee at the sight of the Holy Cross engraved thereon. Whenever it rings may the enemy of the good take flight, the Christian people hear the call to faith, the empire of Satan be terrified, your people be strengthened as they are called together in the Lord, and may the Holy Spirit be with them as He delighted to be with David when he played his harp.[1]

Thus, when blessed bells resound, these realities echo into the cosmos—and this is what the demon hears and reacts to. To wit, "the evil powers of the air" are punished as they feel "the power of [God's] hand" causing them to "tremble at the sound of this bell . . . [and to] flee at the sight of the Holy

---

1 Weller, *Roman Ritual*, 324.

Cross engraved thereon." Thus, the consecrated bells have the same effect as when David played, heard in the words of the blessing: "and may the Holy Spirit be with them as He delighted to be with David when he played his harp." This invokes their defeat in the events of salvation history, as when David played the harp for the diabolically afflicted King Saul: "And when an evil spirit came upon Saul, David would take up the harp in his hand and play a psalm, and it refreshed Saul, and brought good to him, and the evil spirit departed from him" (1 Sm 16:23).[2] Bells, like other sacramentals, draw the demons out of hiding and into the open, forced to recall their defeat, and cause them to flee. The result is refreshment of soul and goodness. This is how sacramentals work. Prayer begets what it signifies. Why do you think the demon works so diligently to convince us to remove the "smells and bells" of Catholicism?

If humanity is in a fight with an ancient adversary, then we must look to the ancient, and proven, ways of Tradition for answers. This means that a return to Scripture and Tradition in both theology and praxis is our surest path to victory—that is, a full embrace of the *depositum fidei* (CCC 84). Thus, we summarize by suggesting seven principal elements of a truly Catholic model of deliverance which are found interwoven throughout this book and the Liber Christo method in general:

1. a *high ecclesiology*, that is, an emphasis on the Church, and working under the authority of the local bishop, as opposed to a reduction to individual charisms. This ecclesiology means the engagement of the entire Mystical Body: Church Militant, Suffering, Triumphant;

---

[2] My translation from the LXX.

2. a *primacy of sacerdotal ontology*, that is, emphasis on the office, to include requisite power and authority, proper to the *tria munera* of ministerial priesthood;
3. an understanding of the *authority structure* as determined by natural law and divine positive law which delimits the right to command the demon for both priests and lay people;
4. the use of approved liturgical rites, including sacraments and sacramentals, the goal of which is to lead the afflicted to *sacramental reconciliation with God the Father*. This reconciliation is sustainable only through holiness of thought, word, and deed;
5. a *high Mariology*, as opposed to a Marian minimalism found in Protestant and charismatic models. This is to acknowledge that sustained liberation is possible only through true devotion to the one prophesied to "crush the head of the serpent" (Gn 3:15) due to her unique privileges and role in salvation history and in the Mystical Body;
6. the importance of a *life ordered to prayer* and a healthy and ordered interior life; and finally,
7. a *centrality of redemptive suffering* that involves atonement and reparation for sin as central to our reconciliation with Christ, as well as in breaking spiritual affliction.

The demon responds as much to the imposition of order as he does to the prayers themselves. Most people search for *a way out* (a special prayer that will free them from the influence of evil spirits) rather than *the way up*. You certainly can find groups who are willing to pray over you in the local area, but these modalities that focus on charism are often plagued with recidivism and other problems. That is, although some models of deliverance may stir up the demon and bring some emotional satisfaction or temporary relief, often the liberation is not lasting. The demon returns, and with a vengeance, as Jesus warned:

> When an unclean spirit goes out of a person it roams through arid regions searching for rest but finds none. Then it says, "I will return to my home from which I came." But upon returning, it finds it empty, swept clean, and put in order. Then it goes and brings back with itself seven other spirits more evil than itself, and they move in and dwell there; and the last condition of that person is worse than the first. Thus it will be with this evil generation. (Mt 12:43–44)

In this metaphor, the "house" is the person's interior self. What the expelled demon finds is that it is "swept clean." A curious word for the evangelist to use, the Greek word (*skolazo*) can have a positive connotation as in leisure or stillness (cf. Ps 45:11) or a negative connotation as in idleness or laziness (cf. Ex 5:8, 17). Thus, the expelled demon finds the soul idle, vacant, and unoccupied and returns to punish with vengeance and retaliation.

There is no neutrality in the spiritual life. If spiritual voids created by the liberation of a soul are not filled by the things of God, the demon will happily return with a sevenfold vengeance. Sevenfold is a biblical symbol of perfection, so unless the soul is filled to perfection with the presence of God, the demon fills the soul with his evil presence, "and the last condition of that person is worse than the first." *Freedom from* (the influence of evil spirits) always means *freedom for* (a radical change of life which opens us to union with God). This is why a disciplined prayer and sacramental life that focuses on the basics of Catholicism is essential to lasting liberation.

We can take a lesson from two famous Catholic football coaches. Recognizing the need for fundamentals after a stinging loss that ended the previous season, Vince Lombardi began the new year with, "Gentlemen, this is a football." In other words, we need to get back to basics. He was said to be a devout Catholic and daily communicant, which undoubtedly influenced his philosophy of coaching. In speaking of winning and losing on the playing field, he once said that winning is an ongoing reality, not "a sometime thing." That is, he said, "You don't win once in a while; you don't do things right once in a while; you do them right all of the time." The mark of a champion is the development of the habits of success through a daily discipline. Thus, the coach famously once said that "winning is a habit. Unfortunately, so is losing."

Another famous Catholic football coach, Woody Hayes, once told his team, "If we practiced half as hard as the marching band, we'd be champions." Hayes favored a style of play called "smashmouth" football, which the famous coach described as a "crunching, frontal assault of muscle against muscle, bone upon bone, will against will." This adjective—smashmouth—describes a tough inner disposition that endures suffering, a commitment to the fundamentals, and proposes nothing fancy such as trick-plays and intricate schemes. Simply stated, it is being content with just "grinding it out" as the pathway to victory.

By way of analogy, the playbook for the spiritual combat in which we find ourselves in this modern era can be described as smashmouth Catholicism. This means a disciplined, orderly return to the basics of the Catholic faith as the way to spiritual victory. This approach means avoiding evil and living a clean life, while doing the spadework necessary to root out vices from the soul, because these attachments to the unholy are a pathway to the diabolic. Winning is a habit, but so is losing. Virtues and vices are both habits, or repeated acts, which make for either success or failure in the spiritual life. The *Catechism* teaches that virtues are "acquired by education, by deliberate acts and by a perseverance ever-renewed in repeated efforts." Our efforts become "purified and elevated by divine grace" and with His help, "they forge character and give facility in the practice of the good" (CCC 1810).

Champions do the work even when no one is looking. The imposition of order includes the daily grind of a life ordered to prayer, and the traditional prayers and devotions like litanies, Eucharistic adoration, the Angelus, a daily Rosary, mental prayer, and daily reading of Sacred Scripture. For priests, this means additional vocational obligation, such as praying the Office and saying Holy Mass. When combined with regular confession and Holy Mass, divine grace slowly transforms the soul. These ancient weapons of Catholicism are found to be the most effective. This means filling the mind and soul with the things of God, and when it comes to the spiritual life, this also means a spiritual version of a "crunching, frontal assault of muscle against muscle, bone upon bone, will against will." This is Catholic spiritual combat, and it has produced champions (the saints) from its inception.

An Historical Note: A Lesson from the 82nd Airborne

In the ancient mind, "history" (Greek, *historein*) was understood differently than the mere categorizing of events and people of the past, as in the popular and modern usage of the term. For them, "history" meant either 1) *to investigate* and inquire into the meaning of past events or 2) *to remember* the great deeds of the heroes of our past so that they and the lessons from their lives are not forgotten. In that sense, then, this has been a work of history. If we forget the heroes of our past, the saints who battled and defeated Satan in their flesh by means of the ancient weapons of tradition, we are doomed to repeat the mistakes of the past. A phrase attributed to medieval philosopher Bernard of Chartres describes what the force of a living tradition can bring to bear to the modern world: *nanos gigantum humeris insidentes* ("We are dwarfs, sitting on the shoulders of giants"). Without the help of those who have gone before us, we will never discover the truths needed for today, for the battle that lies ahead. Military and law enforcement tacticians know this instinctively. They adapt their strategies to a shifting battle plain, while never forgetting that the basics of combat never change.

We must remember, then, that we fight an ancient enemy who seems to be resurfacing with renewed vigor in our time. The enemy wants us to battle him on his terms, obscuring from us the power of the full weight of the Church and all the weapons at our disposal. This book has attempted to show Catholics the spiritual weapons they have at their disposal. For this reason, as we have hoped to show that to defeat the enemy today, we must invoke the weight of tradition.

Among warriors, there is a phrase from the ancient world that still rings true: "A Spartan's greatest weapon is the Spartan to his left." This means we must stand courageously together, knowing that a fellow warrior is next to me who is just as committed as I am to bring victory. If that "Spartan to your left" is your spouse, you are most blessed indeed. If you are a parish priest and that "Spartan to your left" is a widow who sits quietly in the back of the church, rosary in hand and directly engaging the enemy for you, you are blessed. If you have a men's prayer group with whom you have accountability and prayer support in your struggles, you are most blessed indeed. Even better if the "Spartan to your left" is a monastery of cloistered nuns who pray for you and your spiritual battles. What the Church needs today, Saint John Paul II said, "is not more programs, but more saints." That is, a true Spartan militates from his or her purity of thought, word, and deed. We defeat the enemy through courage and sanctity and our unity as warriors—all fueled and sustained by the sacraments and prayer life of the Catholic Church.

Combat is combat. There are rules, strategies, and tactics which develop over time, but certain parts of combat are timeless. Modern warfare has seen the first use of paratroopers, who live the modern-day Spartan code. When a paratrooper jumps in, everything he needs to survive and fight is strapped to his body. A final story from American military history teaches us what is needed in today's spiritual battlefront. Before the Americans defeated the Nazis in World War 2, the Germans made one last push through the Allied lines beginning in 1944, known as the Battle of the Bulge. Like me, many of you had family members who fought in this bloody and decisive battle. One thing I can say of the Airborne, whose silver wings are almost as dear to me as my aviator wings, is their courage and confidence in the face of overwhelming odds. A paratrooper remembers his first jump like a schoolboy his first kiss. I remember donning the parachute for the first time and reading a poster that hung on the wall inside of the rigger's hangar as I prepared to make that long waddle to the C-130 that awaited. On the poster was depicted a paratrooper at the Battle of the Bulge. Mean, nasty, and determined, the soldier walked alone down a snow-covered road. He had a rifle over his shoulder, an anti-tank bazooka in hand, a K-bar knife on his belt, a bayonet strapped to his leg, and a few rations. The Allies were retreating beneath the Nazis' fierce counterattack. As the Germans were closing in, an American tank commander named Rogers was leading his column of beleaguered tanks and soldiers in retreat when they came upon this paratrooper. While the picture says it all, the poster recounted the events:

> There they found a lone soldier digging a foxhole. Armed with bazooka and rifle, unshaven and filthy, he went about his business with a stoic nonchalance. They pulled up to him and stopped. He didn't seem to care about the refugees. "If yer lookin' for a safe place," he said, "just pull that vehicle behind me. I'm the 82nd Airborne. This is as far as the bastards are going."
>
> The men on the tank destroyer hesitated. After the constant retreats of the last week, they didn't have much fight left in them. But the paratrooper's determination was infectious. "You heard the man," declared Rogers. "Let's set up for business!" Twenty minutes later, two truckloads of GIs joined their little roadblock. All through the night, men trickled in, and their defenses grew stronger.
>
> Around that single paratrooper was formed the nucleus of a major strong point.

The rest is, as they say, history.

To the reader of this book, we recall the words spoken to Queen Esther by her uncle Mordecai when the People of God were confronted with annihilation. She was tempted to be silent out of fear of reprisal, but her uncle encouraged her to act. "Who knows," he told her, "but that it was for such a time like this that you obtained the royal dignity" (Est 4:14). Like Esther, "you were born for such a time as this," and as a baptized Christian, you also have a royal dignity. God has airdropped you behind enemy lines at this particular time in history so that you can do your part in the battle. In the words of Saint Paul, "Bear your share of hardship along with me like a good soldier of Christ Jesus" (2 Tm 2:3). We invite you to gear up and engage in battle, and armed with the weapons of holiness and truth, say with us:

> I am the Church Militant, and this is as far as the bastards are going.

Appendix A
AUTHORITY CHARTS[1]

[1] The prayers and charts are taken from Schneider, *The Liber Christo Method* and Ripperger, *Deliverance Prayers for the Laity, Minor Exorcisms, Holy Hour of Reparation*. Used with permission.

Authority for Right to Command Demonic

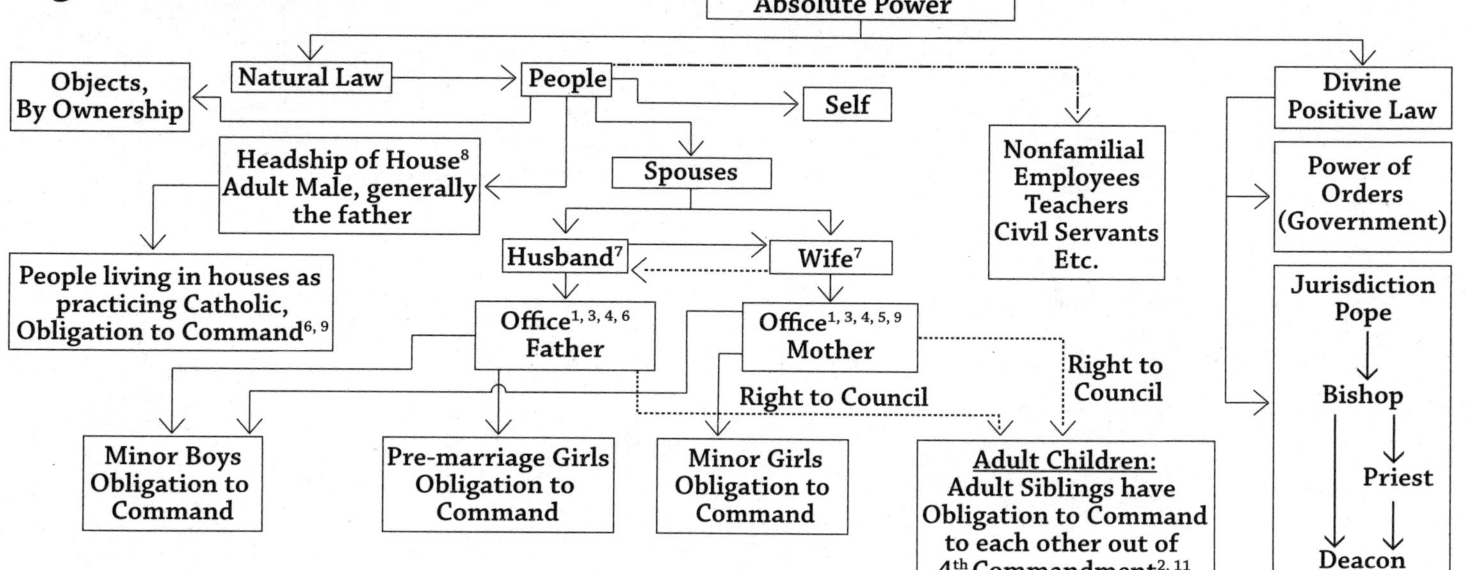

Figure 01

1. Biological Father or Legally Adopted
2. 4th Commandment, Subjection out of piety, giving honor to their parents.
3. Office of Father primarily to protect and provide; Mother, household/children
4. Office gives a right and a duty to command
5. Natural right to command however Father can counter command Mother with reason.
6. Obligation to Command through Office as head of household, (a house divided is an open door to demonic so all in house should be participating in the Sacraments and submit to authority of head of household).
7. Solemn contract is more than an oath or a vow, (Both parties of a solemn contract are bound to the contract even if other party does not abide by it.) This gives the right to give a command over the body, physical healing, not spiritual commands other than in retaliation to demons.
8. If the Father dies then the oldest adult son's obligation of support for the other siblings until age of majority, includes the obligation to command, according to Natural Law.
9. Office of Mother acts as Head of House when Father is absent unless the Father commands otherwise, (absence is different than death).
10. Without Authority may allow demonic affliciton
11. Piety is made manifest toward the aged and infirmed patents by the discharge of the obligation to offer and provide temporal and spiritual support including the obligation to command evil spirits.

Authority
Right to Give Blessing
God
Absolute Authority
Absolute Power
Natural Law
People
Objects,
By Ownership
Self
Nonfamilial
Employees
Teachers
Civil Servants
Etc.
Divine
Positive Law
Jurisdiction
Pope
Bishop
Priest
Deacon
Father,
Office
Wife
Mother,
Office
Children
Grandchildren
Command ≠ Blessing
Command is Imprecatory.
Without Authority blessing
is not valid, superstition.
Petition is deprecatory,
anyone can do.

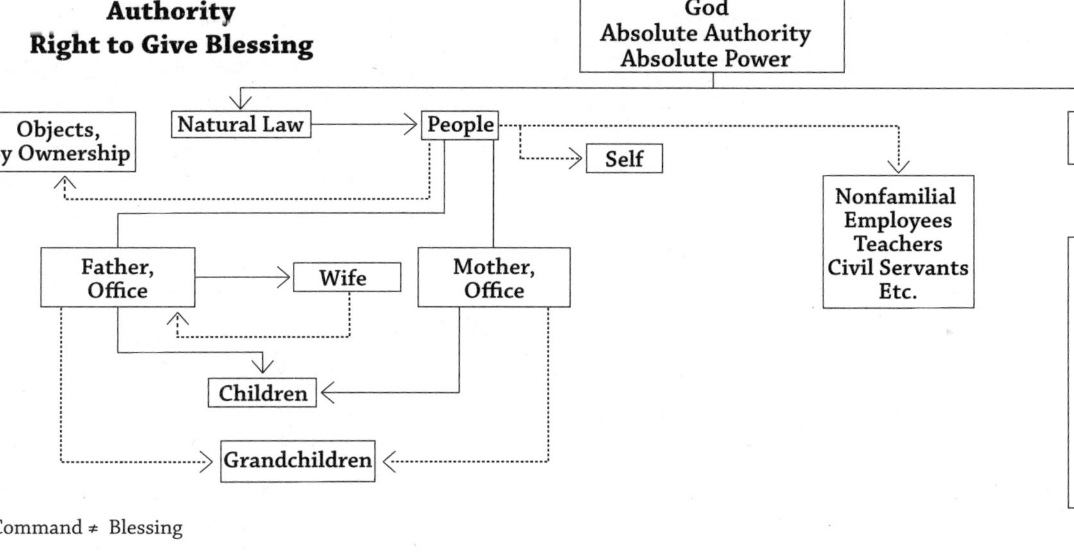

Figure 02

Appendix B

THE LIBER CHRISTO THIRTY-DAY PRAYER REGIMEN

The purpose of this initial period (minimum thirty consecutive days) is to establish a baseline of prayer and discipline through which extraordinary diabolical activity becomes much easier to identify. It also aids in identifying whether the core issue is primarily psychological and/or stemming from character defects/excesses. These tend to have a greater impact on quality-of-life issues than does extraordinary diabolical activity. The latter responds adversely to ongoing conversion or advancement in the spiritual life. The demonic responds negatively to prayer and discipline as you engage your will and a holy desire for union with God. The operative definition of healing in this process is "reconciliation with God the Father through Jesus Christ and His Church through the sacraments."

The initial prayer prescription is based on your formal, sacramental relationship with God and the Church:

Non-baptized, (the baptism must be in the Trinitarian form):

- Angelus three times per day at 6 a.m., 12 p.m., 6 p.m.

Baptized:

- above Angelus plus *Auxilium Christianorum* prayers three times daily[1]

Baptized and first Communion:

- above plus *Confiteor* at noon

Fully initiated (Baptism+Communion+Confirmation):

- above plus Act of Contrition at 6 p.m.

Fully initiated, non-practicing (in habitual mortal sin):

- above plus pray Psalm 130 three times daily

Other prayers, disciplines, devotions as indicated can be used. In addition:

- Media fast, no social media, internet, games, television, etc. Media use is restricted to those activities related to work, vocation, and school, etc.
- Gregorian chant 24/7 at low volume (we recommend the Benedictine monks of Santo Domingo de Silos)
- No reading other than daily Mass readings, that day only, as many times as one wants.
- Pray the Rosary daily.
- Burning of blessed candles to dispel night terrors or evil presence(s) as needed.
- Sacred art and images should replace secular magazines and images.

---

[1] These prayers can be found at http://auxiliumchristianorum.org/, and Ripperger, *Deliverance Prayers for the Laity*, 89–98.

If you are using this as part of a diagnostic prayer due to suspected diabolic affliction, this regimen should be done under the supervision of your parish priest, confessor, or spiritual director. For those who are doing this as a private devotion, the set prayers/hours should be met, but the other disciplines may be done according to one's prudential judgment.

Appendix C

PRAYERS OF PROTECTION FOR PRAYING AT AN ABORTION CLINIC

To be prayed upon arrival:

Sealing Prayer of Protection (n.b. This prayer **seals the faculties**, which the demon uses to gain access via sight, smell, and hearing, and thus will help when you inevitably get drive-by curses, sagers,[1] satanic rock music, etc.)

The person seals himself with Holy Oil:

I ask Jesus to seal me in His Most Precious Blood against any and all incursions of the evil one, and particular against any clinging, familial, familiar or retaliating spirits, in the name of the Father, and of the Son ✠ and of the Holy Spirit. Amen.

Perimeter Prayer (n.b. Based on recent experience from pro-lifers, this prayer helps to shut down harassment. A priest can pray this for a group, or if no priest is present, the laity should pray this prayer for themselves.)

Lord Jesus Christ, in Thy love and mercy, establish a perimeter of protection around (n.) and myself, and all our loved ones, those

[1] Those who use sage as an occult practice.

who pray for us and their loved ones. May the Holy Angels guard us and all of our possessions, establishing a perimeter of protection around (n.), rendering him/her/us immune from any kind of demonic influence. I ask that no demonic bondage, door, portron, demonic entity, portal, astral projection, or disembodied spirit may enter the space of 100 yards in all directions of us. I ask that any demons within this vicinity, or any that should try to enter here, be rendered deaf, dumb, and blind, that Thou would strip them of all weapons, armor, power, illusions, and authority, that Thou would bind, rebuke, and disable them from communicating or interacting with each other in any way. Remove them, sending them directly to the foot of Thy Cross. Jesus, Son of the Most High, I ask this in Thy glorious and Most Holy Name. Amen.

Carmelite Invocation

Come, Holy Spirit with Thy sevenfold gifts and anoint us with Thy divine light, wisdom and power. Come, Lord Jesus Christ and anoint us with Thy Precious Blood, freeing us from every snare and stronghold of the principalities and powers of darkness. O Mother of God, glorious, and Immaculate ever Virgin Mary, come and crush the head of the ancient serpent. O great father St. Joseph, terror of demons, come and annihilate the enemies of our souls. St. Michael, great prince and commander of the heavenly army, strike down the insidious foes who destroy us who seek to destroy us. Come glorious band of Apostles, come, great patriarchs and prophets; come, white, robbed army of Martyrs, pure and nobles, throng of virgins. Come to our aid Holy Mother St. Teresa, our Holy Father St. of the Cross, St. Elijah, St. Elisha, St. John the Baptist, St. Therese, all you Saints of Carmel, St. Pio, St. Isaac Jogues and companions, St. Faustina, St. Benedict, St. Francis, St. Anthony, St. Claire, our Guardian Angels,

Archangels, and all you Holy Angels and Saints, come repulse the attacks and deceits of our wicked enemies; render them impotent and helpless. Let God arise; let His enemies be scattered and all those who hate Him flee before Him. As smoke is driven away, so are they driven away; as wax melts before the fire, so the wicked perish at the presence of God.

Prayer to be prayed by laity upon leaving:

Prayer Against Retaliation

Lord Jesus Christ, in Thy love and mercy, pour Thy Precious Blood over me, so that no demon or disembodied spirit may retaliate against me. Virgin Mary, surround me with thy mantle, blocking any retaliating spirits from having any authority over me. St. Michael the Archangel, surround me with thy shield, so that no evil spirit may take revenge on me. Queen of Heaven and St. Michael, send down the legions of Angels under your command to fight off any evil spirits that would seek to harm me. All you Saints of Heaven, impede any retaliating spirit from influencing me. Lord Jesus Christ, Thou art the Just Judge, the Avenger of the wicked, the Advocate of the Just, we beg, in Thy mercy, that all we ask of the Virgin Mary, the Angels, and the Saints of Heaven, be also granted to all of our loved ones, those who pray for us and their loved ones, that for Thy glory's sake, we may enjoy Thy perfect protection. Amen.

If a priest is present, he seals the participants and leads the prayers. He can also pray the following prayers from *Minor Exorcisms and Deliverance Prayers:*

- Umbrellino Prayer (This prayer prevents the demons from calling in reinforcements.)

- Litany of Saints (The use of the old form in Latin is best because it includes "from the spirit of fornication.")
- Leo XIII Exorcism Against Satan and the Rebellious Angels (the priest must have permission from his local bishop to say this prayer and should be sure to prepare with fasting and prayer, a Holy Hour, etc.)
- Binding Prayer (n.b. This prayer is a prayer against retaliation.)

Appendix D
DESTROYING CURSED OBJECTS

IF YOU HAVE any cursed or evil objects in your possession, we recommend that you destroy them, specifically that they be "blessed, burned, and buried" by the head of the household, or the owner of the items. After sprinkling the objects with holy water, pray the following:

Prayer of Decommissioning

In the name of Jesus Christ and by the authority as head of household [or, as rightful owner of this object] given to me by God the Father Almighty through natural law, I ask Jesus Christ to bless this item and to decommission any evil from it.[1]

Prayer for Breaking Curses of the Occult

I ask Jesus to bind in Most Precious Blood any and all evil curses, pacts, spells, seals, hexes, vexes, triggers, trances, vows, demonic blessings, or any other demonic bondages sent against (n.) or any of our possessions;

[1] Schneider, *The Liber Christo Method*, 85.

I ask Him to bind them and break them. In the Name of the Father, the Son and the Holy Spirit. Amen.

Prayer Against Every Evil

Almighty God, Father, Son, and Holy Spirit, Most Holy Trinity, Immaculate Virgin Mary, Angels, Archangels, and Saints of heaven, descend upon me. Please purify me, Lord, mold me, fill me with Thyself, and use me. Banish all the forces of evil from me, destroy them, vanquish them, so that I do Thy Holy Will. Banish from me all spells, witchcraft, black magic, malefice, ties, maledictions, and the evil eye; diabolic infestations, oppressions, possessions; all that is evil and sinful; jealousy, perfidy, envy; physical, psychological, moral, spiritual, diabolical ailments. Cast into hell all demons working these evils, that they may never again touch me or any other creature in the entire world. I command and bid all the powers who molest me by the power of God Almighty, in the Name of Jesus Christ our Savior, through the intercession of the Immaculate Virgin Mary to leave me forever, and to be consigned into the everlasting hell, where they will be bound by Saint Michael the Archangel, Saint Gabriel, Saint Raphael, and our Guardian Angels, and where they will be crushed under the heel of the Immaculate Virgin Mary.

In addition, if the object was used in some ceremonious way in violation of the first commandment, one can add a prayer of reparation for the offense that the honoring of false gods is against the true and living God:

Prayer of Reparation

Most loving Jesus, when I consider Thy tender Heart and see It full of mercy and tenderness towards sinners, my own heart is filled with joy and confidence that I shall be so kindly welcomed by Thee. Unfortunately, how many times have I sinned! But now, with St. Peter and with St. Mary Magdalene, I weep for my sins and detest them because they offend You, infinite goodness. Mercifully grant me pardon for them all; and let me die rather than offend Thee again; at least let me live only to love Thee in return. Amen.[2]

Act of Reparation to the Sacred Heart of Jesus

Most sweet Jesus, whose overflowing charity for us is requited by so much forgetfulness, negligence and contempt, behold us prostrate in Thy presence, eager to repair by a special act of homage the cruel indifference and injuries, to which Thy loving Heart is everywhere subject.

Mindful alas! That we ourselves have had a share in such great indignities, which we now deplore from the depths of our hearts, we humbly ask Thy pardon and declare our readiness to atone by voluntary expiation not only for our own personal offenses, but also for the sins of those, who, straying far from the path of salvation, refuse in their obstinate infidelity to follow Thee, their Shepherd and Leader, or, renouncing the promises of their baptism, have cast off the sweet yoke of Thy Law. We are now resolved to expiate each and every deplorable outrage committed against Thee; we are determined to make amends for the manifold offenses against Christian modesty in unbecoming dress and

---

[2] This prayer of reparation taken from Ripperger, *Holy Hour of Reparation*, 21.

behavior, for all the foul seductions laid to ensnare the feet of the innocent, for the frequent violations of Sundays and holydays, and the shocking blasphemies uttered against Thee and Thy Saints. We wish also to make amends for the insults to which Thy Vicar on earth and Thy priest are subjected, for the profanation, by conscious neglect or terrible acts of sacrilege, of the very Sacrament of Thy Divine Love; and lastly for the public crimes of nations who resist the rights and teaching authority of the Church which Thou hast founded. Would that we were able to wash away such abominations with our blood. We now offer, in reparation for these violations of Thy divine honor, the satisfaction Thou once made to Thy eternal Father on the cross and which Thou continue to renews daily on our altars; we offer it in union with the acts of atonement of Thy Virgin Mother and all the Saints and of the pious faithful on earth; and we sincerely promise to make recompense, as far as we can with the help of Thy grace, for all neglect of Thy great love and for the sins we and others have committed in the past. Henceforth we will live a life of unswerving faith, of purity of conduct, of perfect observance of the precepts of the Gospel and especially that of charity. We promise to the best of our power to prevent others from offending Thee and to bring as many as possible to follow Thee.

O loving Jesus, through the intercession of the Blessed Virgin Mary, our model in reparation, deign to receive the voluntary offering we make of this act of expiation; and by the crowning gift of perseverance keep us faithful unto death in our duty and the allegiance we owe to Thee, so that we may one day come to that happy home, where with the Father and the Holy Spirit Thou livest and reignest, God, forever and ever. Amen.

Prayer Against Retaliation

[See Appendix C]

Appendix E

INSTRUCTIONS FOR BREAKING FREEMASONIC CURSES

Who needs to say these prayers of renunciation?[1]

THE FREEMASONRY CURSE passes away after the fourth or fifth generation if the curse is not affirmed. Common ways a curse is affirmed include abortion, contraception, fornication, rape, especially involving virginity. The demon sees all of these as blood and human sacrifice. Do not use these prayers as a precautionary measure "just in case" there is any unknown or unconfirmed Freemasonic membership in the family line. These prayers are only to be prayed when there is a religious context involved. This is compared to a peanut allergy in that the allergy can lay dormant and unknown until one is exposed to peanuts. In other words, once a person moves toward a true relationship with the Catholic Church, the penalties invoked may appear. Typical events that trigger retaliation:

---

1 The full ritual can be found at https://liberchristo.org/resources/printed-material/ and Ripperger, *Deliverance Prayers for the Laity*, 122–35.

- Pursuit of vocation within sacramental construct (religious life, ordination, matrimony)
- Minor children approaching sacraments of Baptism, Holy Communion, or Confirmation
- Adult conversion to Catholicism

Prayers Follow the Blood Line

In the case of a descendant whose father, grandfather, and/or earlier generation of grandfathers were practicing members of Freemasonry, the oldest living patriarch should pray the prayers for the family line. Should this oldest living patriarch be unwilling or unable to pray these prayers, then the next oldest son could do so. If there is no living patriarch, then the oldest living daughter can pray these prayers. Note that the male spouse of a descendant daughter would not have the authority to pray the prayers on behalf of his wife and her family. In kind, a woman would not have the authority to pray these prayers on behalf of her husband and his family line. Again, the prayers follow the blood through the male line. They (husband and wife) pray the prayers together in the case of a wife descendant of Lodge member with non-compliant or deceased male's superior in the line to her.

We are finding that the husband's prayers on her behalf are not effective. If she prays the prayers herself, with her husband's assistance and participation, the curse is severed in her and coming through her, and the renunciation is effective in stopping the effects in her and her minor children. When determining the bloodline, consider this in the same way as a legal claim to inheritance. Example: If a man (being the Freemasonic member) were to die without a will, who would be his "blood" descendant to inherit his estate? First, the living sons and daughters, (not stepchildren), then the grandchildren would be the order for inheritance. If all sons and daughters of the Freemasonic father or grandfather were deceased, it would be the living grandson or granddaughter who would pray the renunciation prayers.

How To Engage in Praying the Prayers

The prayers can be found in appendix III at the back of the prayer book *Deliverance Prayers for Use by the Laity*. This may be purchased at www.sentradpress.com It is advisable to read the prayers through first so that you know what is involved so to affirm your resolve to renounce and break the oaths involved.

Active or past members of a Masonic or secret organization must pray the prayers in a sacred space (church or chapel,) in the presence of a priest. The original Freemasonic oaths were taken in an institutional setting (Freemasonic Lodge) in front of members and hierarchy. Therefore, a renunciation must follow in like manner with a Catholic institutional presence and authoritative response in the following manner:

1. To be prayed once a week for a total of three weeks (Rare exception would be that the prayers be prayed over a course of five days with one day between each prayer session.)
2. It is strongly advised for the efficacy of your prayers that all those in attendance are in and sustain a state of grace during this entire protocol. One should confess any involvement in Freemasonry or other secret society/fraternity prior to the sessions. If you are married, your spouse should also be present during these prayer sessions.

3. A witness should be advised to take note of any resistance or affects the person may experience or display while praying these prayers and report these to the priest on the third week. As well, the witness should have holy water available to offer the person praying the prayers so they can bless themselves should any affliction develop in response to the prayer.
4. At the end of each session, the priest has specific prayers to pray while laying his stole on the client's head. These prayers are not found in the book for the laity. They are as follows:

Priest Prayers: (said at the end of EACH session) The descendant says the following three times, as the priest places the stole on the client's head:

In the name of Jesus Christ, I break the power of everything that I have renounced, and I command it to leave me now and go straight to the foot of Jesus to do with as He desires. Amen.

The priest then says three times:

In the name of Jesus Christ, I break the power of everything that (n.) has renounced, and I command it to leave him/her now and go straight to the foot of the Cross for Jesus to do with as He desires.

The priest now asks the Holy Spirit for an infilling of grace into the person.

Non-Member But Descendant

If you never participated in any Masonic organization but you are a descendant of someone who was, it is recommended that the appropriate member in the family blood line pray these prayers as stated above with the only exception being that the prayers are not required to be recited in the presence of a priest.

Appendix F

PROTOCOL FOR DECOMMISSIONING OF TATTOOS

TATTOOS, PIERCING, SCARRING, body alteration, cosmetic surgeries.

In a strict sense, our bodies are the visible manifestation of our invisible soul inasmuch as we are created in the image and likeness of God; He creates both allowing us the free will to conform the gifts of eternal soul and temporal flesh to His divine will. We are "fruit of the earth and work of human hands." Our flesh and what we do with it is either at the service of the soul or a prison in which the soul is held hostage. In a biblical sense, our bodies are the mode and method of our demonstration of our fidelity to God. We make manifest our desires through our flesh and our actions/inactions which shape our flesh.

Any of the practices above, which have no curative or medicinal purpose, are an alteration of the body as God gave it. We are saying that we, rather than God, determine the appearance of our body through unnatural means and procedures.

Addressing tattoos and ritualistic scarring, specifically: determine if the tattoo/scar is an intended symbol of covenant relationship or group affiliation. Does the tattoo/scar represent a deity, god, idol, cult, or religious affiliation? If so, the affiliate relationship must be renounced and all association severed. Formal renunciation of the affiliation should be repeated seven times and all items and articles associated with the affiliation and its members should be destroyed.

Use the language of their initiation in the renunciation. There is a strong possibility that the ink, images, patterns, and the elements of the tattoo/scar are cursed to make the tattoo/scar addictive and/or commemorate a sinful act(s).

The sinful acts must be renounced as well as the practice of tattooing/scarring. If you have a tattoo that requires decommissioning, you will need a priest to obtain the proper prayers by registering on the www.montechristo.net website and accessing the "Printed Material" tab. If a priest has any questions, he may submit an inquiry to info@montechristo.net for further information.

Appendix G

SUGGESTED PRAYERS FOR PRIESTS

Perimeter Prayer

A. *I* ADJURE *all you evil spirits, in the name of the spotless Lamb of God, Jesus of Nazareth to depart from here. I cast you out, every unclean spirit, every phantom, every encroachment of the devil. Yield then to God! You are vanquished in your citadel, all you vile demons. The most Sovereign Queen of Heaven, the glorious and ever Virgin Mary, through her immaculate purity drives you out; before her countenance you must flee. Give way, you evil spirits, to the Queen of Heaven. She is destined by Almighty God to crush your head with her heel.*

Or,

B. (See Appendix C)

Carmelite Invocation

(See Appendix C)

The Light of Christ Prayer

May the light of Christ be on (n.), so that they see themselves as the Heavenly Father sees them; and that I see them as the Heavenly Father sees them.

Latin Binding Prayer

The following Latin prayer may be used in conjunction with the names of the sins, vices, or spirits involved. A few of the spirits have been listed here.

Spiritus (n.), ego te ligo in nomine Jesu, potestate Crucis sancti, potestate pretiosissimi Sanguinis Domini nostri Jesu Christi, auctoritate sacerdotii mei et per intercessione beatissimae Mariae Virginis, sancti Michaelis archangeli, beatorum Apostolorum Petri et Pauli, et omnium Sanctorum et te impero recedere (n.) (nomen personae aut objecti) et ire ad pedem Crucis sancti sententiam tuam recipere, in nomine Patris, et Filii, et Spiritus Sancti. Amen.

Spirit of (n.), I bind you in the Name of Jesus, by the power of the Holy Cross, by the power of the most Precious Blood of Our Lord Jesus Christ, by authority of my priesthood and by the intercession of the Blessed Virgin Mary, St. Michael the Archangel, the blessed Apostles, Peter and Paul and all of the saints, and I command you to leave (n.) (Name of person or object) and go to the foot of the Holy Cross to receive your sentence, in the Name of the Father, the Son and the Holy Spirit. Amen.

astrology	*astrologiae*
binding (holding)	*praestigiae (also the same word for deception)*
depression	*tristitiae (aut depressionis)*
despair	*desparationis*
domination	*dominationis*
effeminacy	*effeminatiae (aut molitiis – if connected to masturbation)*
fear	*timoris*
fornication	*fornicationis*
fortune telling	*praestigii, divinationis*
incantation	*carmenis, incantationis*
lust	*luxuriae*
illness	*aegrotudinis*
incubus	*incubi*
mental illness	*amentis, furiosis (see also obsession)*
mimicking	*simulationis*
necromancy	*nigromantiae*
obsession	*obsessionis*
Odin	*Odin*
Ouija board	*geomantiae*
oppression	*oppressionis*
pacts	*pacti*
pain	*doloris*
palm readings	*chiromantiae*
scratching	*scabri, fricae*
sloth	*acediae*
succubus	*succubi*
superstition	*superstitionis*
witchcraft	*veneficii (aut artis magicae)*

Prayer Against Retaliation

[See Appendix C]

BIBLIOGRAPHY

Agasso, Domenico. *Fr. Gabriele Amorth: The Official Biography of the Pope's Exorcist.* Gastonia, NC: TAN Books, 2021.

Aland, Kurt, and Barbara Aland, eds. *Novum Testamentum Graece,* 28th edn. Stuttgart: Deutsche Bibelgesellschaft, 2012.

Amorth, Gabriele. *Exorcist Explains the Demonic: The Antics of Satan and His Army of Fallen Angels.* Manchester, NH: Sophia Institute, 2016.

———. *An Exorcist Explains the Demonic: The Antics of Satan and His Army of Fallen Angels.* Manchester, England: Sophia, 2016.

———. *An Exorcist: More Stories.* San Francisco: Ignatius, 2002.

———. *An Exorcist Tells His Story.* San Francisco: Ignatius, 1999.

Anonymous. *Physiologus.* Translated by Michael J. Curley. Chicago: University of Chicago Press, 2009.

Aquinas, Thomas. *Summa Theologica,* 5 vols. Translated by the Fathers of the English Dominican Province. Notre Dame, IN: Christian Classics, 1981.

———. *Catena Aurea: Commentary on the Four Gospels Collected Out of the Work of the Fathers, Volume III – Part I.* Albany, NY: Preserving Christian Publications, 1999.

———. *Commentary on the Letter to the Hebrews.* Translated by Fabian R. Larcher. Steubenville, OH: Emmaus Academic, 2018.

———. *De Malo*. Translated by Richard Regan. Oxford: Oxford University Press, 2001.

———. *Commentary on the Sentences*. https://aquinas.cc/la/en/~Sent.IV.

Arndt, William. *The Gospel According to St. Luke*. Saint Louis, MO: Concordia Publishing House, 1956.

Augustine of Hippo, *Against Julian*. Translated by Matthew A. Schumacher. In *The Fathers of the Church, vol. 35*. Washington, DC: The Catholic University Press of America, 1957.

———. *Answer to the Pelagians III*. Edited by Philip Schaff and Peter Holmes. Translated by Robert Ernest Wallis. In *Nicene and Post-Nicene Fathers*, vol. 5 Buffalo, NY: Christian Literature Publishing Co., 1887.

Aumann, Jordan. *Spiritual Theology*. New York: Continuum, 2006.

———. *On the Front Lines: The Lay Person in the Church After Vatican II*. New York, NY: Alba House, 1990.

Baglio, Matt. *The Rite: The Making of a Modern Exorcist*. New York, NY: Double Day, 2009.

Baltimore Catechism. *The Catholic Primer's Reference Series: The Baltimore Catechism of 1891*. Washington, DC: Catholic Primer, 2015.

Bamonte, Francesco. *Diabolical Possession and the Ministry of Exorcism*. Translated by Cliff Ermatinger. Milan: Paoline, 2014.

Beal, John P., et al., eds. *The New Commentary on the Code of Canon Law*. New York: Paulist, 2000.

Benedict XVI. *Verbum Domini*. London: Catholic Truth Society, 2010.

———. General Audience (26 May 2010). https://www.vatican.va/content/benedict-xvi/en/audiences/2010/documents/hf_ben-xvi_aud_20100526.html.

———. *Message of His Holiness Benedict XVI for Lent 2009* (11 December 2008). https://www.vatican.va/content/benedict-xvi/en/messages/lent/documents/hf_ben-xvi_mes_20081211_lent-2009.html.

Biblia Sacra: Iuxta Vulgatam Versionem. Translated by Bonifatius Fischer, Roger Gryson, and Robert Weber. Stuttgart: Dt. Bibelges, 2007.

Bonaventure. *De Perfectione Vitae Ad Sorores*. Edited by Mel Wilfred. Translated by Laurance Castello. Potosi, WI: St. Athanasius Press, 2014.

Budiselić, Ervin, "The Impartation of the Gifts of the Spirit in Paul's Theology," in *Kairos: Evangelical Journal of Theology*, 5.2 (2011): 245–270.

Cabading, Winston Fernandez, and Jose Francisco C. Archdiocese of Manila Office of Exorcism (AMOE), Philippine Association of Catholic Exorcists (PACE), Instituto Sacerdos San Miguel Arcángel (Revised 23 September 2021). https://www.amoe.ph/faqs.pdf. Accessed 3 September 2023.

Cameron, Peter John. "What is Meditation," in *Magnificat* 16, no. 7 (September 2014).

Catechism of the Catholic Church. Liguori, MO: Liguori Publications, 1994.

Catholic World Report. "US Exorcists: Demonic Activity is on the Rise" (15 March 2017). https://www.catholicworldreport.com/2017/03/15/us-exorcists-demonic-activity-is-on-the-rise/. Accessed 28 August 2024. Top of Form.

Chrysostom, John. *Third Homily on Demons*. Translated by T. P. Brandram. In *Nicene and Post-Nicene Fathers, First Series*, vol. 9. Edited by Philip Schaff. Buffalo, NY: Christian Literature Publishing Co., 1889.

Conferencia Episcopal Española. *Su misericordia se extiende de generación en generación (Lc 1,50 nota doctrinal sobre la práctica de la "sanación intergeneracional"* (1 de noviembre de

2024). https://www.conferenciaepiscopal.es/nota-doctrinal-sanacion-intergeneracional/. Accessed 18 December 2024.

Congregation for the Doctrine of the Faith. *Letter to Ordinaries Regarding Norms on Exorcism (29 September 1985).* https://www.vatican.va/roman_curia/congregations/cfaith/documents/rc_con_cfaith_doc_19850924_exorcism_en.html. Accessed 21 February 2021.

Congregation for the Doctrine of the Faith. *Declaration on Masonic Associations* (November 26, 1983). https://www.vatican.va/roman_curia/congregations/cfaith/documents/rc_con_cfaith_doc_19831126_declaration-masonic_en.html. Accessed 21 February 2021.

———. *Inter Insigniores: On Admission of Women to the Ministerial Priesthood.* https://www.vatican.va/roman_curia/congregations/cfaith/documents/rc_con_cfaith_doc_19761015_inter-insigniores_en.html.

———. *Letter to Ordinaries Regarding Norms on Exorcism.* https://www.vatican.va/roman_curia/congregations/cfaith/documents/rc_con_cfaith_doc_19850924_exorcism_en.html. Accessed 21 February 2021.

———. *Letter to the Bishops of the Catholic Church on Some Aspects of Christian Meditation* (October 15, 1989). https://www.vatican.va/roman_curia/congregations/cfaith/documents/rc_con_cfaith_doc_19891015_meditazione-cristiana_en.html. Accessed 4 January 2021.

Cyprian of Carthage, *Epistle LVI.* In Roberts, Alexander, James Donaldson, and A. Cleveland Coxe, eds. *Ante-Nicene Fathers: The Writings of the Fathers down to A.D. 325,* vol 5. Peabody, MA: Hendrickson, 1995.

Degrandis, Robert. *Intergenerational Healing: A Journey to the Depth of Forgiveness.* Totowa, NJ: Praising God Catholic Association Publishing, 1989.

De Montfort, Louis. *True Devotion to Mary*. Rockford, IL: TAN Books, 1941.

———. *The Secret of the Rosary*. Bay Shore, NY: Montfort Publications, 1954.

Encounter Ministries, "Is it legitimate to speak of 'Impartation' of the Holy Spirit?" https://encounterministries.us/wp-content/uploads/2020/09/Is-Impartation-Legitimate-ICCRS.pdf. Accessed 5 June 2023.

Escriva, Josemaría. *The Forge*. New York, NY: Scepter, 1988.

Flannery, Austin, ed. *The Documents of Vatican Council II: The Conciliar and Post-Conciliar Documents*. Dublin: Dominican Publications, 1996.

Gregory the Great. *Homily XXXIII Patrologie cursus completus: series latina*. vol 76, col. 1239A. Paris: Imprimerie Catholique, 1845–55.

Grob, Jeffrey. "A Major Revision of the Discipline on Exorcism: A Comparative Study on the Liturgical Laws in the 1614 and 1998 Rites of Exorcism." PhD diss., St. Paul University, 2013.

Hahn, Scott, ed. *Catholic Bible Dictionary*. New York: Doubleday, 2009.

Hampsch, John. *Healing the Family Tree*. Goleta, CA: Queenship Publishing Company, 1986.

Hardon, John. *Modern Catholic Dictionary*. New York: Doubleday, 1980.

———. *Moral Theology*. https://www.therealpresence.org/archives/Moral_Theology/Moral_Theology_009.htm. Accessed August 29, 2024.

Hippolytus of Rome. *On the Seventy Apostles of Christ*. In Roberts, Alexander, James Donaldson, and A. Cleveland Coxe, eds. *Ante-Nicene Fathers: The Writings of the Fathers down to A.D. 325*, vol 6. Peabody, MA: Hendrickson, 1995.

International Association of Exorcists. *Guidelines for the Ministry of Exorcism: In the Light of the Current Ritual.* Rome, Italy: Edizioni Messaggero Padova, 2020.

John of the Cross. *The Collected Works of St. John of the Cross.* Translated by Kieren Kavanaugh and Otilio Rodriguez. Washington, DC: Institute of Carmelite Studies, 1979.

John Paul II. *Rosarium Virginum Mariae.* https://www.vatican.va/content/john-paul-ii/en/apost_letters/2002/documents/hf_jp-ii_apl_20021016_rosarium-virginis-mariae.html.

Justin Martyr. *First Apology.* Edited by Alexander Roberts, James Donaldson, and A. Cleveland Coxe. *Ante-Nicene Fathers: The Writings of the Fathers down to A.D. 325,* vol 14. Peabody, MA: Hendrickson Publishers, 1995.

Kittel, Gerhard, ed., and William W. Bromiley, trans. and ed. *Theological Dictionary of the New Testament, Volume II.* Grand Rapids, MI: William B. Eerdmans Publishing, 1964.

Leo X. *Sermon* 95, 8–9. In Migne, J. P., ed., *Patrologie cursus completus: series Latina,* vol 54. Paris: Imprimerie Catholique, 1845–55.

———. *Exsurge Domine: Condemning the Errors of Martin Luther. https://www.papalencyclicals.net/leo10/l10exdom.htm.*

Lefebvre, Gaspar. *Saint Andrew Daily Missal with Vespers for Sundays and Feasts.* St. Paul, MN: E. M. Lohmann, 1953.

Lewis, Charlton T. and Charles Short. *An Elementary Latin Dictionary.* Oxford: Oxford University Press, 1963.

Liber Christo. *The Liber Christo Method: Phase 2 Manual for Mentors, Case Facilitators, and GP Priests.* Self-published: Liber Christo, 2023.

———. "Freedom Through Christ Companion Guide: The Catholic Approach to Liberation." Self-published: Liber Christo, 2019.

Liddell, Henry George, Robert Scott, Henry Stuart Jones, and Roderick McKenzie, eds. *A Greek-English Lexicon*. Oxford: Clarendon Press, 1985.

Liguori, Alphonsus Marie. *Dignity and Duties of the Priest: The Aesthetical Works, Volume XII*. Washington, DC: Kassock Bros. Publishing, 2015.

———. *The Glories of Mary*. Rockford, IL: TAN Books, 1982.

———. *Six Discourses on Natural Calamities, Divine Threats, and the Four Gates of Hell*. London: Aeterna, 2015.

Lozano, Neal. *Unbound: A Practical Guide to Deliverance*. Grand Rapids, MI: Chosen Books, 2010.

Manly, Carla Maria. "The Pros and Cons of Having a Soul Tie Relationship in Your Life." Genesis Rivas. *Yahoo! News*. Accessed April 24, 2022. https://nz.news.yahoo.com/pros-cons-having-soul-tie-144155513.html. Accessed 10 May 2022, and on 4 February 2022.

McHugh, John A. and Charles J. Callam. *Moral Theology: A Complete Course Based on St. Thomas Aquinas and the Best Modern Authorities*. New York, NY: Joseph F. Wagner, Inc., 1929.

Metzger, Bruce M. *A Textual Commentary on the Greek New Testament*. 2nd edn. Stuttgart: German Bible Society, 1994.

Moorman, George. *The Latin Mass Explained*. Gastonia, NC: TAN Books, 2007.

Ott, Ludwig. *Fundamentals of Catholic Dogma*. Rockford, IL: TAN Books, 2009.

Pitre, Brant. *Catholic Productions*. "The Laying on of Hands." https://www.youtube.com/watch?v=Yp7h4wRV2Mo. Accessed 3 September 2024.

Pope, Charles. "Can laypeople lay hands on others during prayer?" In *Our Sunday Visitor* (April 18, 2022). https://www.oursundayvisitor.com/can-laypeople-lay-hands-on-others-during-prayer/. Accessed 3 September 2024.

Pacwa, Mitch. *Catholics and the New Age: How Good People Are Being Drawn Into Jungian Psychology, the Enneagram, and the Age of Aquinas*. Ann Arbor, MI: Servant, 1992.

Phipps, Kevin. "Freedom Church: The Principle of Impartation." https://freedomchurchweb.com/blog/2020/04/02/the-principle-of-impartation#:~:text=Others%20are%20watching%20us%20and,cultivate%20and%20develop%20within%20ourselves. Accessed 18 July 2024.

Pio of Pietrelcina. *100 Letters For You*. Edited by Francesco D. Colacelli. Rome, Italy: Ediozioni Padre Pio da Pietrelcina, 2010.

Pontifical Council for Culture and Pontifical Council for Interreligious Dialogue. *Jesus Christ, the Bearer of the Water of Life: A Christian Reflection on the "New Age."* New York, NY: Pauline Books and Media, 2003.

Rahlfs, Alfred, ed., *Septuaginta*. 2 vols. Stuttgart: Wurttembergischen Bibelanstalt, 1935.

Ripperger, Chad. *Deliverance Prayers for Use by the Laity*. Denver, CO: Sensus Traditionis, 2020.

———. *Dominion: The Nature of Diabolic Warfare*. Keensburg, CO: Sensus Traditiones, 2022.

———. *Holy Hour of Reparation to the Sacred Heart of Jesus: For Neglect of and Negligence in Priestly and Religious Vocations*. Denver, CO: Sensus Traditionis, 2004.

———. *Introduction to the Science of Mental Health*. Denton, NE: Sensus Traditionis, 2013.

———. *Minor Exorcisms and Deliverance: For Use by Priests*. Keensburg, CO: Sensus Traditiones, 2016.

———. *The Nature and Psychology of Diabolic Warfare*. Keensburg, CO: Sensus Traditiones, 2022.

Rorate Caeli, "Dubia Answered: Warning for priests treating afflicted souls, guidance on blessings by deacons." https://rorate-caeli.blogspot.com/2018/01/dubia-answered-warning-for-priests.html. Accessed 29 August 2024.

Rossetti, Stephen. *The Pope's Exorcist: 101 Questions about Fr. Gabriele Amorth*. Manchester, NH: Sophia Institute Press, 2022.

———. "Frequently Asked Questions." St. Michael Center for Spiritual Renewal https://www.catholicexorcism.org/frequently-asked-questions. Accessed 3 September 2024.

———. "Guidelines for Deliverance Prayers for the Laity." St. Michael Center for Spiritual Renewal. https://www.catholicexorcism.org/. Accessed 27 October 2023.

Schneider, Daniel. *The Liber Christo Method: A Field Manual for Spiritual Combat*. Gastonia, NC: TAN Books 2023.

———. "*Non Specie Tibi Aestimandus, sed Munere*: Sacerdotal Office, Invisible Fire, and the (Royal) Priestly Ministry of Exorcism." Paper Presentation to the Aquinas Center for Theological Renewal at Ave Maria University and the School of Theology, St. Mary's University ("Christian Know Your Dignity: The Royal Priesthood and the Renewal of the Church"). London, England: June 2024.

Simon, G. A. *Commentary for Benedictine Oblates on the Rule of St. Benedict*. Eugene, OR: Wifp&Stock, 2009.

Smit, Johannes. *De Demoniacis in Historia Evangelica*. Rome: Pontifical Biblical Institute, 1913.

Spicq, Ceslas, *Theological Lexicon of the New Testament*, vols I–III. Peabody, MA: Hendrickson Publishers, 1996.

Thérèse of Lisieux, *The Story of a Soul: The Autobiography of Saint Terese of Lisieux*. Washington, DC: ICS Publications, 2017.

Thigpen, Paul. *Manual for Spiritual Warfare*. Charlotte, NC: TAN Books, 2014.

United States Conference of Catholic Bishops. "Exorcism." https://www.usccb.org/prayer-and-worship/sacraments-and-sacramentals/sacramentals-blessings/exorcism. Accessed July 28, 2024.

———. *Guidelines for Evaluating Reiki as an Alternative Therapy* (25 March 2009). https://www.usccb.org/resources/evaluation-guidelines-finaltext-2009-03_0.pdf. Accessed 21 April 2021.

-----. *The Roman Ritual: Book of Blessings*. New York: Catholic Book, 1989.

Vianney, Jean Baptiste Marie. *The Sermons of the Cure of Ars*. Translated by Una Morrissy. Charlotte, NC: TAN Books, 1995.

Weller, *Roman Ritual, vol 2: Christian Burial, Exorcism, Reserved Blessings, Etc.* Boonville, NY: Preserving Christian Publications, 1952.